Dialect in Film and Literature

Dialect in Film and Literature

Jane Hodson

palgrave
macmillan

First published 2014 by
PALGRAVE MACMILLAN

Palgrave Macmillan in the UK is an imprint of Macmillan Publishers Limited, registered in England, company number 785998, of Houndmills, Basingstoke, Hampshire RG21 6XS.

Palgrave Macmillan in the US is a division of St Martin's Press LLC, 175 Fifth Avenue, New York, NY 10010.

Palgrave Macmillan is the global academic imprint of the above companies and has companies and representatives throughout the world.

Palgrave® and Macmillan® are registered trademarks in the United States, the United Kingdom, Europe and other countries.

ISBN 978–1–4039–3708–7

This book is printed on paper suitable for recycling and made from fully managed and sustained forest sources. Logging, pulping and manufacturing processes are expected to conform to the environmental regulations of the country of origin.

A catalogue record for this book is available from the British Library.

A catalog record for this book is available from the Library of Congress.

Printed in China

For Del

Contents

Acknowledgements

Extract from *Nil by Mouth* (Oldman 1997) reproduced by permission of Douglas Urbanski, SE8 Group.

Extracts from Tony Harrison poems 'Them & [uz]' and 'The Rhubarbarians' published in *Tony Harrison Collected and Selected Poems* (London: Penguin, 2006) reproduced by permission of Tony Harrison.

Poem by Ian McMillan 'Norman Stopped Me on the Street' from *This Lake Used to be Frozen: Lamps* (Sheffield: Smith/Doorstep, 2011) reproduced by permission of The Poetry Business.

Extracts from *Howards End* (Ivory 1992) reproduced by permission of Merchant Ivory Productions.

Extract from screenplay of *Four Weddings and a Funeral*, pp. 58–9 Richard Curtis, *Six Weddings and Two Funerals: Three Screenplays by Richard Curtis* (London: Michael Joseph, 2006) Copyright (c) Richard Curtis, 2006 reproduced by permission of Penguin Books Ltd. (World rights, excluding US and Canada.) and by permission of St. Martin's Press (US and Canadian Rights). All rights reserved.

Extract from Tom Hague *Totley Tom: Tales of a Yorkshire Miner* (Kineton: Roundwood Press, 1976) reproduced by permission of Sharon Hall and Russell Hague.

Extract from David Dabydeen *Slave Song* (Sydney: Dangaroo Press, 1984) reproduced by permission of David Dabydeen.

Extract from Willy Russell *Educating Rita* (London: Methuen, 2007) reproduced by permission of Willy Russell.

Extract from *East is East* (O'Donnell 1999) reproduced by permission of Film Four Limited.

Extract from *Ladybird, Ladybird* (Loach 1994) reproduced by permission of Ken Loach, Sixteen Films and Film Four Limited.

Preface

I have been extraordinarily fortunate over the years to work with many colleagues and postgraduate students who have shared my interest in the representation of dialect. From research seminars, to supervisions, to conversations in the corridor, they have all made the University of Sheffield an excellent place to work on this project and my book would have been much poorer without their input. I would particularly like to thank Sylvia Adamson, Joan Beal, Alex Broadhead, Paul Cooper, Hugh Escott, Susan Fitzmaurice, April McMahon, Julie Millward, Emma Moore, Chris Montgomery and Jonathan Rayner. Above all, however, I would like to thank Richard Steadman-Jones for listening, critiquing and encouraging at all the right moments.

I have also been privileged to be part of a broader intellectual community thinking about these issues. I have benefited from these academics at conferences, reading their work and communicating by e-mail. Specific mention goes to Taryn Hakala, Jackie Labbe, Phil Leigh, Carol Percy, Lauren Stewart, Ingrid Tieken Boon von-Ostade and Katie Wales, but I am grateful to everyone who participated in the very productive sessions at the International Conference on Dialect and Literature in Sheffield in 2011. I would also like to thank Mary Bucholtz for allowing me to see an early draft of her work on Hollywood white African American English.

Many thanks to all my students on 'Language and Power' and 'Dialect in Literature and Film'. I have learned much from working with them and hearing what they thought of the material we have discussed together.

Very special thanks to Peter Stockwell, who generously read this in draft form not once but twice, and whose thoughtful and perceptive comments have gone some way to correcting earlier weaknesses in its structure and argument. All remaining failings are of course my own. Thank you also to Aléta Bezuidenhout, who is finally shepherding this manuscript through to production with efficiency and good humour.

Many thanks to my parents who have always provided warmth, stability and encouragement in everything I do. They can also take credit for kickstarting my interest in language variety, by moving the family when I was 8 from Middlesbrough to Surrey, where none of the other children in the playground could understand a word I said.

Thank you to my two daughters, Anne and Esther. Reading books to them has given me lots of opportunities to think about how dialects are represented in children's books, and also forced me to acknowledge my complete inability to perform any kind of accent out loud. In addition, Anne has provided valuable insights into how a Yorkshire child perceives my Southern English accent: I have learnt that in my accent *cut* sounds like 'cat', and a good spelling of my *last* is 'larst'.

Most importantly, thank you to my husband, Del, who has listened to me talk about dialect and literature a lot over the last few years, and who has various provided coffee, meals and space to work. I'm not sure that you want a book about dialect representation, but this is for you.

JANE HODSON

A note on transcription

This book contains several transcriptions of film scenes. I have not attempted to represent anything about the accent of the speakers in the transcription. This is because a full phonetic transcription would be difficult for those without linguistic training to read, while a transcription that uses some respelling to indicate pronunciation is problematic for reasons that are discussed in Chapter 5. In the transcriptions I have therefore used standard spelling for all words, regardless of the pronunciation the actor uses. I then pick out the specific phonetic features of the performance that I wish to highlight in the discussion afterwards. In these discussions I have used the International Phonetic Alphabet (IPA) although I have also tried to describe the features in question. Any reader who would like to get to grips with the IPA is recommended to read J.C. Catford's *A Practical Introduction to Phonetics* (2001).

I have chosen to present the transcripts in a straightforward 'film script' style rather than marking pauses, intonation, etc. as would be appropriate if this were a conversation analysis book. Again, this makes the transcripts easier to read on the page for those unfamiliar with the conventions. In any case, the actors are working to a pre-existing script in most of the films I discuss here, so this style of transcription works better than it would do for natural conversation.

For reasons of copyright I have in one case used a published film script (*Four Weddings and a Funeral*). In all other instances the transcriptions are my own.

1

Why study dialect in film and literature?

This book draws on ideas and approaches from the discipline of linguistics in order to investigate the ways in which different dialects of English are represented in a range of films and literary texts. As I will explore in later chapters, the representation of dialects in both film and literature primarily means the representation of different spoken, rather than written, varieties. Speech has been central to the novel since its emergence as a distinct genre in the eighteenth century, and it has been an integral aspect of film since the invention of the 'talkies' in the 1920s. Both art forms have employed a range of different dialects in their representations of speech throughout their history, in different ways and for different purposes. However, while the analysis of dialect in literature has received some significant critical attention during the last 100 years, the question of dialect in film has largely been ignored, and the two topics have never been considered together. In this chapter I begin by defining what I mean by the term 'dialect' and I present some of the reasons why I think that dialect in film and literature is a valuable field of analysis. I then explain why I have chosen to treat film and literature together in a single book. Finally, I map out the structure of the rest of the book.

Dialect in Film and Literature is designed to be accessible to scholars working at different levels and with a range of different academic backgrounds. With undergraduate students in mind, I have provided exercises and recommended reading at the end of each chapter. However, this book will also be of value to more advanced scholars at postgraduate and postdoctorate levels. Recent developments in linguistics with regards to subjects such as identity, authenticity and metalanguage make this an exciting time to investigate the role that dialect plays in film and literature. I hope that this book will offer some innovative approaches to the field of dialect representation, and assist readers in undertaking their own research.

What is a dialect?

A dialect is a variety of English which is associated with a particular region and/or social class. To state the obvious, speakers from different geographical regions speak English rather differently: hence we refer to 'Geordie' (Newcastle English), 'New York English' or 'Cornish English'. In addition to geographical variation, the social background of a speaker will also influence the variety of English that person speaks: two children may grow up in the same Yorkshire village, but if one is born into a wealthy family and attends an expensive private school, while the other is born into a less well-off family and attends the local state school, the two are likely to end up speaking rather different varieties of English. It is this combination of regional and social variation that I refer to collectively as 'dialect' in this book.

In linguistic terms a dialect is a combination of regional pronunciation, vocabulary and grammar and can be described at those three levels. A specific regional pronunciation is an accent; hence we can refer to a Geordie accent, a New York accent, or a Cornish accent when we wish to describe the way in which someone pronounces English. In many cases vocabulary, grammar and accent co-occur: a person who speaks with a Geordie accent is also likely to use the vocabulary and grammatical features of Geordie English, in which case we say that they speak in a Geordie dialect. In some circumstances, however, this may not be the case: a speaker may have a Geordie accent without also using the vocabulary and grammar of Geordie English. In this case we say that they speak with a Geordie accent, but that they do not speak in a Geordie dialect. (See Kerswill 2006: 25–7 for a more detailed discussion of the definition of 'accent' and 'dialect'.)

Standard English is the dialect of English used by 'educated' people. It is the dialect that is taught in schools, and is employed on radio and television for 'serious' programmes, such as current affairs. In the British Isles, the accent most frequently associated with Standard English is termed Received Pronunciation (RP). However, it is possible to find the grammar and vocabulary of Standard English pronounced with different regional accents. This is common, for example, among newscasters who often use regional accents to deliver the news in Standard English. Indeed, Paul Kerswill notes that '[i]ncreased social mobility in the second half of the twentieth century has apparently led to the downgrading of this "standard" pronunciation, RP, in favour of mildly regionally accented varieties such as "Estuary English"' (Kerswill 2006: 25).

Thus far I have suggested that speakers use different dialects of English depending on their social and regional background. However, it must be noted at the outset that matters are rather more complicated. In addition to all the background factors that may govern the variety of English that a person speaks, the context within which he or she speaks and the purpose of the speech will also influence the variety used. All speakers command a range of different varieties of English which they will employ as appropriate, depending upon factors such as: who they are interacting with, what the purpose of the interaction is, and where the interaction takes place. Linguists use the term style to categorize language varieties which can be defined according to the circumstances within which they are employed. I will be focusing on the topic of style and style-shifting in Chapter 9.

Dialect and character

Because different varieties of English are associated with speakers from different regions and social backgrounds it is possible to deduce information about speakers' backgrounds from the way in which they speak. In everyday life, the way in which someone speaks provides clues about where they come from, what social group they belong to, what kind of education they received, and so forth. This is something that authors and filmmakers make use of in various ways, not the least of which is to provide background information about characters and locations. As an example, try watching the first two minutes of *Nil by Mouth* (Oldman 1997) and thinking about what you can deduce about the character of Ray and the setting of the film. Here is a transcription of Ray's speech:

> Can I have a drink mate, mate?
> Can I get served here? Can I have a drink?
> Yeah, I want two, no three, three pints of lager, oh and erm three vodka tonics, and a drop of scotch. Half a lager and lime and all.

Three vodka tonics, yeah, slice of lemon in them. Oh, and erm put an
    olive in that.
You got a tray, mate? Yeah? A tray?
No, I want half a lager. Half a lager. Yeah, a lager and lime that's all.
How much?
Ta.
Ain't you got no ice?
You got no ice?

This is quite a low-key opening for a film, in that all that happens
is that a man orders a round of drinks at a noisy bar. Indeed, the
fact that it is the kind of mundane scene that rarely appears in film
already hints at the fact that this will be a film committed to the realistic depiction of everyday life. The scene is intercut with the film's
opening credits meaning that as we are being given written information about the production and cast of the film, so we are also getting
a first view of one of the central characters in what is to follow. It is
possible to analyse various aspects of filmmaking in the bar scene.
The lighting, for example, is low-key with significant portions of the
image in shadow. The scene is filmed in close-up and has a crowded
composition; backs of other heads move across the screen occasionally, obscuring Ray from view. The camera is handheld, meaning that
it sways throughout rather than being fixed on a tripod. All of these
features tend to provide a naturalistic feel: they give the impression
that someone has wandered in with a single camera and filmed a
real-life event. The music works rather differently. It does not have an
obvious source within the scene (it is not coming from an onscreen
performer or sound system) and there is no evidence that the characters on screen are aware of it. Music without an onscreen source
is called extra-diegetic music by film critics, and its purpose is often
to establish the mood of the scene. In this case, a bluesy guitar piece
is playing, providing a melancholic and downbeat mood which contrasts in interesting ways with the onscreen scenes of people having a
sociable evening out.

Camerawork, lighting and music thus all do important work in
terms of establishing the tone and feel of the film that is to follow. However, it is the dialect of the central character, played by Ray
Winstone, that provides the clearest indications of who this man is and
where he might be. His accent immediately signals that he comes from
South East England: he deletes /h/ at the start of 'half' and 'how'; he
employs TH-fronting so that he says [friː] ('free') for 'three'; he uses

L-vocalization so that he says [ɔʊ] ('aw') for 'all', and T-glottalizes at the end of 'mate' so that it is realized as [meɪʔ]. Several of the vocabulary items that he uses ('pints of lager', 'half a lager', 'lager and lime') are all strongly suggestive of a British setting, as is his repeated use of the address term 'mate'. At the same time some of his grammar, particularly the double negative of 'ain't you got no ice', are stigmatized in the UK, suggesting that he does not come from a socially privileged background and probably does not have a high level of education. Finally, the fact that he is clearly comfortable in the setting of the bar suggests that he is on home turf in London. Thus, even before we move beyond this initial close-up of one character ordering drinks, the speech of the actor has provided the audience with some strong clues as to the background of the character in question, and the social and geographical setting of the movie. Sarah Kozloff notes that one of the chief ways in which language variety is used in film is to provide background for a character without having to laboriously spell it out. She writes that 'Recognizable, clichéd dialects are used on-screen to sketch in a character's past and cultural heritage, to locate each person in terms of his or her financial standing, education level, geographical background, or ethnic group' (Kozloff 2000: 82). Rosina Lippi-Green makes a similar point, noting that 'film uses language variation and accent to draw character quickly, building on established preconceived notions associated with specific loyalties, ethnic, racial or economic alliances' (1997: 81). All of this occurs with the character of Ray in the opening minutes of *Nil By Mouth*.

This is not to say that dialect is the only aspect of a film that provides clues as to the background of the character. In the case of the bar scene of *Nil By Mouth*, for example, we might also deduce information about his social identity from his checked shirt and close-cropped haircut, the fact that he regularly sniffs rather than using a handkerchief, and the fact that he is ordering pints of lager rather than, say, a glass of cabernet sauvignon or a vodka martini. Furthermore, any assumptions drawn from the way a character speaks may sometimes prove to be false. In the case of the opening of *Nil by Mouth* it might, for example, be revealed that the character is putting on the accent because he is a spy; or he might be a Londoner on holiday in Spain; or he might be a university professor who has retained the accent of his childhood. It might even be the case that the film is set thousands of years in the future on a distant planet. Sometimes a deliberate mismatch between the visual and verbal identity of a character might be played for laughs. Most of the time, however, the way in which a character speaks will correlate directly with their social and geographical background, and as audiences or readers we are accustomed to using these clues to help us understand the film or novel.

Quite how much we depend upon dialect to fill in information can be seen when we watch a film where we are not attuned to the dialects in question. I had an experience of this sort recently while watching the French film *A Prophet* (Audiard 2009). In this film a young Muslim man, Tariq, is committed to prison for an unspecified crime. While there he is persuaded by an older man, César, to murder another prisoner, and thereafter he comes under César's protection and begins to rise through the hierarchy of the prison. The film is in French, but is subtitled into English so that even someone who (like me) speaks limited French will find it easy to understand the content of the dialogue. However, I had been watching the film for quite a while before it was explicitly stated that César was from Corsica, and even after that it took a while for me to understand that he was a high-up member of a gang of organized Corsican criminals, and that the Corsican mafia are to be feared every bit as much as the more internationally recognized Sicilian mafia. The film began to make a lot more sense at this point: I had not really understood why César wanted the other prisoner killed, or how he exerted such influence throughout the prison. It is likely that a French viewer would have recognized that César speaks with a Corsican accent immediately, and considered the possibility (particularly in the context of a prison) that he belonged to the mafia. This points to the fact that when analysing dialogue in film it is important to consider not only *what* is said but also *how* it is said. When someone speaks in a dialect with which we have some familiarity, we are able to bring a range of both linguistic and extra-linguistic information to bear in understanding the nuances and implications of their style of speech. If the film had been set in America and César spoke with an Italian-American accent, for example, it is likely that I would have suspected him to belong to the mafia much more quickly because I have seen many American films featuring mafiosi of Sicilian origin speaking with Italian-American accents.

Inter-character relationships and thematic concerns

Thus far, then, I have suggested that it is worth paying attention to the use of different varieties of English in films and literature because of the information that they supply to audiences about character and location. But if dialect were just a static label in this way, it would be of limited interest. As I will explore in this book, dialect can be much more dynamic. Shifts in dialect can, for example, also be used to suggest relationships between characters. Consider, for example, this short scene from Andrea Levy's novel *Small Island*:

> As my feet had set down on the soil of England an Englishwoman approached me. She was breathless. Panting and flushed. She swung me round with a force that sent one of my coat buttons speeding into the crowd with the velocity of a bullet. 'Are you Sugar?' she asked me. I was still trying to follow my poor button with the hope of retrieving it later as that coat had cost me a great deal of money. But this Englishwoman leaned close in to my face and demanded to know, 'Are you Sugar?'
>
> I straightened myself and told her, 'No, I am Hortense.'
>
> She tutted as if this information was in some way annoying to her. She took a long breath and said, 'Have you seen Sugar? She's one of you. She's coming to be my nanny and I am a little later than I thought. You must know her. Sugar. Sugar?'
>
> I thought I must try saying sugar with those vowels that make the word go on for ever. Very English. Sugaaaar. And told this woman very politely, 'No I am sorry I am not acquainted with . . .'
>
> But she shook her head and said, 'Ohh,' before I had a chance to open any of my vowels. This Englishwoman then dashed into a crowd where she turned another woman round so fast that this newly arrived Jamaican, finding herself an inch away from a white woman shouting, 'Sugaaar, Sugaaar,' into her face, suddenly let out a loud scream.
>
> (Levy 2004: 15)

In this passage it is 1948 and the narrator, Hortense, has just arrived in Britain from Jamaica in order to be with her husband, Gilbert. One aspect of the scene that might immediately be noted is that Levy does little to characterize the narrative voice of Hortense as identifiably Jamaican. In part this may be because Levy does not want to make Hortense's first-person narration too difficult for an audience unfamiliar with Jamaican Creole to understand, and this is an issue which will be discussed in much more detail in Chapter 6. However, it would also appear that Hortense's background and education mean that she speaks a prestigious variety of Jamaican English. During the period when Jamaica was a colony of the British Empire, a creole emerged, which is a vernacular that develops under specific circumstances of language contact. Creoles often arose in colonies out of the mixing of the languages used in the colony, including English and the African languages of the slaves who were brought to work the plantations. Given the continued social and economic prestige of the English language, what is now spoken in Jamaica is a post-creole continuum, ranging from the acrolect, which is the variety closest to Standard English, to the basilect, which is the variety furthest from Standard English and containing the highest density of creole forms (for a full account of creoles see Sebba 1997). In Hortense's case, her mother was a poor 'country girl' and her grandmother is shown to have spoken a basilectal form: 'When me mudda did pregnant dem seh smaddy obeah'er' (Levy 2004: 43). However, she is very proud of the fact that her absent father is 'a man of class' and she has been brought up in the family of one of his well-to-do cousins (Levy 2004: 37). She has received a good education at a private school run by a white American couple, and then at a teacher-training college in Kingston. In short, Hortense speaks an acrolectal form of Jamaican English, which marks her out as belonging to a privileged social class within Jamaica.

The English woman only speaks a few sentences, and there is little direct evidence in the scene to mark her language variety. Given that the scene is set in London, it might be assumed that the Englishwoman who accosts her is a Londoner and that she speaks with a London accent. However, it can also be noted that the woman is employing a nanny, which suggests that she belongs to the upper middle classes. Her vocabulary and grammar appear to be Standard English, and, the long second vowel that Hortense describes in 'Sugaaaar' fits with the Received Pronunciation that was characteristic of the upper middle classes during the early part of the twentieth century.

The two women are thus alike in speaking with accents that identify them as belonging to privileged social groups. However, they respond to each others' accents in very different ways. Hortense's immediate response is that she wants to sound like the woman: 'I thought I must try saying sugar with those vowels that make the word go on for ever'. The phenomenon of adapting your style of speech to suit a particular situation is termed convergence by linguists, and it is something that

I will explore in detail in Chapter 9. At this point, however, I will simply note that the style-shifting between the two speakers is distinctly unilateral: Hortense wishes to sound like the Englishwoman, but the Englishwoman makes no effort to be at all polite towards Hortense, let alone to sound more like her. This immediately suggests an imbalance of power between the immigrant Hortense, who is desperate to fit in, and the established Englishwoman who evinces no interest, linguistic or personal, in the newcomer.

Finally, the scene also dramatizes the simplistic ways in which different social groups perceive one another. Hortense thinks of the woman as 'The Englishwoman' and finds her vowels to be 'Very English' because she has not yet learnt to discern the differences in social classes that accents can connote in England. Conversely, the Englishwoman is unaware that there may be any social differences between Jamaican immigrants, and the fact that the she tells Hortense that Sugar is 'one of you' reveals that she lumps all Jamaican immigrants into a single, distinctly subordinate, category. Hortense may pride herself on her family background and education, but in her new home this counts for little among people who see skin colour first. Elsewhere in the novel it is suggested that such generalizations are by no means uncommon across the race divide. For example, Hortense recalls that even the American couple who ran her school were unable to distinguish between varieties of Jamaican English:

> Mrs Ryder, in her movie-star accent, remarked, 'Someone must help these poor negro children. Education is all they have.'
>
> Many people wondered if Mr and Mrs Ryder were aware that their school took only the wealthiest, fairest and highest-class children from the district. Or whether these polite, clean and well-spoken pupils nevertheless still looked poor to them.
>
> (Levy 2004: 44)

Again, the fact that Hortense hears any American voice as having a 'movie-star accent' suggests that she is unaware of the social distinctions that accent can index in America, which is unsurprising given that she has never been to America. Rather more surprising is the fact that the Ryders do not register the social standing of the 'polite, clean and well-spoken' children they work with. Both the Englishwoman at the docks and the Ryders in their school appear to make assumptions about the Jamaicans they encounter based upon race alone: they ignore all other social distinctions which language variety might alert them to.

Thus in the scene on the docks we do not just encounter two different varieties and learn about speakers' identities through the way in which they speak, but we also learn something about the speakers' attitudes and the broader social attitudes they typify. It offers an illuminating insight into Hortense's character by demonstrating how strongly predisposed she is to admire and emulate wealthy, well-educated English people, while at the same time demonstrating how completely uninterested the average wealthy, well-educated English person is in engaging with Hortense. The scene from *Small Island* is a small one, and it is the only time that the character of the Englishwoman appears. Within the context of the novel, however, it offers an example of the casual racism she will encounter repeatedly in Britain and it demonstrates the enormous gulf in expectations that exists between the existing inhabitants of the British Isles and the arriving immigrants: Hortense arrives expecting to make a new home, but the Englishwoman is only interested in finding a domestic servant. It thus highlights some of the wider thematic concerns of the novel.

Text-external reasons for studying dialect in fiction

I have offered two reasons for studying dialect in film and literature: that it can tell us about individual characters and locations, and that it can tell us about relationships between characters, and so highlight broader thematic concerns. Both of these motivations might be characterized as text-internal: pursuing them helps us to understand the texts better. Alongside these motivations, there are also text-external reasons. Text-external reasons for studying the representation of dialects of English in film and literature focus on the way in which such representations interact with the society within which they appear. Thus far I have suggested that readers and filmgoers bring their existing knowledge about language varieties to a film or text in order to interpret the dialects they encounter. In practice, however, it seems unlikely that the situation is this straightforward because as well as bringing existing knowledge *to* a new text or film, readers and audiences also take ideas about language varieties *from* that text or film. Indeed, in some instances their existing knowledge about a particular variety of language may have been acquired from other films and texts rather than from the real world (my own knowledge of Italian-American accents, for example, is entirely based upon media exposure as I have never met a person of Italian-American descent in real life). As Rosina Lippi-Green has argued in her study of language varieties in Disney films:

> For better or worse, the television and film industries have become a major avenue of contact to the world outside our homes and communities. For many, especially children, it is the only view they have of people of other races or national origins.
>
> (Lippi-Green 1994: 81)

In many instances, audiences end up with the impression that they know what a dialect sounds like and what characteristics a speaker of that dialect is likely to have, even though they have no real-life experience of interacting with speakers of that variety. These linguistic impressions form an integral part of their understanding of the social or ethnic group that uses that variety. This highlights a potential danger in the way that filmmakers use dialect as a shortcut to 'sketch in a character's past and cultural heritage': such shortcuts can result in films that reinforce negative stereotypes about particular groups of people, and this is an issue to which I will return in more detail in Chapter 4. Sarah Kozloff has written eloquently about the way in which film dialogue can contribute to the stereotyping of marginalized groups in American film:

> Much scholarship has been devoted to demonstrating the negative portrayals in American film of women, African-Americans, Hispanics, Asian-Americans, and Native Americans. Most of these analyses have concentrated on the level of plot and characterization. What is often overlooked is how much the speech patterns of the stereotyped character contribute to the viewer's conception of his or her worth; the ways in which dialect, mispronunciation, and inarticulateness have been used to ridicule and stigmatize characters has often been neglected. Who gets to speak about what? Who is silenced? Who is interrupted? Dialogue is often the first place we should go to understand how film reflects social prejudices.
>
> (Kozloff 2000: 26–7)

As Kozloff points out, the way in which dialogue and dialect is used in film and literature is a good indicator of our attitudes towards the characters thus portrayed.

To what extent, however, do such portrayals simply 'reflect' social prejudices, as Kozloff suggests, and to what extent do they serve to create and maintain such prejudices, as Lippi-Green suggests? This is perhaps an impossible question to answer because, alongside the films they see and the books they read, individuals are also influenced by, among other things, their family and friends, their education, and their experiences in the workplace, as well as by other media including newspapers, television and advertising. It is simply not possible to isolate out the influences that literature and film have. What is possible, however, is that by examining the way in which varieties of language are represented in film and literature we can become more conscious of the ways in which literature and film depict different social groups, and better able to resist the simplifications that they offer. These are topics I will focus on particularly in Chapters 4 and 6.

Dialect in film and literature versus dialect in real life

In the previous sections I have suggested that our ability to interpret this information rests in large part upon our real-world abilities to make deductions based upon the way in which people speak. However, a central premise of this book is that there are important differences between the way in which language varieties function in a film or literary text and the way in which they function in real-life situations.

In literary texts many of these differences are obvious on the page because audible speech has to be rendered into the visual medium of print. In the first instance, both the Englishwoman's pronunciation of 'sugar' ('Are you Sugar?') and Hortense's ('I must try saying sugar') are presented through exactly the same combination of letters, even though logically we know that there must be differences in the way the two women pronounce this word. Hortense then specifically reflects upon her perception that the Englishwoman pronounces the word with 'those vowels that make the word go on for ever' and the word is respelled as 'Sugaaaar' to indicate this. The repeated 'aaaa' is evidently intended to indicate a lengthened vowel sound, but it is rather a blunt instrument. What kind of /a/ does it represent? In my own accent should I understand the 'a' as in 'ant' [ænt], 'awful' [ɔ:fəl] or 'artful' [ɑ:tfəl]? And what about the fact that the book is liable to be read by people with different accents, who will interpret 'aaaa' in different ways? Also, given that the Englishwoman is from the South East of England, it is extremely unlikely that she would actually pronounce the 'r' at the end of 'Sugaaaar', but it is retained in the spelling by Levy. Does this mean that the Englishwoman pronounces the 'r'? Or is it just there to help the audience see that the word is still 'sugar' (a spelling 'Sugaaaa' might be confusing)? This topic of how we make sense of the orthographic manipulations that writers undertake to indicate accent is something that I will explore further in Chapters 5 and 6. For the time being, it is enough to note the fact that writing an accent down on paper requires the visual representation of an audible sound, and that this is a very inexact process.

In film matters are more straightforward. Because speech is recorded directly as sound, the differences between real speech and the filmic representation of it are less obvious. Nevertheless, as Sarah Kozloff has pointed out, speech in films is still very different from real-world speech:

> In narrative films, dialogue may strive mightily to imitate natural conversation, but is always an imitation. It has been scripted, written and rewritten, censored, polished, rehearsed, and performed. Even when lines are improvised on set, they have been spoken by impersonators, judged, approved, and allowed to remain. Then all dialogue is recorded, edited, mixed, underscored, and played through stereophonic speakers with Dolby sound.
>
> (Kozloff 2000: 18)

In the case of film, as Kozloff has bluntly put it, 'linguists who use film dialogue as accurate case studies of everyday conversation are operating on mistaken assumptions' (Kozloff 2000: 19). This is true even in the case of a film which seems very 'realistic' such as *Nil by Mouth*. In the opening scene, for example, it is noticeable that that although Ray's voice is clearly audible, the voice of the bartender cannot be heard even when Ray is evidently responding directly to something that has been said to him ('No I want half a lager. Half a lager.') In part, this might be because the scene is edited so that we can see Ray's face when he is speaking, and the credits come up when he is silent. However, it is not simply the case that the soundtrack is muted when the credits are on screen because both the extra-diegetic music and the background chatter from the bar can be heard throughout. A deliberate decision has been taken to omit the bartender's voice, either by editing it out of the soundtrack or not recording it in the first place. This was perhaps because the director wanted to ensure that the entire focus is on Ray at this point in the film; if we could hear the bartender it would become an interaction between two characters. This directorial decision highlights the fact that, far from being a raw 'slice of life' that has been captured on film, the speech in the opening scene of *Nil by Mouth* is a highly mediated work of art.

Susan L. Ferguson, in an article in which she analyses the representation of dialect in three Victorian novels, has coined the term 'ficto-linguistics' to describe the way in which varieties of English function within literary texts. She writes:

> I will explore the *narrative consequences* of dialect use in fiction by looking at what might be called the ficto-linguistics as opposed to the socio-linguistics of dialect in the novel. By ficto-linguistics I mean the systems of language that appear in novels and *both* deviate from accepted or expected socio-linguistic patterns *and* indicate identifiable alternative patterns congruent to other aspects of the fictional world.
>
> (Ferguson 1998: 3)

As Ferguson emphasizes, the systems of language that we find in fiction may differ significantly from those we find in real life. The term 'ficto-linguistics' is valuable because it provides a way of talking about the patterns of language variety we find within fictional texts, and using terms and concepts borrowed from linguistics in order to do so, while making it clear that language varieties do not function in the same way as language varieties in the real world. The term thus moves us beyond analysing language varieties in literary texts in order to rate them in terms of their real-world accuracy or consistency, which is what sometimes happens when linguists analyse literary texts, and instead enables us to see that they form an integral part of the fictional world within which they appear. Although Ferguson's article focuses solely upon Victorian novels, the term ficto-linguistics can be extended to include the study of language varieties in all works of fiction, including narrative poetry, film and television.

Why study film and literature together?

One question that I have frequently been asked in the writing of this book is why I am attempting to deal with film and literature together in a single volume. Are they not, as I have already indicated, rather different subjects, and would I not be better off dealing with them separately? There are three main answers that I give to this question.

First, I think there are sufficient similarities for them to be treated as different aspects of the same basic question, which is: how is dialect used in fictional narratives? Furthermore, as I shall be demonstrating in the chapters that follow, some recent developments in the linguistic study of dialects, particularly in fields such as metalanguage, style-shifting and perceptual dialectology, are applicable to the fictionalized presentation of dialects in both media.

Second, I have personally found that considering them together has greatly enhanced my own understanding of dialect representation in both art forms because it has made me aware of what is and is not possible within each. At first sight, as I have suggested, it seems to be much easier for filmmakers to represent dialects then writers, because for filmmakers it is simply a case of setting up a microphone and recording the actors. This is perhaps why dialect in film has been the subject of so little analysis – it is simply too easy and too obvious. And yet, by bringing to bear some insights from the much better established tradition of studying the representation of dialect in literature, such as Ferguson's concept of 'ficto-linguistics', it becomes possible to talk about the fact that films use dialect in highly artificial and purposeful ways. At the same time, comparing film to literature has made me aware of what literature can do that film cannot. As I shall be discussing in more detail in Chapters 7 and 8, literary texts often have narrators who comment explicitly upon the dialects that can be heard, and report how other characters respond to them. One example of this can be seen in the *Small Island* extract where Hortense reports her own response to the Englishwoman's accent. Commentary of this sort allows writers to draw the reader's attention to dialect variation in ways that are much more difficult for film to achieve. This is something I had not thought about until I began working on film and literature together.

A third reason for dealing with film and literature together is that I hope that this book will be useful to teachers and lecturers teaching classes on dialect, as well as to individual readers who wish to learn more about the topic. My own experience of teaching this subject over the past few years is that approaching literature and film together makes for a richer and more rewarding experience than treating the topics separately.

The structure of this book

This book is structured so as to move from a practical investigation of the mechanics of analysing dialect in film and literature, to a broader and more theoretical analysis of some of the underlying issues involved in the representation of dialect in film and literature.

In this first chapter I have argued that the representation of dialect in both film and literature can play an important role in setting the scene, establishing character, showing relationships between characters and highlighting thematic concerns, as well as having implications beyond the text in terms of perpetuating or challenging stereotypes of different kinds of speakers. In the next chapter, Chapter 2, I lay the groundwork for the rest of the book by exploring some of the issues of perception and prestige surrounding dialects of English.

In Chapters 3 and 4 I focus specifically on the analysis of dialect in film. In Chapter 3 I examine a scene from the film *Howards End* (Ivory 1992), showing how to work through the three levels of dialect analysis (accent, vocabulary and grammar) and then considering how these can be related to other aspects of filmmaking, including *mise en scene*, cinematography, editing and sound. In Chapter 4 I explore the issue that I have already raised in this chapter, which is that by using dialect to quickly sketch character, films may reinforce negative stereotypes. Here I take as my core analysis a scene from the film *Four Weddings and a Funeral* (Newell 1994).

In Chapters 5 and 6 I turn my attention to dialect in literature. I start by considering where dialect appears in literary texts (direct speech, narrative voice, etc.) and then consider the question of how dialect is represented, again working through the three levels of analysis (accent, vocabulary, grammar). In Chapter 6 I introduce the notion of 'reader resistance', which is that readers often dislike reading dialect representation because they are accustomed to Standard English. I consider the difficulties that this presents for writers wishing to represent characters speaking dialect, and I look at some of possible solutions to this problem.

In Chapter 7 I bring the analysis of film and literature together, exploring how dialect is represented in the film *Saturday Night and Sunday Morning* (Reisz 1960)compared to the novel on which it was based, and how dialect is represented in E.M. Forster's novel *Howards End* (first published 1910) compared to the film adaptation that I discussed in Chapter 3. I argue that these comparisons demonstrate that there are significant differences in the way in which dialect is handled in film and literature, relating to the treatment of specific linguistic features, narrative voices and the use of metalanguage. However, it is not the case that film always has the advantage over literature.

Chapters 8 and 9 continue from Chapter 7, focusing on linguistic concepts which arise from the analyses in those chapters. Chapter 8 explores the concept of metalanguage, focusing primarily on literature. I take short examples from a range of authors including Angela Carter, Zoe Heller and Nick Hornby and undertake a more extended study of the Thomas Hardy short story 'The Son's Veto' (1891). I then turn to film, looking at scenes from *Howards End* (Ivory 1992) and *Educating Rita* (Gilbert 1983). Chapter 9 takes up the topic of style-shifting. I describe three types of style-shifting that are commonly represented in films: emotional, interpersonal and transformative, taking examples from both film and literature. The chapter concludes with an extended discussion of a scene from the film *East is East* (O'Donnell 1999) which, I argue, demonstrates a variety of types of style-shifting.

Chapters 10 and 11 take different approaches to addressing the relationship between dialect representation in film and literature and 'the real world'. In Chapter 10 I consider the fact that extensive representation of dialect in a film or text often signals a commitment by the filmmakers or writer to representing 'the real world', even though the notion of 'the real world' is inevitably a slippery one. I offer a brief survey of the history of the relationship between dialect and realism in literature, and I explore passages from George Eliot's *Adam Bede* (published 1859) and James Kelman's *How Late It Was, How Late* (published 1994). I then turn to film, again undertaking a short survey of the relationship between dialect and realism in the history of film, and I explore *In Which We Serve* (Coward and Lean 1942) and *Ladybird, Ladybird* (Loach 1994). In Chapter 11 I focus on a question that recurs throughout the book: to what extent is it appropriate to judge literary and filmic representations of dialect on the basis of their 'real world' authenticity? Here I argue that although notions of authenticity have often underpinned approaches to dialect representation, in practice they are hard to sustain in any meaningful way. Nevertheless, authenticity remains an important category because the perception of authenticity is often highly valued by audiences and readers.

Further reading

Joan Beal's *An Introduction to Regional Englishes* (Beal 2010) provides an excellent introduction to the study of dialect, including chapters on accent, grammar and vocabulary. *English Accents and Dialects* by Arthur Hughes, Peter Trudgill and Dominic Watt (Hughes et al. 2012) surveys the main dialects of English in the British Isles, and includes a CD with extracts from speakers from each area. Bernd Kortmann and Clive Upton's edited volume *Varieties of English 1: The British Isles* provides an up-to-date survey of the main dialect regions, featuring chapters by experts on the grammar and sounds of English dialects (Kortmann and Upton 2008). J.C. Wells' three-volume *Accents of English* is 30 years old, but remains a useful reference for anyone wishing to know more about the sound systems of English dialects (Wells 1982a; Wells 1982b; Wells 1982c).

Exercises

Exercise 1

Try imagining the scene from *Nil By Mouth* if it were played by actors speaking with dialects associated with different social classes or regions. What effect would this have both upon how we respond to the character, and how we understand the scene as a whole?

It can be enlightening to imagine the same scene played but with a different actor voicing the character of Ray. What if he spoke like Hugh Grant, George Clooney or Robbie Coltrane?

Exercise 2

Choose any film (preferably one that you are unfamiliar with) and listen to the audio track for the opening few minutes of it without watching the visuals at all (turn off the screen or look away). This can be quite effective if done in pairs or groups, so that some of the participants do not know anything about the film that is being played.

- What speech can you hear? Who do you think is speaking?
- What can you deduce about their nationality and their regional and social background from the way in which they speak?
- Where do you think the film is set?

Pay attention too to any non-spoken elements of the audio track.

- What sound effects and background noises can you make out? Do these suggest anything about the setting of the film?
- Is there any music? Does this suggest anything about character or setting?

Now watch the film with the visuals as well as the audio track. How do the visuals relate to the audio track? Think particularly about the costume and behaviour of the speaking characters, as well as the environment in which they appear. Is it what you expected?

Exercise 3

Now try the same exercise in reverse: watch the opening scenes of a film with the sound turned off. What can you deduce about the characters and setting just by watching it? What kind of voices do you think the characters will have? What music and other audio effects do you think there might be?

Now watch the film with both the visuals and the audio track. How does the audio track relate to the visuals? Do you hear what you expected?

Exercise 4

Take the scene from *Small Island* and imagine how it might play in a number of different ways, changing just one aspect of the scene each time. For example:

- What would have happened if they met at a party or in an exclusive shop?
- What if they had met at a market in Jamaica?
- What if the dock were situated in Jamaica rather than England?
- What if they were old friends?

- What if the Englishwoman was the potential employee and Hortense was the one trying to find her nanny?
- What if Hortense spoke Standard English and the Englishwoman had a Jamaican accent?

In each case, think about: which one would have been trying to impress the other? How polite would each of them have been trying to be? How might this have affected the way in which each of them spoke?

2

Dialects and Standard English

In this chapter I explore the social values that are placed on language varieties in everyday life. I focus in particular on the values that are ascribed to Standard English as opposed to social and regional dialects of English. I explore where these values originate from, and what effect they have upon the way in which speakers of social and regional dialects are perceived.

The value of Standard English

It is a basic principle of linguistics that all varieties of English are qualitatively equal. There are two primary reasons why linguists from Saussure onwards have taken this view. First, linguistics models itself upon empirical science and takes human language as the object of investigation. Linguists therefore take it as an axiom that their role is to *describe* languages, not *prescribe* how they should be used. Second, there is in any case no satisfactory basis on which such judgements could be made. For example, 'we were there' is considered to be Standard English while 'we was there' is not. But can any logical argument be made to explain this distinction? Although it is sometimes claimed that there are reasons why one form of the language is preferable to another form, such claims tend to work only in very specific contexts and are impossible to maintain when extended to the whole language. For example, it may be claimed that 'we was there' is inferior to 'we were there' because in English the verb inflects to agree with the subject, so that in Standard English we say 'I was there' and 'we were there'. But how then do we account for the fact that Standard English has 'I went there' and 'we went there'? There is no objective argument that can be used to explain why it is good that *was* inflects but *went* does not. It is impossible to argue on language-internal evidence alone that any one variety is consistently superior to all other varieties.

Of course, outside the discipline of linguistics this value-neutral view of language variety has little influence. As the Milroys have noted, 'There is apparently a yawning gap between what linguists profess to think about language and what ordinary people assume in their daily use and observation of language' (Milroy and Milroy 1999: 11). People continually make the assumption that some language varieties are to be preferred over others: some dialects are considered to be innately 'warm' or 'comforting' while others are 'harsh' or 'ugly'; some speakers are described as 'well spoken' while others are found to be 'slovenly' in their speech habits; some words are considered to be 'proper English' while others are 'just slang'.

Tony Harrison dramatizes the experience of being on the receiving end of such judgements in his poem 'Them & [uz]'. In this poem the schoolboy (who appears to be an autobiographical version of Harrison himself) is chastised by his schoolmaster for the way he reads the first line of John Keats's poem 'Ode to a Nightingale':

> 4 words only of *mi 'art aches* and . . . 'Mine's broken,
> you barbarian, T.W.!' *He* was nicely spoken.
> 'Can't have our glorious heritage done to death!'
>
> I played the Drunken Porter in *Macbeth.*
> 'Poetry's the speech of kings. You're one of those
> Shakespeare gives the comic bits to: prose!
> All poetry (even Cockney Keats?) you see
> 's been dubbed by [ʌs] into RP,
> Received Pronunciation, please believe [ʌs]
> your speech is in the hands of the Receivers.'
>
> 'We say [ʌs] not [uz], T.W.!' That shut my trap.
> I doffed my flat a's (as in 'flat cap')
> my mouth all stuffed with glottals, great
> lumps to hawk up and spit out . . . *E-nun-ci-ate*!
>
> *from* 'Them & [uz]' by Tony Harrison
>
> (Harrison 2006: 122)

According to the schoolmaster, Received Pronunciation (RP) is the only accent that can do justice to 'our glorious heritage' and the schoolboy's

northern accent marks him out as a 'Barbarian' who is only fit to perform 'the Drunken Porter in Macbeth'. In the schoolteacher's view RP
is cultured, prestigious and aesthetically pleasing, while a northern
English accent is at best comic and at worst worthless ('your speech
is in the hands of the Receivers'). As Harrison observes in 'Them &
[uz]', by the twentieth century the belief had taken hold that all 'great'
poetry must properly be spoken in RP even if, as in the case of Keats,
the poet themselves may have spoken with a social or regional accent:
'All poetry (even Cockney Keats?) you see / 's been dubbed by [ʌs] into
RP'. But how did this situation come about?

A brief history

The language that we now think of as English first arrived in the British
Isles with the Angles, Saxons and Jutes who invaded as the Romans
withdrew (starting around 500AD). These newcomers spoke a number
of closely-related Germanic languages which are generically referred
to as Anglo-Saxon or Old English, and Celtic speakers were pushed out
to the edges of the British Isles (Wales, Cornwall, Scotland, Ireland).
Between 700 and 900AD another wave of invasions, this time from
further North (the Vikings), brought another Germanic language, Old
Norse, to Britain. Old Norse is very closely related to Anglo-Saxon,
however, and the two were generally mutually intelligible. In 1066 the
Norman invasion led by William the Conqueror saw the influx of a
number of French-speaking feudal overlords, as William rewarded his
followers with parcels of territory in Britain. This meant that the language associated with secular power was French, while Latin carried
prestige because it was the language of the Church. However, most
of the inhabitants of the British Isles continued to use English, with
the particular linguistic variety depending upon the history of settle-
ment in that area. In the absence of any socially endorsed national
variety, poets writing in English used the version of the language they
were personally familiar with; for example, John of Trevisa employed
a Cornish dialect, the anonymous author of *Gawain and the Green
Knight* used a Northern English dialect, and Geoffrey Chaucer wrote in
a South East English dialect. There was no sense at this time that any of
these regional varieties were 'the language', or that other varieties were
subsidiary to them.

   Over time, however, the loss of Continental territory by the Kings
of England meant that the ruling classes came to increasingly identify

themselves as English rather than French, and they began to use English for legal and political purposes. At the same time, power and prestige began to be concentrated in London on account of its role as the emergent legal, political and commercial centre of the country. In particular, the chancery scribes who wrote the laws of England were situated in London, and it was here that the idea of a written standard began to emerge most strongly. With the advent of printing, the desirability of having a standard form of the language became ever more pronounced, and the fact that the majority of the publishing trade made its home in London ensured that it was the language of the South East which was the variety that took on this role.

The flourishing of learning referred to as the Renaissance saw a growing sense of pride in the English language, and an insistence by some writers that it was every bit as good as French or Latin for the purposes of literature and scholarship, which they set out to prove by writing major works in English. This period saw many words of Latin origin being borrowed into the English language, resulting in the fact that high register vocabulary items are often Latinate, while colloquial vocabulary items are Anglo-Saxon (think, for example, of *inexpensive* versus *cheap*, *employment* versus *job*, and *equine* versus *horsey*). In due course demand for dictionaries and grammars which would make publicly available the 'correct' form of the language emerged, and during the eighteenth century these completed the process of codifying the written form of the English language. It was not until the nineteenth century, however, that the idea of having a standard pronunciation really gained ground, and as Lynda Mugglestone recounts, Received Pronunciation emerged at the end of the nineteenth century out of public schools and was in due course promoted by the BBC and radio (Mugglestone 2003, chs 7–8).

English has thus followed the same set of processes that historical linguists have found in almost all languages that become standardized: first the variety to be standardized is selected from among all other varieties (in the case of London English, because of its location in the emerging centres of power); then it takes on an increasing number of functions (for example, lawmaking, business contracts, artistic and scholarly endeavours); because of its increasing association with government and the law it acquires prestige; concerns grow about ascertaining and ensuring its correct use which leads to increasing prescription; finally the acceptable 'standard' form is codified in grammars and dictionaries. As Giles and Coupland note, the prestige that the standard language acquires 'is due to historical influence rather than intrinsic value'(Giles and Coupland 1991: 38). Before London English underwent the process of standardization, other dialects of English shared similar histories, possessed similar qualities, and would have been equally suitable for standardization. For example, if the city of York emerged as the legal, political and commercial centre of England during the late medieval period, then doubtless Standard English today would have been based upon Yorkshire English. It is only after the process of standardization is well under way that people begin to believe that the standardized variety is self-evidently superior to all other varieties.

The prestige of Standard English

The emergence of a single dialect as 'the standard' thus had implications for all other varieties of English: every process of standardization is also a process of de-standardization for those varieties that are not selected to serve in this way. Once London English had been singled out as the language of the court and lawmakers, all other dialects of English began to be considered as inferior. John Joseph describes this process as follows:

> Once a dialect has achieved this level of dominance, it is a short step for people both within and outside the region to consider it to be the dialect proper, with the dialects of other communities relegated to the status of variants or subdialects. In European usage, the 'dialect proper' comes to be called the language, and subdialects are called dialects (or patois, Mundarten, etc.).
>
> (Joseph 1987: 2)

This distinction between 'the language' and 'dialects' suggests a hierarchical structure, leading to a widespread popular belief that whatever is held to be 'the language' was the original form, and that regional dialects are lazy corruptions of it. In fact, as I have described, the inverse is closer to the truth: originally there were many equally valid dialects, out of which one was selected through a gradual process to serve as the standard.

As Pierre Bourdieu has noted, once 'the standard' exists, the ability (or, to use his term, the 'competence') of speakers to use this 'legitimate language' confers immense social and economic benefits, enabling them to make their views count much more than those who do not speak the 'legitimate language'. He writes:

> The competence adequate to produce sentences that are likely to be understood may be quite inadequate to produce sentences that are likely to be *listened to*, likely to be recognized as *acceptable* in all situations in which there is occasion to speak. Here again, social acceptability is not reducible to mere grammaticality. Speakers lacking the legitimate competence are *de facto* excluded from the social domains in which this competence is required, or are condemned to silence. What is rare, then, is not the capacity to speak, which, being part of our biological heritage is universal and therefore essentially non-distinctive, but rather the competence necessary in order to speak the legitimate language.
>
> (Bourdieu 2003: 55)

In other words, the ability to use language may be universal among human beings (excepting only those with certain types of mental disability, and rare cases when children are brought up in extreme social isolation) but the ability to use the most prestigious variety of the language is restricted to those who acquire it by birth or education.

Researchers have explored the attitudes that listeners have towards different language varieties through 'matched guise' tests. In such tests, listeners are played audio recordings of a number of different speakers, and asked to rate them for characteristics such as intelligence, friendliness, ambition, etc. What listeners are not told is that some of the 'different' speakers are actually the same speaker using a different dialect. This allows researchers to compare directly how listeners respond to different dialects. What researchers have found is that there is in fact a remarkably high degree of consistency concerning attitudes towards standard languages across cultures and countries. Giles and Coupland summarize the findings of such studies as follows:

> Empirical studies spanning a range of speaking situations and communities around the world have produced a generally consistent pattern of results relating to the social evaluation of standard and non-standard speakers. A standard variety is one that is most often associated with high socioeconomic status, power and media usage in a particular community. Its particular form is due to historical

influence rather than intrinsic value ... yet because of its extrinsic associations it is typically evaluated more favourably on traits relating to competence (such as intelligence, confidence and ambition) in comparison with other (regionally marked, non-standard urban, and minority ethnic) varieties. Even speakers of such non-standard 'subordinate' varieties will themselves tend to downgrade them.

(Giles and Coupland 1991: 38)

As Giles and Coupland note, standard varieties are associated with power and status. Speakers of standard varieties *on the basis of their accents alone* are found by listeners to be more intelligent, more confident and more ambitious than non-standard speakers. It is perhaps not surprising to find that speakers of the standard variety rate other standard speakers more highly than speakers of other varieties. What is surprising is that, as Giles and Coupland report, these studies have repeatedly found that speakers of non-standard varieties also rate the intelligence, confidence and ambition of standard speakers more highly than speakers of their own variety. In other words, non-standard speakers have internalized the judgements about their own language variety. This is hinted at in Harrison's poem when the schoolboy narrator notes of the schoolmaster that '*He* was nicely spoken.' This statement implies by opposition that the schoolboy believes that his own speech is 'not nice'.

As this suggests, questions of language variety are closely tied to issues of prestige and power. Ryan, Giles and Sebastian summarize the relationship between language variety and social advantage as follows:

In every society the differential power of particular social groups is reflected in language variation and in attitudes toward those variations. Typically, the dominant group promotes its patterns of language use as the model required for social advancement; and use of a lower prestige language dialect or accent by minority group members reduces their opportunities for success in society as a whole.

(Ryan et al. 1982: 1)

Speakers of the standard variety often have an advantage because, as we have seen, listeners associate Standard English with higher levels of intelligence, confidence and ambition. This means that speakers of

Standard English are more likely to be perceived as successful in contexts which value such qualities, such as the media, education and business, while speakers of non-standard English may find themselves discriminated against in these contexts. Rosina Lippi-Green, for example, has explored a number of legal cases in the United States where complainants felt that their language variety was being used as a pretext for other kinds of discrimination. In one case, for example, a school librarian was dismissed from her job for her poor English. When the case came to trial, one of the pieces of evidence submitted by the prosecution was a note written by the school administrator: 'Mrs. Sparks has a language problem. She cannot help the negro dialect, but it is certainly bad for the children to be subjected to it all day' (cited in Lippi-Green 1994: 179). In this case the racist basis of the supposedly linguistic comment was fairly transparent and the court found in favour of Mrs Sparks. Nevertheless, as Lippi-Green records, there have been many other cases where the evidence is less clear-cut, or where the Judges have favoured their own 'common sense' interpretation of the evidence over the expert opinion of linguists. The Milroys summarize the situation as follows:

> Although discrimination on the grounds of race, religion, gender or social class is not now publicly acceptable, it appears that discrimination on linguistic grounds *is* publicly acceptable, even though linguistic differences may themselves be associated with ethnic, religious and class differences (see further J.R. Edwards, 1979; Hudson, 1980). In effect, language discrimination stands as proxy for discrimination on these other grounds (for a fuller discussion see Lippi-Green, 1997) and may be openly used to discriminate against lower class or minority speakers while avoiding direct reference to class or ethnicity.
>
> (Milroy and Milroy 1999: 2–3)

In short, it is much more socially acceptable to complain about someone's 'poor English' or 'thick accent' than it is to complain about their ethnicity, religion or socioeconomic background. However, this means that people in positions of power may use apparently descriptive observations about an individual's dialect as a means to discriminate against them. This constitutes another compelling reason why it is important to be conscious of the way in which speakers of English dialects are depicted in film and literature, because such depictions can have the effect of reinforcing stereotypes about speakers of non-standard varieties, and so encouraging this kind of discrimination.

Attitudes have to some extent moved on from the times described in 'Them & [uz]', in part perhaps because they have been challenged by writers such as Harrison. It is, for example, now possible to find BBC newsreaders with regional accents, and the theatre company Northern Broadsides performs Shakespeare in northern accents to critical acclaim. Nevertheless, many of the assumptions identified by Harrison remain in place, and it is worth reflecting on the fact that while a Welsh accent may now be acceptable for newsreaders, any hint of Welsh English grammar or Welsh English vocabulary most certainly is not. Moreover, not everyone believes the increased acceptance of regional accents to be a good thing. In a recent article for the respected television and radio guide the *Radio Times*, veteran broadcaster Stuart Hall lamented that a BBC director, Jana Bennett, had promised that many more regional accents would be heard on BBC networks. Hall wrote 'If you imagine I am proposing the death of regional accents, let me put it in perspective. I value them in context. Give me Charlotte Green [who speaks with an RP accent] for my news, Alan Green [who speaks with a Northern Irish accent] for my sport' (Hall 2010: 65). The problem with restricting regional accents to specific 'contexts' as Hall proposes is that regional accents cannot be detached from speakers. By insisting that only RP speakers can deliver the news Hall proposes keeping journalists who might otherwise be very well qualified for the role but who speak with a regional accent away from the news desk.

It can be argued that there are good reasons for having an agreed-upon variety of English for use in situations when maximum clarity and comprehensibility are required, because in some instances differences between dialects can result in dangerous misunderstandings. James and Lesley Milroy refer to the story of a Yorkshire car-driver who was run over by a train after obeying a sign which read 'Wait while the red light flashes'. In most of the UK the sign would mean 'wait here *during the time* that the red light flashes', but in Yorkshire, where *while* has a slightly different meaning, the sign would mean 'wait here *until* the red light flashes'. The story is, as the Milroys point out, probably apocryphal, and in fact very little research has been undertaken to establish the extent to which dialectal differences really result in miscommunication (Milroy and Milroy 1999: 21). Nevertheless, such considerations do provide some justification for having a standardized language variety that can be used in situations when clarity is

paramount, for example, when laws are being written or business contracts exchanged. The problem is that a practical need for an agreed
standard so easily becomes the basis for personal judgements such as
the schoolmaster's 'you're a barbarian'.

The prestige of non-standard Englishes

The question may arise as to why anyone continues to speak a non-
standard variety of English if they believe it to carry such negative
connotations. Why does not everyone simply adopt Standard English,
thereby obliterating some of the social barriers that stand in their
way? This is certainly the account that Stuart Hall offers of his own
acquisition of an RP accent. He tells us that after listening to a visiting RP speaker he approached his headteacher, who 'established a
small group of those who wished to throw off native Derbyshire and
Lancashire and embrace English' (Hall 2010: 65). It is worth noting
how in this anecdote 'native Derbyshire and Lancashire' are opposed
to simple 'English' and how the native dialect is figured as something
constraining which is to be 'thrown off'. This idea that Standard English
can be easily acquired by anyone was held out by some early teachers of elocution, including Thomas Sheridan in his *General Dictionary
of the English Language. One main object of which, is to establish a
plain and permanent Standard of Pronunciation* (1780). Among a list
of rhetorical questions that Sheridan asks in the preface in order to
highlight the advantages that would be accrued to the nation if a single
standard of pronunciation could be agreed upon, he asks:

> Whether it would not greatly contribute to put an end to the odi-
> ous distinction kept up between the subjects of the same king, if a
> way were opened, by which the attainment of the English tongue in
> its purity, both in point of phraseology and pronunciation, might
> be rendered easy to all inhabitants of his Majesty's dominions,
> whether of South or North Britain, of Ireland, or the other British
> dependencies?
>
> (Sheridan 1780, Preface)

Sheridan thus believed that establishing a single 'plain and permanent Standard of Pronunciation' would be a politically levelling act that

would put an end to 'odious' social distinctions. As Lynda Mugglestone has observed, however, in reality the outcome was rather different:

> while non-localized forms of speech did indeed succeed in transcending indications of 'the place of a man's birth', just as Sheridan had originally wished, they did so by placing prominence in terms of social meaning on the possession of an accent without regional markers as a signifier of social level ... Regionalized speakers were, in consequence, to be doubly proscribed – first by the fact of their localized forms of speech, and second by the widespread notion that such markers were incompatible with any sign of status at all.
>
> (Mugglestone 2003: 40–1)

Far from eradicating the connection between accent and social difference, the rise of Received Pronunciation served to reinforce it. But why did not Sheridan's predictions of a single, non-localized accent come true?

The first explanation is that it is just not that easy. The variety of English that a person speaks is largely determined by the language that they hear at home and among their immediate peer group. This is the variety that they encounter continually from birth, and they acquire it automatically as part of the process of acquiring language. When children who speak Standard English with an RP accent at home go to school, they have to acquire the complex skillset necessary to read and write, and they have to learn the styles appropriate for written communication. By contrast, when children who speak a non-standard variety at home go to school, they have to learn the skillset necessary to read and write, they have to learn the styles appropriate for written communication AND they have to do this while also acquiring a new accent, new grammatical rules and new vocabulary items. The children who already speak Standard English are thus at a significant educational advantage, and given the existing correlation between Standard English and social background, this serves to further reinforce social inequalities. It is telling that in Stuart Hall's anecdote, he felt able to approach the headmaster and that the headmaster was able set up a group of like-minded students. Not all children will feel able to approach a headmaster in this way, not all schools will be able to field a group of eager pupils, and not all headmasters will have the resources to be able to staff such a group. While some highly motivated students with supportive teachers may be able to learn to speak Standard English with an RP accent, it is unrealistic to assume that this option is equally available to all.

The second reason why people continue to use non-standard varieties of English despite the fact that it can work to their disadvantage concerns 'covert prestige'. This term was coined by Peter Trudgill in his study of Norwich English to explain why it was that men in some working-class areas consistently claimed to use more non-standard features than they did. He argued that it was because when some people were asked to report on their own language variety, they tended to describe themselves as using the variety they believed to be desirable, that is, they reported how they would like to be perceived as speaking rather than how they actually speak. He found that working-class men often over-reported their use of non-standard features, and he argued that this indicated that for these men the non-standard variety carried prestige within the communities in which they lived (Trudgill 1972). The non-standard variety may not carry the institutionally endorsed prestige of Standard English, but for these speakers it carries important social connotations of identity and community. Acquiring an RP accent might make sense for someone who moves to London and pursues a career in a field where a regional accent may be perceived as a disadvantage, but it makes much less sense for someone who remains in their home town and pursues a career working with local people. Indeed, in the latter case acquiring a 'posh' accent may be a positive disadvantage because regional varieties of English carry very real positive values for the communities who use them. Indeed, Penny Eckert argues that it may be a mistake to assume that only Standard English requires conscious effort: 'While formal style certainly involves greater attention to speech, and while speakers have to pay careful attention when they're speaking in the most extremely standard end of their repertoire, there is every reason to believe that a similar effort is required at the extremely non-standard end of their repertoire as well' (Eckert 2000: 18). It may, in fact, be unhelpful to think of the phenomena that Trudgill describes as 'covert prestige'; it is simply a different prestige from that most commonly recognized at a national level.

Harrison deals with issues of prestige and identity in his poetry, not least in the title 'Them & [uz]' where the typographical presentation of [uz] is being used to indicate that the word should be pronounced with a Yorkshire [u] and [z] rather than the RP [ʌs]. In this way [uz] carries a double meaning: at a semantic level it is the pronoun that is used

to refer the group to which the speaker belongs, while at a phonological level it specifically rejects the admonishment of his teacher that
'We say [ʌs] not [uz], T.W.!'. In the second part of the poem Harrison
writes:

> I chewed up Littererchewer and spat the bones
> into the lap of dozing Daniel Jones,
> dropped the initials I'd been harried as
> and used my *name* and own voice: [uz] [uz] [uz],
> ended sentences with by, with, from,
> and spoke the language that I spoke at home.
> *from* 'Them & [uz]' by Tony Harrison

(Harrison 2006: 123)

The schoolboy in the poem comes to reject the rules he has been taught
at school, and decides to use his own variety, which he describes pos-
sessively as 'my *name* and own voice'. He refuses to emulate the RP of
his teacher and instead embraces 'the language that I spoke at home'.
Although not all dialect speakers will conceive of their decision in this
way, for many an attempt to adopt a more standard accent would
involve a rejection of the language of home and self. It should not be
assumed that those children who chose not to join Stuart Hall's group
to 'throw off' their regional accents were acting against their own best
interests.

Furthermore, regional dialects not only have positive associations
for individuals and the communities to which they belong, but also
more broadly at a national level. As I have already discussed, matched
guise tests demonstrate that speakers of Standard English are typically
rated more highly than non-standard speakers in terms of intelligence,
education and ambition. However, studies have shown the attitudes
that people have towards different language varieties work on three different factors: superiority (e.g. educated, intelligent, organized); attractiveness (e.g. friendly, warm, honest) and dynamism (e.g. active, enthu-
siastic, confident) (Zahn and Hopper 1985). While speakers of Standard
English typically score highly on the superiority factor, they score less
well on the attractiveness factor. In fact, it has been repeatedly found
that speakers of non-standard varieties are rated more highly than
standard speakers in terms of trustworthiness, warmth and friendliness. This is one of the reasons why call centres are often located in
regions where the local dialect is found to have particularly positive
connotations, such as Newcastle or Scotland, and also one of the reasons why certain regional accents are often favoured in commercials

where advertisers wish consumers to form an emotional attachment to the product in question. Thus, although there are situations in which speaking Standard English will confer greater prestige, there are also situations in which using Standard English may put speakers at a social and/or economic disadvantage.

It should by this point go without saying that, despite the consistency with which listeners tend to rate Standard English speakers as more intelligent and regional dialect speakers as more friendly, there is no inherent quality in any variety that guarantees that the speaker will really possess these qualities. It is as easy to find unintelligent and unambitious speakers of Standard English as it is to find untrustworthy and unfriendly speakers of regional dialects. Indeed, studies have shown that when listeners are played a range of varieties of a language with which they are entirely unfamiliar, they do not find that the standard variety is obviously more 'beautiful' than the others, and they do not judge standard speakers as being self-evidently more intelligent than non-standard speakers. In other words, if you were to play an extract of the schoolmaster's RP accent and the schoolboy's Leeds accent to someone who has never encountered either variety before, they would be unable to deduce which variety is the more culturally prestigious. I have already discussed a fictionalized instance of this phenomenon in Chapter 1 with reference to the scene from *Small Island*, where the Ryders, the American teachers at Hortense's school, are unable to distinguish between the basilectal English spoken by genuinely poor Jamaicans, and the acrolectal English spoken by their wealthy students. Because they are unaware of the social and linguistic nuances of the different varieties of Jamaican English, the Ryders are unable to recognize which variety is deemed the most prestigious. It is thus important to remember that whatever judgements are passed on different varieties of English, and however widespread such judgements may seem, they are always socially determined and not based upon internal qualities of the varieties themselves.

Written English and Standard English

James and Lesley Milroy have pointed out that standardization is inextricably linked to the writing system, and that standardization is as much an ideology as a reality:

Standardisation is motivated in the first place by various social, political and commercial needs and is promoted in various ways, including the use of the writing system, which is relatively easily standardised; but absolute standardisation of a spoken language is never achieved (the only fully standardised language is a dead language). Therefore it seems appropriate to speak more abstractly of standardisation as an *ideology*, and a standard language as an idea in the mind rather than a reality – a set of abstract norms to which actual language usage may conform to a greater or lesser extent.

(Milroy and Milroy 1999: 19)

Modern literate societies place a lot of emphasis on writing: business contracts are entered into through the signing of documents; qualifications are earned through written examinations and conferred through certificates; information is recorded and transmitted though writing. Although speech is central to many of our daily activities, writing is associated with legality and permanence. To become literate is to learn Standard English. Although, as I noted in the previous chapter, it is possible to read a text written in Standard English with a regional accent, a strong association between Standard written English and an RP accent remains entrenched.

As such, it can be difficult to remember that speech comes before writing, and that when children learn language, they learn to speak first and acquire reading and writing skills later, as well as the fact that historically, speech came first and writing was a secondary development. Walter Ong writes:

It is demoralizing to remind oneself that there is no dictionary in the mind, that lexicographical apparatus is a very late accretion to language as language, that all languages have elaborate grammars and have developed their elaboration with no help from writing at all, and that outside of relatively high-technology cultures most users of languages have always got along pretty well without any visual transformations whatsoever of vocal sound.

(Ong 1988: 14)

It is thus important to bear in mind that the rise of Standard English is a very recent event in terms of human history, and that prior to that humans successfully used language for all kinds of social interactions without feeling the need for a written standard.

Nevertheless, when we think of 'English' we tend to think first of written English which is, of its nature, much more standardized than spoken English. This is one of the primary reasons why we tend to believe that Standard English is so much more fixed than other varieties: we automatically equate it with the written form of the language, which is much more stable and fixed than any spoken form (including spoken forms of Standard English). It also means that any deviation from the fixity of the written forms – such as respellings to indicate dialect – strike readers very forcibly. Dennis Preston has put it thus:

> English has been spelled for so long, and we literates have read it for so long in one shape, that its very appearance has taken on significance beyond the message. I find it difficult to think of a respelling (except such trivial, nonattributed ones as nite) that I do not feel to be critical of the speaker. Generally, that criticism is in the direction of lower social status, lack of education, illiteracy, boorishness or thuggishness, or rusticity (though I know that all these 'criticisms' are open to romantic interpretations).
>
> (Preston 1982: 322)

In other words, when we learn to read we learn to associate a particular set of spelling practices as being 'correct' spelling and to see all other spellings as 'bad' spelling. This means that any respellings carry the message that the person whose speech is being represented in this way is ill-educated and of low social status.

But does this association between alternative spelling and illiteracy make any logical sense? In most cases, any attempt at representing non-standard varieties of English will be predicated upon a knowledge of Standard English. This point is emphasized by a sign that I recently came across in the Lake District:

TEK CARE
LAMBS
ONT ROAD

By altering the standard orthography of English, the sign aims to capture a flavour of the local dialect and impart a greater sense of 'local colour' than a Standard English equivalent such as 'Take care: lambs on the road'. In this context the 'romantic interpretation' (as Preston puts it) of the non-standard spelling seems to predominate, and the appeal of the sign to tourists is testified to by the fact that a photograph of it is widely available as a postcard. However, it should be noted that, far from being the spontaneous oral creation of a local farmer writing in his native dialect, there is something very literate about it. In particular, it can be argued that anyone who knows to include the silent 'b' in 'lambs' has received enough education in Standard English to know that *take* is not normally spelled 'tek'. Moreover, this respelling is in any case unnecessary for Cumbrian speakers because they would automatically pronounce 'take' as 'tek': the respelling is aimed at showing how Cumbrian English differs from RP. The sign can thus be understood either as a deliberate rendition of Cumbrian English for non-Cumbrian readers, or as an affectionate in-joke among Cumbrian speakers. Either way, it represents a deliberate choice by someone who could have used the standard spelling if they had wished to do so.

For Tony Harrison, then, there is something of an underlying contradiction in trying to *write* 'in my own voice', because this inevitably demands an engagement with Standard English. Indeed, the poem as a whole refers mainly to spoken contexts, but he has to utilize a broad set of resources in order to represent the audible in print. When he attempts to render Keats's line 'my heart aches' so as to give the reader a sense of a northern schoolboy's pronunciation, he uses italics and semi-phonetic respellings to do so ('*mi art aches*'). He employs another semi-phonetic respelling to represent the Northern pronunciation of 'us' as [uz] and employs a symbol borrowed from the International Phonetic Alphabet in order to render the Southern pronunciation of 'us' as [ʌs] (presumably on the basis that for a Northerner there is no satisfactory way to represent the fact that Southerners insist upon distinguishing between two different phonemes for /u/). He captures the fact that the schoolteacher does not articulate as perfectly as he might believe, by contracting 'has' in the sentence and using an apostrophe in the lines 'All poetry (even Cockney Keats?) you see / 's been dubbed by [ʌs] into RP'. He also describes some features, as in 'You can tell the Receivers where to go (and not aspirate it)' where the phrase alluded to is presumably 'Go to Hell!' and the desired lack of aspiration (H-deletion) means it should be pronounced as 'Go to ell!'. All of these orthographic manipulations resist the easy association between Standard English and an RP accent, but all require a highly literate and engaged readership who are also familiar with some basic linguistic terminology. While Harrison prides himself on writing in 'my own voice', his poems are not easily accessible to those who have not benefited from the same level of education. This is a contradiction he addresses in other poems. In 'The Rhubarbarians', for example, he writes:

> Finale of ACT II. Though I resist
> Blurring the clarity of *hanba* (shame)
> not wanting the least nuance to be missed
> syllables run to rhubarb just the same . . .
>
> Sorry, dad, you won't get that quatrain
> (I'd like to be the poet my father reads!)
> *from* 'The Rhubarbarians' by Tony Harrison

(Harrison 2006: 114)

Here he acknowledges that the people at home are not the audience for his poetry and they will not understand some of the poetic and linguistic playfulness and allusions. For some critics, however, Harrison's poetry fails because his account of his own education into a new social class depends upon a negative portrayal of his working class background:

> Harrison colludes in the myth of the inarticulacy of the working classes since, for him, they remain 'tongue-tied', '*a very Bad Hand at Righting*', 'clumsy talker[s]': in Harrison's poetry the working classes have not travelled far enough from the 'mute, inglorious' figures whom Thomas Gray patronises in his eighteenth-century 'Elegy'.

(Lyon 2005: 88)

Whether or not we agree with Lyon's assessment depends, I think, on if we believe that Harrison is 'colluding' with the myth of inarticulacy, or if we believe that he is exploring and critiquing the ways in which that myth functions. This points us towards one of the recurrent questions of this book: given that in modern literate societies most readers and filmgoers are completely encultured into accepting the dominance of Standard English, is it possible to represent non-standard voices in film or literature that does not automatically depict them as inarticulate?

Conclusion

In this chapter I have shown that dialect is strongly connected to issues of power and prestige. Listeners often make judgements about speakers on the basis of the way they speak, judging Standard English speakers to be more educated and intelligent, and dialect speakers to be more friendly and trustworthy. As I began to discuss in Chapter 1, and shall discuss further in the next chapter, this means that dialect can be a convenient tool for communicating information about characters in films. At the same time, however, it means that using dialects in this way can be a way of simply reinforcing stereotypes and discrimination, a topic I shall explore in Chapter 4.

Further reading

James and Lesley Milroy's book *Authority in Language* (3rd edition, 1999) provides a much fuller account of prescription and standardization than I have had space to provide here. Lynda Mugglestone's *Talking Proper: The Rise of Accent as Social* Symbol is a highly readable account that traces the rise of RP (2003). Paul Kerswill's chapter on 'RP, Standard English and the standard/non-standard relationship' (2006) provides a good account of the complex issues surrounding the definition of 'accent', 'dialect,' 'Standard English' and 'RP'. There are several good guides to the history of the English Language. I particularly recommend *The English Language: A Historical Introduction* (Barber et al. 2009).

Exercises

Exercise 1

Make a collection of five different television advertisements (you might do this by recording a commercial break section from the television, or collecting a few from YouTube). Listen to all the voices that you hear in the advertisements carefully, both character voices and voiceovers, and try to identity the accents you hear. Can you detect any patterns in your collection? Are certain kinds of accents associated with particular types of products or brands? If so, why do you think this might be?

Exercise 2

Read the following poem by Ian McMillan. Don't worry too much about *how* dialect is being represented as this is a topic we shall turn to in Chapter 5, but do think about the following:

- What impressions do you form about the two characters, Ian and Norman, from this poem?
- Why is going to the theatre such a big event for Norman? Do you think Ian has been to the theatre? Do you think Norman will ever go? Does it matter?
- Can you identify what prompts you to formulate these impressions?
- How do you as a reader respond to this poem? How might readers from different social groups respond? If possible, ask some friends and family to read the poem and ask them about their responses to it.
- What view do you think this poem takes of the social divisions that mean that some people go to the theatre and others don't? In your opinion does the poem reinforce social divisions, or does it question them?

Norman Stopped Me on the Street

Norman stopped me on the street
And he said
Hey, Ian lad

Ah cud gu t't theatre
If ah wanted, ah reckon.

Ah cud sit theer an clap
At end an shart moor

An then ad gu om and say
Wheer hev yore bin?

T't shop? T't bus stop?
T't wall? T't shed?

Ah bin t't theatre.
Ay gorra programme.

Ah cud du that Ian.
Now stopping mi, is there?

(McMillan 2011: 8)

3

Analysing language variation in film

There is considerable general interest in topics related to film and dialect. A quick trawl of the internet, for example reveals numerous blogs and newspaper articles discussing topics such as which actors have succeeded in mastering new accents for film roles, which films feature famously bad accent performances, and why Hollywood villains so often speak with English accents. But despite this popular interest, the analysis of dialect in film has been the subject of very little serious study. Indeed, although spoken dialogue has been an integral part of almost all commercially produced films for 80 years, the topic as a whole has attracted little critical attention during this period. Sarah Kozloff, author of the only full-length study in English on dialogue in film, argues that the main reason for this neglect is because film has been seen primarily as a visual medium. She cites as examples John Ford's observation that 'When a motion picture is at its best, it is long on action and short on dialogue' and Ephraim Katz's definition of the word 'dialogue' in his popular *Film Encyclopedia*, in which he pronounces that 'Since the cinema is essentially a visual medium, dialogue is, or should be, used more sparingly than in the theater, supplementing action rather than substituting for it' (Kozloff 2000: 4–8). Kozloff finds that this kind of resistance to film dialogue is in part a result of the silent origins of film, and in part a result of the fact that from the beginning film has been defined in opposition to the 'talkiness' of theatre (as Katz's definition itself attests). More broadly, she argues that films that are perceived as 'talky' 'come with the connotations of 'trivial' and 'idle' and that 'dialogue has been continually discredited and undervalued in film because it is associated with femininity' (Kozloff 2000: 13).

Given that the entire field of film dialogue has received so little critical interest, it is unsurprising to find that the way in which varieties of English are represented in film has been virtually ignored. There are a few good chapters and articles, including Rosina Lippi-Green's excellent chapter on language variety and stereotyping in Disney films in her book *English with an Accent* (1997), Stephanie Marriott's article on language variation in the film *In Which We Serve*, 'Dialect and Dialectic in a British War Film' (1997) and Barbara Meek's exploration of the representation of what she terms 'Hollywood Indian English' (2006). On the whole, however, the issue of dialect in film has been largely ignored within film studies.

Kozloff herself is sensitive to the functions of dialect in film, although she deals with the topic relatively briefly as part of her much broader exploration of the role of dialogue in film. Her central thesis is that the filmgoer can best be understood as an 'eavesdropper' to the on-screen dialogue. She argues that film dialogue 'has been purposely designed for the viewers to overhear' in order to enable them to comprehend the onscreen action, even though the film simultaneously does its best to disguise the fact (Kozloff 2000: 15). This creates the situation where dialogue has two recipients: the onscreen characters who are ostensibly being spoken to, and the unacknowledged filmgoer who is the real audience. As she puts it 'each word does double duty, works on double layers' (Kozloff 2000: 19).

Dialect is one way in which the double duty of film dialogue can be carried out, as I began to explore in Chapter 1. While the content of the dialogue may serve any number of purposes for its onscreen and offscreen recipients, the dialect in which that content is delivered can itself communicate meaning. Of course, this does not happen in isolation from the rest of the film: the verbal soundtrack is just one part of the audio-visual experience that makes up a film, others including the *mise-en-scène*, cinematography, editing, and the rest of the soundtrack. In this chapter I focus on exploring the dialect that is represented in the film *Howards End* (James Ivory, 1992). I begin by focusing on a single scene and exploring in detail the dialects of two characters. I then consider what other aspects of filmmaking are relevant to interpreting the scene. Finally, I broaden my analysis out to consider the film as a whole, and the way in which focusing on dialect and accent in film may help our approach to critical questions.

Language variation in a scene from *Howards End*

The 1992 film *Howards End* is based upon E. M. Forster's 1910 novel of the same name. Like the novel, the film explores the connections between different social classes in early twentieth-century England.

The film focuses on two sisters, Margaret and Helen Schlegel, played by Emma Thompson and Helena Bonham Carter respectively. Margaret and Helen come from a privileged English background, although their father was German and they maintain extended family connections on the continent. They are broadly liberal in their political outlook, having an interest in art, philosophy and literature and showing a benevolent concern for the lower classes. At various points in the film they become involved with the Wilcox family, who have made their money through colonial trade and are primarily interested in finance, cars and progress. At the same time, the sisters become involved with Leonard Bast, a bank clerk who aspires toward middle-class culture, but is dragged downwards by his poverty and his relationship with Jacky, an older woman with a dubious past. The Schlegels attempt to befriend and assist Leonard but they inadvertently pass on poor employment advice from Henry which leads to Leonard's financial ruin.

The scene in question takes place relatively early on between Leonard and Jacky, when Leonard arrives home after attending a lecture and meeting the Schlegel sisters for the first time (Helen accidentally picked up his umbrella, and he followed her in order to retrieve it). Leonard is played by Sam West, the son of two well-known British actors, Prunella Scales and Timothy West. West attended an independent school in London, and graduated from Oxford University (IMDb 2013a). Given this privileged background, it seems probable that his own natural accent is close to RP. Little background information is available about Nicola Duffett, the actress who plays Jacky, other than the fact that she was born in Plymouth. However, the fact that she has regularly played working-class characters from the South East of England (including stints in the soap operas *EastEnders* and *Family Affairs*) suggests that casting directors find her convincing when she uses this kind of accent (IMDb 2013b). The scene starts at 20 minutes.

JACKY:	Is that you Len? Where have you been? I'm off my head with worrying.
LEONARD:	About what?
JACKY:	About you.
LEONARD:	Let go Jacky. Every time I'm five minutes late you see me lying dead in the road crushed and killed in a gruesome accident.

JACKY:	Well, people do get killed in accidents and don't come home no more.
LEONARD:	Any more, Jacky. I told you I was going to a lecture on music and meaning. I lost my umbrella. It's all right I got it back.
JACKY:	You had your tea? I kept you a bit of tongue and jelly.
LEONARD	No.
JACKY:	Sure? I'll have it then. Funny isn't it. Every time I worry I get starving hungry. Thoughts that go through my head. You'd laugh. You listening Len? Not only accidents but that you'll get wet in the rain. Did you?
LEONARD:	No.
JACKY:	You said you lost your umbrella. I think, Lord, he'll catch cold. It'll go to his chest. And where's the money to come from for the doctor? And what if he is in an accident. And they take him to the hospital in the ambulance. And him with holes in his socks.
LEONARD:	Jacky!
JACKY:	I want to see
LEONARD:	What?
JACKY:	If there's holes in your socks.
LEONARD:	Stop it Jacky.
JACKY:	Len. Come to bed?
LEONARD:	Just finish this chapter.
JACKY:	Len. You love your Jacky do you Len?
LEONARD:	Let me read.
JACKY:	Len? Are you going to make it all right?
LEONARD:	You're not starting on that again. I told you a hundred times if I've told you once. We'll get married the day I'm twenty one. I'd do it before if it weren't for my brother would come and put a stop to it. What's it to him? What's he ever done for me?
JACKY:	That's right. What's anyone ever done? It's just you and me. And if you was to go and leave me I don't know what I'd do. I truly don't.

When analysing a scene for its dialect representation, it is worth watching the scene several times, focusing in turn upon accent, vocabulary and grammar. Indeed, it can also be worth focusing on a single phonological feature (such as H-deletion or T-glottalization) at a time, and watching the scene more than once for each feature.

Accent

Jacky has a marked London accent. She categorically deletes /h/ (for example, 'off my **h**ead with worrying'), glottalizes /t/ in word-final and intervocalic positions (for example, 'a bi**t** of tongue and jelly') and realizes the velar nasal /ŋ/ as [n], for example 'I get starvi**ng** hungry'. (Note: this final feature is popularly referred to as 'g-dropping' even though, from a linguistic point of view, the [g] exists only in the spelling 'ing'. A better description of the feature from a linguist's perspective is 'develarization of word-final nasals', although of course that is a bit of a mouthful.)

In terms of vowel sounds, it is slightly harder to identify characteristic London features in Jacky's speech. She does sometimes produce the diphthong /əʊ/ in GOAT words with a more open first vowel than RP, closer to the London /aʊ/ (e.g. in 'Thoughts that **go** through my head'). Similarly, she sometimes pronounces the diphthong /eɪ/ in FACE words closer to the London /aɪ/ (e.g. in 'wet in the **rain**'). However, these pronunciations are not consistent: the vowels in '**go** to his chest' and 'That's **right**' are considerably closer to the RP pronunciation. Stephanie Marriott, in her study of *In Which We Serve*, finds a similar pattern for some of the actors, and suggests that it is typical of prolonged attempts to produce vowels which are not the speaker's own, which may suggest that the broad London accent that the actress is attempting to portray is not her natural accent (Marriott 1997: 178).

In terms of accent, Leonard's speech is closer to RP than that of Jacky. As a general rule, he does not delete /h/ and does not realize /ŋ/ as [n]. He does, however, sometimes glottalize /t/ in word-final position, particularly in very short utterances (for example, 'Abou**t** wha**t**?', and 'Wha**t**?'). His vowel sounds, like Jacky's, are rather inconsistent. Overall there is a somewhat nasal quality to his speech, another quality that is often associated with a London accent. One noticeable feature of the scene is that Leonard's accent briefly becomes less standard when he is upset about his brother: he deletes /h/ in 'I told you a **h**undred times' and glottalizes word-final /t/ in the middle of a longer sentence: 'I'd do i**t** before'. This fits with observations by sociolinguists.

For example, William Labov found that if he asked an informant to describe occasions when he felt that his life had been in danger, '[o]ften he becomes involved in the narration to the extent that he seems to be reliving the critical moment' with the result that his speech becomes much more casual and spontaneous (Labov 1966: 107). Overall, this scene suggests that Leonard is particularly careful to avoid stigmatized features such as H-deletion and double negatives, perhaps suggesting that he has become conscious of these linguistic markers through his education.

Vocabulary

Jacky does not use any specifically dialect words, but does use some colloquial phrases, such as 'off my head' and 'starving hungry' as well as the vocative 'Lord!' Leonard does not generally use colloquial vocabulary, although his use of 'starting on' in 'You're not starting on that again' is arguably colloquial. Again, it is noticeable that this happens during his outburst of frustration.

Elsewhere in the film, it is made evident that Leonard can also use a much more formal and Latinate register than he does here. For example, when Helen attempts to send Leonard a large sum of money via her brother Tibby, Leonard returns the cheque with the following letter (which is read in voiceover as he composes it). The scene begins at 1 hour 41 minutes:

'Dear Mr. Schlegel

I acknowledge receipt of your letter dated second of October enclosing a cheque for 5,000 pounds. I am very grateful for your concern, but having no immediate necessity I have the honour to return your cheque herewith.

Yours sincerely, Leonard Bast.'

As the polite formulae of this letter reveal ('acknowledge receipt', 'immediate necessity' and 'herewith') Leonard has the ability to command a formal written register when occasion requires, as might be expected of a clerk. Equally, of course, it is to be expected that he does not use this vocabulary to talk at home when talking to Jacky.

Grammar

Jacky uses several non-standard grammatical features in this scene, including double negatives (e.g. 'do**n't** come home **no** more'), and non-standard subjunctive forms (e.g. 'if you **was** to go and leave me'). By contrast, even when he is upset Leonard still uses the standard form of the subjunctive ('if it **were**n't for my brother'). He also shows that he is conscious of Jacky's grammar: when Jacky uses the double negative 'Well, people do get killed in accidents and do**n't** come home **no** more.' Leonard automatically corrects her: 'Any more, Jacky.'

Film analysis

Following Bordwell and Thompson's seminal book on analysing film, I have here broken the analysis of the scene down into *mise-en-scène*, cinematography, editing and sound (Bordwell and Thompson 2008). Again, when analysing a scene it is worth watching the scene several times, focusing on each aspect in turn.

Mise-en-scène

Mise-en-scène, which means literally 'arranged on stage', refers to everything that appears within the camera shot. This includes the set, the props, the costume, appearance and movement of actors, the lighting and the overall colour scheme. Here are a few things to note about the *mise-en-scène* in this scene from *Howards End*.

The lighting is high-key, with multiple light sources used to create a scene in which everything is clearly illuminated and nothing is in shadow. Indeed, throughout the film the scenes are brightly coloured and composed to create a visually pleasing effect. If you contrast the lighting in this scene with the lighting in the opening scene from *Nil by Mouth* that I discussed in Chapter 1, for example, it is possible to see the difference that lighting can make to the feel and tone of a scene. It is important, however, to note that this is not because more thought has gone into the lighting of *Howards End* than *Nil by Mouth*: a great deal of craft has gone into the lighting of both films, but in the pursuit of very different visual styles.

The scene takes place in Jacky and Leonard's apartment. When Leonard first steps inside the house the primary colour we see is red.

The set has lots of red tones and draped fabric, with highlights of white lace. This creates quite a rich and bohemian impression. Some of the props support this impression. For example, there is plenty of bread, meat and pears on the table, and Jacky eats some of the ham when Leonard declares that he is not hungry. Although the apartment is not cramped, it is shown to be quite small – the dining table and sitting chairs are in the same room, and an unmade bed is visible in the background. All of this underscores the fact that, although the Basts are in no imminent danger of starving to death, their living environment is very different from the airy spaciousness of the Schlegels' apartment from which Leonard has just come.

Finally, there are striking contrasts between the two characters in terms of their appearance. Leonard has just been to a lecture and is wearing a respectable suit and tie. Jacky on the other hand is wearing indoor clothes of a rather bohemian style, with multiple layers of fabric, a heavily cantilevered bosom and lots of jewellery. She has big, frizzy hair that is dyed an unnatural shade of orange. While Leonard appears to be aiming for quiet middle-class respectability, Jacky is loudly less respectable.

Cinematography

Cinematography refers to all the choices made about the way that the camera is used in shooting the scene. This includes the type of film stock used, the framing of shots, the perspective, whether the camera is static or mobile, and the length of shots. Here are a few things to note about the cinematography of this scene.

This is an interior scene between the two characters. The camera is static. The sequence begins with some close-ups of Jacky and Leonard as Leonard enters the room and hangs up his coat. There is then a wide shot as they stand by the table. This wide shot is what allows the viewer to see most of the apartment simultaneously, and to catch a glimpse of the bed in the background. There are then alternate mid-shots of the two of them as Jacky continues to stand at the table, while Leonard sits down and attempts to read his book. Finally there is a midshot of the two of them as Jacky starts by Leonard's feet, teasing him about holes in his socks, then moves up to sit on his knee. This single take lasts for 1 minute 30 seconds, which is significantly longer than any other shot in the sequence. By keeping the camera still while

Jacky progresses slowly up Leonard's knee it focuses attention on the physical interaction between them.

Editing

This refers to the way in which shots are put together in a sequence. Editing can create a particular rhythm to a scene, establish spatial and temporal relationships between shots and above all create a sense of logical continuity for the viewer (or sometimes a deliberate sense of discontinuity).

In the case of this scene it is worth noting that it occurs immediately after we have seen Leonard striding through some dark, blue-toned scenes. The cut to the red-toned interior scenes immediately alerts us to the fact that he has arrived home, and helps to establish a sense of warmth and interiority as opposed to the cold outdoors. The way in which the scenes are edited together maps out the space of the apartment: as I have already noted, the wide shot of the apartment allows us to get an understanding of the space within which Jacky and Leonard live.

Sound

The soundtrack of the film includes the dialogue, the nonverbal noises and any music. Sometimes sounds have a visible onscreen source. For example, we see that Jacky is wearing a lot of jewellery and we hear it jingling as she moves. At other times their source may be offscreen, but the fact that we can hear them provides information about the setting of the scene or offscreen activity. In the case of this scene, for example, we see a train and hear the noise of it as Leonard walks home, and we also hear such noises as he hangs up his coat even though we can no longer see the train. This informs us that the apartment is close to the railtrack, suggesting that this is not a 'good' location. Sound can be an important part of editing, alerting the viewer to something that is about to happen (e.g. there is a noise of a car offscreen and then a car appears) or indicating that something is continuing even if it is no longer in-shot (as in the case of the trains).

The use of music in a film is a significant academic field in its own right. As I discussed in the previous chapter, film analysts draw a distinction between music with an onscreen source (diegetic music) and music from outside the world of the film (extra-diegetic music). There is no music playing during this scene from *Howards End*, although it is used frequently throughout the film. Diegetic music occurs during the wedding of Percy and Evie, and extra-diegetic music is used to heighten the emotional impact of the scene on the river between Helen and Leonard later in the film. The composer of the film's score, Richard Robbins, made use of two piano pieces by the Edwardian composer Percy Grainger in addition to his own compositions to create a score in keeping with the period setting of the film.

Putting it all together

As the film shows, Leonard is teetering on the brink of outright poverty, as evidenced by his small flat in a poor location. Leonard's style of speech suggests that he is someone who yearns for middle-class respectability and stability, but that he struggles to maintain his claims to such status. Most of the time, he is fussily pedantic about grammar and stigmatized variables such as H-deletion. Nevertheless, the fact that when he is surprised or angered some stigmatized features appear in his speech suggests that these features may be a part of his 'natural' variety of English, and that the more formal speech he employs the rest of the time is a later acquisition.

In some ways, Jacky appears to come from a similar background to Leonard: her father was 'a clerk in an export business', which implies that in marrying a bank clerk she is marrying within her social class. However, Jacky shows none of Leonard's concern with avoiding stigmatized variables, and she makes no response to his attempt to 'improve' her grammar. Taken together with her flamboyant style of dress, this suggests that she is much less concerned with acquiring the trappings of middle-class culture than he is, despite her insistence that Leonard 'make it all right' by marrying her.

Dialect also provides some insight into their relationship. Jacky evidently irritates Leonard with her demands for attention when he would rather be reading, although there is also some warmth between them and they are physically affectionate. However, the differences in their styles of dress and their styles of speech signals that there is a gulf between them in terms of social identity and aspirations, and this is of course underscored by their language. An interesting feature to note about this scene is that, although the two of them are alone, they both resolutely stick to their own linguistic identities: there is no evidence of aligning their speech with each other. For example, even when Jacky is attempting to engage Leonard's attention, she still deletes /h/ from 'If there's **h**oles in your socks' and when joining in with Leonard's indignation about his brother she uses the non-standard subjunctive 'if you **was** to go and leave me' even though it is apparent from the scene as a whole that Leonard can be very pedantic about such points. Conversely, even though Leonard is attempting to mollify Jacky after coming home late, he still corrects her grammar. From a sociolinguistic perspective, this is rather odd behaviour: as I shall discuss further in Chapter 9, we would expect two people in close proximity to take on aspects of each other's speech. From a ficto-linguistic perspective, however, this decision to draw a clear line between the language varieties of the two characters makes sense: Leonard's pedantic speech with occasional slips sketches in a lot of information about his character, background and aspirations, while the difference between his speech and Jacky's reinforces the sense of the wide gulf that lies between them.

Broadening the perspective: critical questions

A major critical question that exists for the film *Howards End* is whether it should be read as a conservative drama which celebrates English culture and countryside as timeless and stable, or as a more politically engaged piece of filmmaking that tackles issues of identity and change. In his extended study of the politics, marketing and reception of the film, Andrew Higson outlines these two approaches to the film as follows: 'On the one hand, there is this potentially conservative "surface of elegant gentility". On the other hand, if we probe beneath the surface, we find a much darker narrative exploring social inequities of the period in a way that makes the film relevant to the 1990s' (Higson 2003: 184). According to Higson, the visual qualities of the film – its painstaking attention to period details and costumes, its obsessive framing of English landscapes and houses, its beautiful cinematography – promote a conservative reading of the film, and it was this kind of reading which much of the marketing of the film tended to encourage. However, a focus on the narrative of the film highlights the fact that much of the apparently time-less Englishness of the film rests upon change and hybridity. Higson writes:

By the end of the film, a new, national community has been imagined, potentially consensual, but clearly a hybrid intermixing of different social groups. New class liaisons have been established, and new social groups have been invited into the centre of this community, to inhabit and inherit Howards End – and England. Other social groups, previously central, have been marginalized. Thus the errant sister, now a single parent, is in, as is her illegitimate son from her union with the lower class Leonard Bast.

(Higson 2003: 150–1)

Higson declines to choose between these two possible readings of the film, concluding instead that the film is 'multivalent'. Indeed, he argues, it was the fact that the film could mean different things to different parts of the audience that enabled such a small and apparently niche-market film to become a broad commercial success.

How might a focus on language variety help to address the question of whether the film of *Howards End* should be read as a conservative or more radical piece of filmmaking? The first point to make is that in *Howards End* the range of social classes depicted is very narrow. This is not a film that is concerned with the lives of the very rich or the very poor. The Schlegels and Wilcoxes are certainly wealthy, but they have no pretensions to gentility, and while Howards End is a desirable country property, it is not particularly ostentatious. At the other end of the social spectrum within the film, the Basts are far below the Schlegels and Wilcoxes but they do not belong to the labouring classes: Leonard has a white-collar job in a bank and his wife does not appear to do paid work. Servants are periodically depicted in the film, but they appear mainly to offer refreshments to the Wilcoxes and Schlegels, and they hardly ever speak. One exception occurs when the Schlegels' housekeeper, Annie, informs Margaret that someone is at the door. This turns out to be Jacky looking for Leonard under the mistaken impression that he must be visiting the Schlegels. The scene starts at 45 minutes 30 seconds:

ANNIE:	There's a woman to see you ma'am.
TIBBY:	A woman and not a lady, Annie?
ANNIE:	She won't give her name.
MARGARET:	Ask her to come up.
ANNIE:	She says she won't come up.
MARGARET:	Then we shall have to go down.

Annie speaks in short, matter-of-fact sentences, with some features of London English (for example, she deletes /h/ in 'She won't give her name'). However, far from being at all dissatisfied with her position in life, this interchange with Margaret reveals Annie to be very class conscious, labelling the visitor pejoratively as a 'woman' rather than a 'lady'. By contrast, Margaret shows considerable politeness towards Jacky in the ensuing scene, and refers to Jacky as a 'lady' when talking about her afterwards. It is typical of the film as a whole that, on this rare occasion when a servant gets to speak, she proves to be even more conservatively defensive of the social order than her employers. Indeed, Annie's views align her with Henry Wilcox who, after a brief encounter with Leonard at the Schlegels' London home, suggests to the Schlegels that 'Your servants should not let such people in.'

The narrowness of the range of social classes represented in the film means that the range of different varieties of English represented is also quite narrow, being comprised chiefly of the Standard English and Received Pronunciation of the Schlegels and Wilcoxes, and the more London English of Jacky and Leonard. Nevertheless, as I have shown, differences in dialect are employed in the film to indicate differences between characters. Leonard's encounters with the Schlegels provide further examples of the interaction between speakers of different dialects. When Leonard makes his first visit to the Schlegels in order to retrieve his umbrella the Schlegels attempt to be welcoming, but he finds them overwhelming and quickly retreats. During this visit Margaret gives him her card, which Jacky later finds. When Leonard then goes missing one night (he is in fact walking in a wood looking at stars) Jacky assumes that he must be with the Schlegels, and calls on them to try to retrieve him. Leonard then makes a second visit to the Schlegels' house in order to try to clear up the confusion and embarrassment caused by Jacky's visit. This time, rather than attempting to persuade Leonard to stay by offering him hospitality, Helen challenges him about some of the inconsistencies in his story, which prompts Leonard to say rather more in his defence. The scene starts at 49 minutes:

| MARGARET: | Oh, I see. So the mistake arose out of my card, did it? The lady who called here yesterday thought that you were calling as well and that she would find you here. |
| LEONARD: | In the afternoon, I said to my wife ... I said to Mrs. Bast, 'I have to pay a call on some friends.' |

and Mrs. Bast said to me 'Do go.' But while I was gone, she wanted me, on important business, and thought I had come here, owing to the card and I beg to tender my apologies and hers too for any inconvenience we may have caused you.

MARGARET: None at all, truly.

HELEN: I still don't understand. When did you say you paid this call, this afternoon call?

LEONARD: In the afternoon, of course.

TIBBY: Saturday afternoon or Sunday?

LEONARD: Saturday.

HELEN: Really? And you were still calling on Sunday when your wife came here? A long visit.

MARGARET: It was very good of you to come and explain, Mr. Bast. The rest is naturally no concern of ours. We are going to go upstairs for coffee. I do hope that you will join us. Annie, pour the coffee, please.

LEONARD: It's not what you think. I was … I left my office and walked. Right out of London. I was walking all Saturday night.

HELEN: All night? In the dark?

LEONARD: Got so dark I couldn't see my own hand.

MARGARET: Mr. Bast you must be a born explorer.

LEONARD: I tried to steer by the Pole Star but once outdoors everything gets so mixed and I lost it.

HELEN: Don't tell me about the Pole Star. I know its little ways. It goes round and round and you go round with it.

To begin with Leonard uses a similar variety of English when talking to the Schlegels as he does when talking to Jacky, apparently carefully policing his speech to minimize the appearance of low-prestige markers such as H-deletion and T-glottalization. He also introduces some polite formulae into his speech, such as 'I beg to tender my apologies and hers too for any inconvenience we may have caused you.' In the context of a face-to-face discussion, these formulae, which are more appropriate to a written rather than spoken mode, sound stilted and even slightly comic. When Leonard is finally pressed into offering the real explanation as to where he was, more London English features appear in his speech, just as during his outburst about his brother when talking to Jacky. For example, he glottalizes word-final /t/ in 'I left my office and walked. Right out of London' and realizes /ŋ/ as [n] in 'walking all Saturday night'. At one level the effect of this is to point up the social differences between Leonard and the Schlegels. However, it is also at this moment that Leonard connects with the Schlegels and gains their full attention: the following scene sees Leonard ensconced in their drawing room, talking animatedly with them about literature. This points towards an underlying irony about Leonard's speech: when he tries to use the kind of English he believes appropriate for talking to the Schlegels, he only succeeds in sounding stiff and uncomfortable. When he speaks in what appears to be his more 'natural' variety of English, a more interesting and authentic version of him appears.

Dialect is used in *Howards End* to highlight the impossibility of Leonard's position. He longs to participate in middle-class culture and yet is excluded both by his financial situation, which denies him the necessary leisure time, and by his social standing, which makes it difficult to converse even with the sympathetic Schlegels on equal terms. His determination to better himself means that he sounds pedantic compared to Jacky, but uncomfortable and strained compared to the Schlegels. His accent provides a constant reminder that no matter how many lectures he attends, or how much Ruskin he reads, the social gap between him and the Schlegels will always remain. At the end of the film this problem is translated into a visual image: when Leonard suffers his heart attack, he grasps hold of a bookcase for support, which then topples over on top of him so that he dies amid a rain of books. Leonard is quite literally finished off by the weight of unattainable middle-class culture.

In many ways, therefore, the film offers an analysis of the problem of a class-bound society, but it offers no solution. However much it may be tempting to read the film as being about hybridity and change, it is also about the fixity of class relations. Leonard is locked out of both the financial and cultural wealth of the Schlegels. 'The poor are poor,' says Henry Wilcox in the film, 'one feels sorry for them, but there it is.' The film does not endorse Henry's position, but it offers no better solution either. Leonard's child will eventually inherit Howards End but, unlike Higson, I find it difficult to read this as any kind of lower-class victory. The child may have a mixed social parentage, but it will be raised with all the privileges of class, culture and money that the combined Schlegels and Wilcoxes can offer. There can be no doubt but that the child will speak Standard English with an RP accent.

At the same time, however, the film does hold out some possibility for communication across the classes, particularly in the moments when Leonard's accent shifts when talking to the Schlegels. From a sociolinguistic point of view there is perhaps something rather unexpected about the fact that characters are able to connect most strongly at moments of linguistic divergence, but from a ficto-linguistic point of view within the film it makes sense.

Conclusion

At the start of this chapter, I drew on Kozloff's idea that filmgoers take the position of 'eavesdroppers', listening to dialogue which has been written specifically so that they can comprehend the onscreen action, even as that dialogue disguises its genuine recipients by taking the form of conversation between onscreen characters. Dialect, I argued, is one of the key ways in which dialogue performs this 'double duty', communicating information about characters, relationships and themes. I focused on a single scene from *Howards End* in order to demonstrate how dialect analysis and film analysis can be brought together, before broadening my analysis to the film as a whole. Overall, I found that *Howards End* makes subtle use of dialect to highlight some of the social issues that the film addresses, even if the film does not finally offer a solution to those issues.

In the next chapter I turn to some of the problems inherent in relying upon dialect to fulfil the 'double duty' of screen dialogue. These relate to the fact that, in using dialects to communicate background information about characters, filmmakers can perpetuate negative stereotypes of dialect speakers.

Further reading

Sarah Kozloff's *Overhearing Film Dialogue* (2000) provides an excellent introduction to thinking about the role of language in film, particularly the introduction and first three chapters. Bordwell and Thompson's textbook on the analysis of film, *Film Art: An Introduction* (2008), will provide a solid grounding in the analysis of film.

Exercises

Exercise 1 offers a generic approach to analysing dialect in film and can be applied to any scene. Exercises 2 and 3 suggest scenes from specific films that can be analysed using this approach.

Exercise 1

Choose a scene from a film to explore:

(1) Create a simple transcript of the scene by writing down all the words you can hear and who speaks them.
(2) Watch the scene several times, paying attention to the different dialect elements (accent, vocabulary, grammar). Annotate the text with your findings.
(3) What have you learned about the use of dialect in the film? Which characters use dialect? How do they interact with other characters? Is this use of dialect consistent or does it change?
(4) Now, watch the scene several times, paying attention to the different film elements (*mise-en-scène*, cinematography, editing and sound). Annotate the text with your findings.
(5) What have you learned about the scene as a piece of filmmaking? What is the overall tone of the scene? Which elements contribute to this tone? Are there any important changes during the course of the scene?
(6) Now, think about your two set of annotations together. How does the use of dialect function within the scene as a whole?

Exercise 2

Watch the scene from *Kes* (Loach 1969) where the teacher reads the register and Billy unthinkingly responds with part of the shipping forecast. The scene runs from 10 minutes 40 seconds to 12 minutes 20 seconds. Analyse it in accordance with the approach outlined in Exercise 1 above, but think particularly about these questions:

• In the classroom, how does Billy's accent compare to the teacher's?
• How does Billy's dialect change when he gets out into the corridor and starts talking to his friends?
• Why has Loach chosen to represent dialect in this way?

Exercise 3

Watch the scene from *Four Lions* (Chris Morris 2010) where the potential terrorists survey Faisal's bleach stockpile. The scene runs from 21 minutes to 22 minutes 50 seconds. (N.B. this scene was released online as part of the marketing for the film, so it is easy to find on YouTube, etc.) Analyse it in accordance with the procedure outlined in Exercise 1 above, but think particularly about these questions:

- There are two different cameras present – the film camera plus onscreen videoing by one of the team. How does the film make use of the two sets of footage?
- What different dialects can you hear? You might in particular think about the relationship between ethnicity and region, Northern British English versus Southern British English.
- Faisal attempts to perform a series of different identities. Can you hear any change in his dialect as he does so?
- Why has Morris chosen to represent dialect in this way?

4

Stereotyping and film

As I discussed in Chapter 1, language variety is often used by filmmakers to quickly sketch in character. I quoted from Sarah Kozloff, who writes that 'Recognizable, clichéd dialects are used on-screen to sketch in a character's past and cultural heritage' (Kozloff 2000: 82) and Rosina Lippi-Green who writes that 'film uses language variation and accent to draw character quickly, building on established preconceived notions associated with specific loyalties, ethnic, racial or economic alliances' (Lippi-Green 1997: 81). As well as being descriptive of film's use of dialect, these quotations should also alert us to a potential problem with the use of accent to sketch in character, which is that such use can quickly slide into stereotyping. As both Kozloff and Lippi-Green recognize, the varieties that films use are often considerably indebted to tradition: they are 'clichéd' and rely upon 'established preconceived notions'. Over-reliance upon such linguistic clichés often goes hand-in-hand with crude stereotyping of particular social groups. Kozloff writes:

> Thus, screen dialects lead directly into the problems of stereotyping. Hollywood cannot be charged with inventing this ill (vaudeville and radio skits are even more blatant in their racial and ethnic carica-tures), but the film industry has exacerbated negative stereotypes, and instead of being sensitive to the accuracy of non-standard dialects, movies have historically exploited them to represent char-acters as silly, quaint, or stupid.
>
> (Kozloff 2000: 82)

In the following sections, I consider this problem of stereotyping more fully. First, I make the point that for various reasons associated with the production and consumption of film, completely true-to-life accents are never captured on film. Then I offer a basic definition of stereotyping, and I argue that when it comes to dialect in films there are two different issues to address: the representation of some groups of characters as 'silly, quaint, or stupid' (character stereotyping) and the inaccurate rendering of non-standard dialects by films (linguistic stereotyping). As Kozloff suggests, these two issues are often tied together because linguistic stereotyping feeds directly into character stereotyping. Nevertheless, as I shall argue, it is useful to recognize them as two separate phenomena because they require different modes of analysis, and may at times operate separately. I focus on a scene from *Four Weddings and a Funeral* (Newell 1994) in order to consider the extent to which the use of language variety in this scene shows simply characterization, or might be considered to be an instance of stereotyping through language.

The limits of dialect representation in film

Before discussing the issue of stereotyping it is important to recognize that there are some very genuine limitations on how accurate filmmakers are able to be in representing dialects in film. Broadly speaking these can be divided into production issues, reception issues, and the general 'tidying up' of real language that takes place in film scripts.

Firstly, practical production issues limit the extent to which complete accuracy can be achieved. A major issue concerns the original accents of the actors in question. Filmmaking is expensive, and investors want to maximize the chance of achieving a return on their money. This often means the casting of 'star' actors into major roles, and those 'star' actors may be cast into roles which require a dialect very different from their own natural voice. While dialect coaches will work with actors to help them to produce the desired accent, the success of such coaching depends upon the time and money available to spend on the project, as well as the natural aptitude of the actor to acquire a new accent as required.

Secondly, filmmakers may choose not to aim for a fully accurate rendition of dialect speech because of audience comprehension. For example, there is a scene in the film *The Full Monty* where four unemployed steelworkers sit around chatting in a job centre (Cattaneo 1997). I analysed this scene in seminars with my students for several years before one of my Sheffield-born students pointed out something to me that I had never noticed: that while there is nothing really wrong with the actors' dialect performances, all of their dialects are much closer to Standard English than would be the case in real life. As she pointed out, if four ex-steelworkers were really having a private conversation, listeners from outside Sheffield would find it very difficult to understand what they were saying. The filmmakers have chosen to strike a balance between allowing the characters to speak with enough of a dialect to sound convincing, while still being comprehensible to a national (and indeed international) audience. A useful way to think about this balance is in terms of Allan Bell's 'Audience Design' framework, which he originally formulated to explain why newsreaders changed their style of speech depending upon which radio station they were broadcasting on. Bell argued that was because style is essentially interactive and social, so that even though the radio audience were not physically present, the newsreaders still adapted their speech style to suit their intended audiences (Bell 1984). As Kozloff notes, speakers in films have two audiences: their onscreen interlocutors and the offscreen audience. Hence any performance must be a compromise, designed to suit both audiences.

Kozloff discusses some of the difficulties inherent in finding a suitable compromise between authenticity and comprehension in relation to foreign languages. She notes that in films foreign languages are often recast into English 'spiced with some of the accent and idioms of the original language to foreground the fact that the characters are foreign' (Kozloff 2000: 81). This practice can easily be criticized as Anglo-American cultural imperialism, but, as Kozloff argues, the alternative is not always preferable:

> In David Lean's *Bridge on the River Kwai* (1957), the brutal Japanese commandant of the prisoner of war camp, who (rather unrealistically) speaks perfect English, is a major character, and the audience is encouraged to develop some measure of understanding for his predicament. However, in Michael Cimino's *The Deer Hunter* (1978), when the protagonists are captured and tortured by a group of Viet Cong, the latter's dialogue is left totally untranslated. The foreign dialogue serves primarily as a marker of Otherness, and the fact we, like the American characters, don't understand anything that the Vietnamese characters are wildly 'jabbering' further vilifies them.
>
> (Kozloff 2000: 81)

Presenting foreign characters as speaking in foreign languages may appear to be a culturally sensitive choice, but in practice it can create barriers between the foreign characters and the audience, because viewers feel alienated by the fact that they do not understand what is being said. As Kozloff notes, an alternative is to use subtitles, which she argues 'allow foreign languages their integrity and expressiveness, while still preserving the dialogues' narrative functions' (Kozloff 2000: 81).

In the case of non-standard varieties of English, giving characters such strong dialect that audiences may find it incomprehensible can similarly create barriers between the characters and the audience. At times this may be played for laughs, as happened with the film *Hot Fuzz* where one of the farmers speaks in such a strong rural accent that cannot be understood by either his onscreen listeners or most of the offscreen audience (Wright 2007). Most of the time, however, filmmakers prefer to avoid the situation where the audience do not understand what a character is saying. In some cases, different versions of a film may be released in different parts of the world in order to ensure that the language is comprehensible. For example, some of the dialogue in the film version of *Trainspotting* (Boyle 1996) was re-recorded by the actors in order to make the Glaswegian accents more accessible to an American audience (Smith 2002: 22). An alternative option is to use subtitling, which was apparently considered for the American release of *Trainspotting*. However, subtitling itself presents at least two further difficulties: first, audiences can be resistant to subtitling because it splits the attention between the visual image and the text at the bottom (this is particularly true of Anglophone audiences who are often unaccustomed to watching subtitles); and second, subtitling can be perceived as an insult to the dialect group in question because it implies that their variety is as incomprehensible as a foreign language. For example, when the speech of Scottish trawlermen was subtitled by the BBC in a 2006 documentary, it created outcry in the Scottish parliament, with one MSP demanding that if Scottish dialects were to be subtitled by the BBC, all dialects of English should be subtitled, including, for example, *EastEnders* ('Subtitle Decision "Puzzles" Scots', 2006). If the makers of *The Full Monty* had chosen to represent the characters as speaking with very strong Sheffield accents and then subtitled the dialogue it would undoubtedly have created a similar public outcry in Yorkshire. By employing a variety which references the target dialect but is still comprehensible to a general audience the filmmakers avoided such problems.

Finally, it should be borne in mind just how different most film speech as a whole is from real-life conversation. Take for example this broad transcription of a real mealtime conversation between four people. Andrew and Barbara are the hosts and they have invited their friends, Chris and Diane, round to dinner. I have used | to indicate an interruption.

Barbara	right, who wants – erm – trifle
Chris & Diane	yeah
Andrew	trifle	
Barbara	|right there's – erm – ice cream there – don't know what that little bit of red stuff is on it [laughing] probably from the last time we had the ice-cream [general laughter]
Andrew	right – can't really see too much what's going on there cause there's rather a lot of – erm – ger- do you want some of this
Chris	ooh yeah
Andrew	have that bit to start off with then we'll see if you want some more cause it's all so covered over it's a bit difficult	to tell what you're
Barbara	|oh it is you can|
Andrew		dishing out
Chris	wow that looks good

There are several ways in which this differs from film dialogue, most of which derive from the fact that everyday speech is unplanned and spontaneous. For example, there are several pauses and several uses of 'erm' to fill in a pause while the speaker thinks of the next word. There are two points when Andrew and Barbara speak at the same time as they both try to take charge of serving the dinner: Andrew comes in to say something about trifle but stops as it becomes clear that Barbara has not finished speaking; Barbara starts to say something about the pudding but then stops in turn as Andrew continues speaking. Andrew switches topic mid-utterance: he begins to explain why he is finding it difficult to serve the pudding, but without completing this utterance he then asks his guests if they want some. There is also some repetition: for example, Andrew twice mentions the fact that there's something covering the rest of the pudding although he does not specify what it is.

By contrast, the dialogue in the scenes from most if not all of the films I discuss in this book are much tidier: there are few pauses, few erms, no overlaps, no one gets stuck for a word, and each sentence is complete and coherent without obvious repetition. These differences arise partly for practical reasons (in most cases the actors are working from a written script that they have memorized, so it is unsurprising to find that their speech has quite a 'written' quality), partly for narrative reasons (the hesitancies, repetitions and overlaps make everyday speech both longwinded and difficult for a non-participant to follow: film dialogue tends to streamlines matters so that the main plot point of a particular scene is arrived at quickly and clearly); and partly for aesthetic reasons (there is a general audience expectation that dialogue, particularly in comedies, is fast-moving and delivers regular laughs). A counter-example to this is provided in a scene from *Four Weddings and a Funeral* when Charles declares his love for Carrie. In this case, the hesitancies, repetitions and digressions are played up beyond those normally found in everyday speech in order to create a comic moment. However, this hesitancy is still a deliberate decision on the part of the filmmakers. As Kozloff reminds us about film language: 'The actual hesitations, repetitions, digressions, grunts, interruptions, and mutterings of everyday speech have either been pruned away, or, if not, deliberately included' (Kozloff 2000: 18). In the case of *Four Weddings and a Funeral*, Charles's hesitations and digressions are a key part of his characterization.

Taken overall, dialects in film will always be some distance removed from dialects in real life. But does this mean that dialects in films will always be guilty of stereotyping?

What is stereotyping?

The subject of stereotyping is a broad one, and it has been approached from a number of different disciplinary perspectives, including psychology, political science, sociology and media studies. A basic definition of stereotyping is that it occurs when a group of people are characterized as possessing a homogeneous set of characteristics on the basis of, for example, their shared race, gender, sexual orientation, class, religion, appearance, profession or place of birth. Stereotypes take a single aspect of a person's identity and attribute a whole set of characteristics to them on the basis of it, presenting these characteristics as being 'natural' and 'innate'. Stereotypes can be enormously influential, colouring the way that we see and understand the people thus stereotyped, as numerous studies have demonstrated. For example, in one study subjects were shown a picture of a basketball player and then asked to rate his abilities on the basis of listening to a commentary of a game he had played in. When the subjects had been shown a picture of an African American player, they typically rated the player as having greater athletic ability and playing a better game than when they were shown a picture of a white player, but they also rated the white player as having greater basketball intelligence and showing more 'hustle'. In other words, the stereotype that African Americans are more athletic but less intelligent than European Americans affected the way that listeners interpreted the basketball match (J. Stone et al. 1997).

Such studies point towards the fact that stereotypes are inflexible. Michael Pickering distinguishes between stereotypes and categories on this basis: 'Categories are not fixed for all time. They can be used flexibly and their designations can be disputed.' Stereotyping, by contrast, 'attempts to deny any flexible thinking with categories' (Pickering 2001: 3). In other words, people do not assess the information they receive in order to judge whether it confirms or contradicts the stereotypes they hold; rather, they unconsciously interpret the information they receive in light of the stereotype. When evidence appears to contradict the stereotype, it is either ignored or treated as though it does fit the stereotype. Pickering argues that one of the reasons for this is because stereotyping is fundamentally about power. He writes: 'The comfort of inflexibility which stereotypes provide reinforces the conviction that existing relations of power are necessary and fixed' (Pickering 2001: 3). For example, if a society broadly accepts the stereotype that people of black African descent are better at sport but less intelligent than people of white European descent, then that society will be less inclined to look for social and economic explanations as to why people of black African descent are underrepresented in well-paid professional jobs, and will be less likely to try to take action to challenge the status quo.

Language variety is one of the ways in which such stereotypes can be triggered. As I discussed in Chapter 2, 'matched guise' tests demonstrate that listeners have strong associations between particular varieties of English and the personal qualities of individuals. This explains why filmmakers find language variety such a convenient tool for sketching in character background: it exploits the audience's existing preconceptions about the people who use that variety. However, it also explains why using language variety in this way can so quickly slide into character stereotyping.

Stereotyping and *Four Weddings and a Funeral?*

63. INT. CHARLES'S BEDROOM. DAY.

His door opens. It is Scarlett. She carries a tray.

SCARLETT: Morning, Charles – breakfast's up. Sorry it's a bit burnt.

Charles wakes. They both settle down to breakfast on his bed, eating toast and sipping tea.

SCARLETT: What are you up to today?

CHARLES: I'm taking advantage of the fact that for once in my entire life it's Saturday and I don't have a wedding to go to. All I have to do is not be late for David.

Charles opens a big white letter.

SCARLETT: I thought I might go for a job. There's this new shop called Spank that wants a sales assistant. I think I'd be great. They sell all this funny rubber stuff.

CHARLES: O no – another wedding invitation. And a list – lovely!

SCARLETT: They say rubber's mainly for perverts – I don't know why – I think it's very practical actually. I mean you spill anything on it and it just comes off. I suppose that could be why the perverts like it. Are you all right?

Charles isn't concentrating. He's thrown by the contents of the invitation.

CHARLES: Yes ... It's that girl ... Carrie – remember? The American ...

(Curtis 2006: 58–9).

Note: this is taken from the published screenplay. It is very close to the onscreen dialogue in the finished film, except that Hugh Grant uses rather more 'erms' than are represented here. In the film, the scene starts at around 55 minutes 30 seconds.

Four Weddings and a Funeral (Newell 1994) was one of the most successful British films of all time. Although it was made on a small budget, it went on to take over 200 million dollars worldwide, and it remains popular today. It focuses on Charles (Hugh Grant) and his group of friends as they attend the eponymous four weddings and a funeral. The above scene takes place between Charles and his flatmate Scarlett (Charlotte Coleman). It is an interior scene, primarily shot with a fixed camera which is positioned at the end of the bed that Charles is sleeping on. Charles's slumbering form visually parallels the previous scene, where he left Carrie (Andie McDowell) sleeping after they had spent the night together. There is, however, a change in colour. The scene with Carrie had a warm, apricot hue to it, where the scene in Charles's bedroom has a blue, slightly cold hue, hinting at a shift back to reality from the romance of the previous scene. Charlotte enters with the tray and she sets down on the end of the bed. She kneels on the floor to pour the tea and spread the toast. Charles props himself up on one elbow. This means that they are at equal height, in midshot, and each fills approximately half the screen. When Charlotte asks 'Are you all right?' the shot changes to a close-up of Charles's face, indicating that he is shaken by the fact that the wedding invitation is from Carrie.

A noticeable visual aspect of this scene is that although they are physically close they are not directly looking at each other. Charlotte is focused on the breakfast, with only an occasional sideways glance at Charles. Charles is focused on the letter he has received. This means that although this is potentially a very intimate scene – Charles is in bed and his torso at least is naked – there is no suggestion that they are physically attracted to one another. This point is further underscored by the fact that Charlotte is wearing a baggy and very brightly coloured striped jumper, with denim dungarees over the top. It is not an outfit that hints at sexual availability.

Throughout the film much of the characterization of Charles and Scarlett is achieved through their contrasting accents. We learn little directly about Charles's social or economic background. We know that he has a deaf brother, that he went to Cambridge, that he has had a series of neurotic girlfriends, and that he attends lots of weddings, but we are told nothing about where he comes from or what he does for a living. We do, however, know about his language variety, which is Standard English spoken with an RP accent. In the above scene, for example, Charles pronounces phrases such as 'it's Saturday' and 'that girl' with no evidence of glottalization on the /t/; he articulates the

/h/ in '**h**ave'; and he pronounces the final consonants in 'taki**ng**' and 'weddi**ng**' as nasal velars [ŋ]. There is no evidence of non-standard vocabulary or grammar in his speech. It is also worth noting that he speaks in quite a high register, despite the fact that he's just woken up: his vocabulary is Latinate ('advantage', 'entire') and his grammar complex and formal (note in particular the sentence 'I'm taking advantage of the fact that for the first time in my entire life it's Saturday and I don't have a wedding to go to'). This language variety serves to fill in some of this missing background, strongly suggesting that his upbringing was a privileged one, and hinting that he can afford to live in his beautiful flat and attend expensive weddings because he has inherited wealth.

A possible danger for filmmakers of giving a central character like Charles such a 'posh' accent is that audiences may not warm to the character. As I noted in Chapter 2, matched guise studies have demonstrated that RP speakers may be perceived by listeners as intelligent and educated, but not as trustworthy or friendly. In the case of Charles, however, his RP accent is balanced by the fact that he is clearly not very wealthy: his car is shabby and he is horrified at being asked to pay £3,000 for a wedding gift. More importantly, however, his manner is extremely diffident. This shows up in his language, particularly in the way that he often has difficulty starting sentences. At the same time, his discourse strategies tend to be excessively polite and indirect. As I have already discussed, when he declares his love for Carrie midway through the film the declaration is so hedged about and indirect that she does not seem to be quite sure what he has just said. The effect of this is comic, and it plays up the stereotype of the polite Englishman to absurdity. However, it also works to assert Charles's sincerity. Filmgoers are accustomed to lead characters who speak without pause, repetition or digression. In breaking those conventions, Charles seems more honest. Furthermore, it again underscores the fact that, despite his privileged background and circle of friends, Charles lacks self-confidence, and as such it invites the audience to feel sympathy for him.

In the case of Scarlett the audience knows that she has an unsuccessful romantic history and attends lots of weddings. However, as the breakfast scene reveals, she does undertake paid employment, even though the fact she says that she 'thought she might go for a job' rather than 'thought she might go for a **new** job' implies that she is not currently working. In fact, on the basis that she shares a flat with Charles and also attends lots of upmarket weddings despite only occasional and poorly paid employment as a shop assistant, it might be deduced that she too has inherited wealth. Her variety of English makes this seem unlikely, however. Scarlett speaks Standard English, but with a noticeable London accent, including the frequent glottalization of word-final /t/ in phrases such as 'a bit burnt' and 'What are you up to'; the realization of the final phoneme in 'Morning' as an alveolar [n] rather than velar nasal [ŋ] and the vocalization of the /l/ in 'spill anything' so that it is realized as [spiʊ] ('spiw'). She also engages in rather more elision than Charles, with the phrases 'was going to go' and 'don't know why' being reduced to [wəz gənə gəʊ] and [dənəʊ waɪ]. Of course, elision is a natural process that occurs during rapid speech so there's no reason why it should occur more in Scarlett's speech than in Charles's, but it adds to the impression that Scarlett is not as 'well spoken' as Charles. Overall, Scarlett's accent suggests that her upbringing was less privileged than that of Charles, and that she is less likely to have inherited money. The review of the film in *Sight and Sound* notes the apparent mismatch between Scarlett's accent and her social circle: 'Scarlett appears to be a "Sarf" London punkette, so you wonder just how she got in with the independently wealthy crowd' (Myers 1994: 47).

There are of course numerous ways in which Scarlett's friendship with Charles and his group could be explained, and it might be argued that there is something rather snobbish about *Sight and Sound*'s presumption that a real-life Scarlett would find it difficult to 'get in' with them. The film itself makes no attempt to account for the formation of the group, or to explore the implications of their apparently very different backgrounds. Interestingly, one of the deleted scenes on the 2006 Special Edition DVD version of the film reveals that a scene was shot in which Charles tells Carrie how he met his friends. Charles reports that he met Matthew and Fiona at college, Gareth was a professor there, and that he found Scarlett under his kitchen table after a party. The fact that such a scene exists suggests that at some stage the filmmakers considered the need to explain Scarlett's membership of the group, while the fact that the explanation itself proves to be so arbitrary suggests that, as the reviewer for *Sight and Sound* identified, there is no very obvious explanation.

Nevertheless, the fact remains that the language varieties used in the film serve to guide the audience towards making certain assumptions about the characters, and that these varieties were the result of choices, made consciously or otherwise, by the filmmakers. Scarlett is alone in her social group in speaking with a variety that does not immediately suggest that she comes from an upper-middle-class background (Matthew speaks with a Scottish accent, but it is an educated middle-class Scottish accent). It seems plausible, in fact, to argue that the character of Scarlett was included because the group of friends might otherwise appear unattractively elitist. In an article that attempted to account for the international success of the film, Nick Roddick suggested that 'some of the film's appeal has to do with the broad range of characters'(Roddick 1995: 15). However, if Scarlett were to be subtracted from the film, that 'broad range of characters' would narrow sharply. The filmmakers have relied on the fact that, rather than questioning with *Sight and Sound* how such a character came to be part of this crowd, the audience will instead receive the general impression that Charles's friends are a socially diverse group.

Does this mean that the character of Scarlett is being negatively stereotyped, and that one of the ways this is signalled is through the language variety she uses? She is certainly a sympathetic character, but it is difficult to argue against the charge that her London accent goes hand-in-hand with her being represented as, if not silly, quaint or stupid exactly, certainly less serious and less intelligent than most of the other characters. For a start, she is repeatedly shown as lacking the verbal dexterity of the other characters. When Gareth suggests to her in one scene that her purple and orange wedding outfit is symbolic of a union between heathen and Christian traditions, Scarlett's response is baffled and uncertain. At the same time she is portrayed as being open and unworldly to the point of being clueless. Her discussion of the practicality of wearing rubber in the scene cited above is one example, as is the scene in which, after a cancelled wedding, she asserts that the disappointed bride will find her lovely wedding dress useful for parties. It is telling that in both of these instances the audience is invited to laugh *at* her rather than *with* her: she herself is unaware that what she says might be considered humorous. By contrast, although Charles has a talent for saying the wrong thing at the wrong time, he is always immediately conscious of what he has done. For example, when he inadvertently reveals to a recently married man it was rumoured his wife was unfaithful before their wedding, the next scene shows him deliberately hitting his head against a marquee pole. With Charles, the comedy arises from identifying with him as he blunders into unfortunate social situations, whereas with Scarlett the comedy arises from feeling superior to her naïve responses to the world.

It should be pointed out, however, that the issue of character stereo-typing through language variety is perhaps not as clear-cut as I have so far presented. For example, admirers of *Four Weddings and a Funeral* might reasonably point out that the character of Tom (played by James Fleet) is also presented as being less serious and less intelligent than other characters, despite the fact that he is an RP speaker who is described in the film as being one of the richest men in England. (Of course, it may be argued that the posh-but-dim upper-class twit is another stereotype, albeit one that does not serve to reinforce social inequalities in the same way.) Overall, it is not the case that all the standard speakers in the film are smart and articulate, while all non-standard speakers are dense and incoherent. Does this mean that the association between Scarlett's accent and character should be understood as accidental and without broader social meaning?

This is an issue that Rosina Lippi-Green sets out to explore in her study of dialect representation in Disney films. She starts with the complaints that were made about the film *Aladdin* by the American Arab Anti-Discrimination Committee, whose representative argued that the film carried the message that people with foreign accents are bad (in the film the 'good' main characters speak standard American English, while many of the 'bad' and minor characters speak with marked foreign accents). Lippi-Green asks 'Is there truth to this suppo-sition? What are children to take away from ... brutal Arabian palace guards? Is it significant that they see bad guys who sound a certain way, look a certain way, and come from a certain part of town or of the world?' (Lippi-Green 1997: 80). In order to investigate whether there is indeed any systematic pattern to the way in which Disney uses language variety to portray character, Lippi-Green reviewed dialect representation in 24 full-length Disney films, amounting to 371 char-acters in total. What she found was that, while it is certainly not the case that all MUSE (Mainstream US English) speakers are 'good' and all dialect speakers are 'bad', there were nevertheless distinct patterns to be found in the films. She writes:

> Characters with strongly positive actions and motivations are over-whelmingly speakers of socially mainstream varieties of English. Conversely, characters with strongly negative actions and motiva-tions often speak varieties of English linked to specific geographical regions and marginalized social groups. Perhaps even more impor-tantly, those characters who have the widest variety of life choices

or possibilities available to them are male, and they are speakers of MUSE or a non-stigmatized variety of British English.

(Lippi-Green 1997: 101)

She concludes: 'Even when stereotyping is not overly negative, it is confining and misleading'(Lippi-Green 1997: 101). What this means is that although it may be argued that the accents of individual characters do not prove that Disney films stereotype through language variety, the overall pattern of language variety in the films suggests that negative stereotyping is occurring. In the same way, although it may be argued that not too much should be read into the character of Scarlett in *Four Weddings and a Funeral*, if that film is placed alongside the other Richard Curtis-scripted romantic comedies *Notting Hill* and *Love, Actually* (not to mention the sitcom that he created and co-wrote, *The Vicar of Dibley*) then a pattern begins to emerge whereby non-standard speaking characters tend to be quirky and endearing but lacking in brains and seriousness.

Linguistic stereotyping

What Lippi-Green does not explore in any detail, however, is *how* language variety is signalled in Disney films. As she states in her methodology section, 'In cases where an actor is clearly contriving an accent, a decision was made as to what language variety was most likely intended to be portrayed. That is, a poorly imitated British (or other foreign) accent was still counted as such for the creators and (most) viewers' (Lippi-Green 1994: 86). Other academics have been more concerned with exploring the question of how films portray language variety. Mary Bucholtz and Quiana Lopez, for example, have explored the way in which European American actors in Hollywood films use African American English (AAE):

> Similar to traditional theatrical minstrelsy, which used dialect performance in addition to blackface and plantation-style clothing in order to perform exaggerated sketches of southern blacks, the indexicalities of white mediatized performances of AAE are produced not only through language but also through European American actors' entire embodied performances of (meta)stylized blackness, including clothing, gestures, facial expressions, and

other semiotic resources stereotypically associated with African American culture … In keeping with dominant mediatized representations of AAE, European American actors' use of variety is typically limited to the non-fluent and often inaccurate use of a restricted set of stereotypical lexical, phonological, and grammatical features.

(Bucholtz and Lopez 2011: 684)

In other words, what is represented as AAE is a narrow and stereotyped caricature of the 'real world' variety, or as Bucholtz puts it in another article 'a stereotyped and highly simplified fiction' (Bucholtz 2011: 259). Bucholtz and Lopez survey the performance of AAE by European American actors in 59 films, and then focus on two films: *Bulworth* (1998) and *Bringing Down the House* (2003). They conclude that the representations of AAE in these films 'not only reduce the linguistic complexity of the variety and reproduce racial divisions but also perpetuate seemingly positive yet essentializing language ideologies of AAE' (Bucholtz and Lopez 2011: 702). Bucholtz and Lopez thus take the argument a step further than Lippi-Green, arguing not only that dialect can be used to stereotype, but showing how a stereotyped performance of dialect can be directly implicated in reinforcing racist ideologies.

Barbara Johnstone, Jennifer Andrus and Andrew E. Danielson have written very interestingly about the way in which people become conscious of dialectal differences, with particular reference to the variety of English spoken in the North American city of Pittsburgh (Johnstone et al. 2006). The article begins with the apparently paradoxical heading 'Why Globalization Collapses Regional Linguistic Distinctions and Creates Regional Dialects' (Johnstone et al. 2006: 79). By this, the authors explain, they mean that an increasingly globalized economy and the resulting need to communicate across wide geographical areas tends to reduce the linguistic differences between regions (a process sometimes described as 'dialect levelling'). But these same factors also mean that people increasingly come into contact with groups of people speaking dialects different to their own, which raises linguistic awareness and makes them particularly conscious of what is distinctive about their own way of speaking. Drawing on the work of both William Labov and Michael Silverstein, Johnstone et al. propose that there are three different levels at which relationships between linguistic form and social meaning exist (in their terms, three different 'orders of indexicality', indexicality being the process by which a particular set of linguistic features become associated with a particular social group). With first-order indexicality, a relationship exists between a group of linguistic features and a particular geographical area, but no one is particularly conscious of it, perhaps because a lack of geographical mobility means that there is nothing to compare the local dialect with. With second-order indexicality, speakers begin to notice some of the linguistic features that make their own dialect distinctive, and to attribute meanings to do with social class and correctness to these features: attention may be drawn in print to the peculiarities of the local dialect, but often only to point out their undesirability. With third-order indexicality, a subset of the linguistic features which are to be found in the local dialect becomes widely recognized as marking that particular dialect, and these linguistic features may be listed together in popular local dialect dictionaries for the area, and it becomes possible for people to reference that dialect simply by using a few features in isolation (in England, for example, 'Away!' pronounced in a specific way signals a Newcastle dialect, while 'a lorra fun' indicates a Liverpudlian dialect). At this point these forms may be said to have become enregistered as typical of that dialect. In fact, it may be that some of the identified linguistic forms have ceased to be current within the geographical area in question, or that they show considerable variability among speakers within the region. As such there is often a mismatch between the actual linguistic practices within a region and the perception of the dialect of that region in the popular imagination. When outsiders from the speech community try to imitate the speech they associate with the area or social group in question, they will often mis-use or over-use the features in question. For example, Bucholtz finds that white Hollywood AAE 'is often liberally peppered with profanities, especially *fucking* and *motherfucker*, which together with many of the slang terms ideologically represents hip hop culture as misogynistic, violent, and aggressive' (Bucholtz 2011: 260).

A revealing example of the kind of problems that swirl around the characterization of such varieties is offered by Quentin Tarantino's film *Pulp Fiction* (1992). When this film was released, Tarantino was criticized by African American film director Spike Lee for the fact that one of his African characters used the word 'nigger' around 50 times in the course of the film. The word 'nigger', unsurprisingly in the light of America's history, is a controversial word. It is deemed highly offensive when used by European Americans in any context, but is used among African Americans to mark in-group identity. At the time of the release of *Pulp Fiction* Lee was reported as saying: 'I'm not against the word, and I use it, but not excessively. And some people speak that way.

But, Quentin is infatuated with that word. What does he want to be made – an honorary black man?' (Archerd 1997). Lee clearly has some doubts about the word, as evidenced by his comment that 'I use it, but not excessively'. What angers him, however, is Tarantino's appropriation of the word, and his feeling that by using it Tarantino is trying to be made an 'honorary black man'. What makes Lee's critique particularly interesting here is the fact that the character in *Pulp Fiction* who uses the word is African American, and was played by African American actor Samuel Jackson. Nevertheless, Lee is made uncomfortable by the fact that he knows that the lines Jackson is speaking were written by a European American. In addition, Lee seems to feel that even by the standards of AAE speakers, Tarantino is overusing the word in his script ('Quentin is infatuated with the word'). This harks back to Bucholtz's point that when AAE is rendered by non-African Americans, what is produced is often 'a stereotyped and highly simplified fiction'. In the case of Tarantino, it might be argued that he has picked up on this single word and over-generalized its use.

Barbra Meek offers a detailed study of the linguistic stereotyping that occurs in the representation of American Indians in fictional film and literature. She argues that there is a speech style that is used in films, television and literature to depict fictional American Indian speech, and she terms it 'Hollywood Injun English' (HIE) (Meek 2006). Features of HIE that she identifies include long, oddly positioned pauses; a lack of tense marking; a lack of contraction; the deletion of various grammatical elements, including determiners, pronouns and auxiliary verbs; specialized vocabulary including 'chief', 'how', 'peace pipe' and 'wampum'; the use of elaborate 'courtly' speech; and the frequent use of metaphors drawn from nature. These linguistic features, Meek argues, present the speakers simultaneously as disfluent, childlike and 'foreign', and as timeless and 'in tune with nature', thus creating a linguistic stereotype of the 'noble savage'. Meek writes:

> this 'abnormal' linguistic style is an iconic representation of real-life American Indian speech that indexes an image of Indians as foreign victims, eloquent yet unsocialized. Additionally, these linguistic images perpetuate the historical placement of Native Americans as characters who exist only in a national past and not in a modern present.
>
> (Meek 2006:121)

Meek further points out that, despite the uniformity implied by HIE, there are in reality many different varieties of English spoken by different communities of real American Indians. While some features of HIE may be found in some varieties of American Indian English, these features are always over-generalized and therefore unrepresentative of any real AIE speech. She concludes that the use of HIE in popular films, television and literature is 'covertly racist' (Meek 2006: 121).

A final example of the way in which a few features of non-standard English can form the basis of a stereotype is provided by the film *Star Wars: The Phantom Menace* (Lucas 1999). The original three *Star Wars* films (*Star Wars*, *The Empire Strikes Back* and *The Return of the Jedi*) were released between 1977 and 1983. In 1999, *The Phantom Menace* was released as the first of a new trilogy of films telling the story leading up to the events of the original three films (thus forming an extended prequel). *The Phantom Menace* was hotly anticipated by audiences and achieved enormous box office success, but critical reception of the film was lukewarm. In particular, hostile commentary quickly focused on the character of Jar Jar Binks, a computer animated character integrated into the live action of the rest of the film. In the film Jar Jar is a swamp-dwelling creature from the planet of Naboo who becomes involved in the main story through a series of accidents. Jar Jar was found to be irritating by many filmgoers, and an unauthorized version of the film with all of Jar Jar's scenes edited out proved popular on the internet. More significantly, however, some critics found the depiction of Jar Jar to be inherently racist and it was argued that the character harked back either to 'Jim Crow' stereotypes of African Americans prevalent in popular culture during the nineteenth and early twentieth centuries, and/or that it uncomfortably echoed popular stereotypes of Jamaicans. Alan Stone, for example, wrote that 'as soon as I saw Jar Jar Binks I knew why my student, an African-American, felt betrayed. Jar Jar Binks, like all fun-loving Gungans, is child-like, spontaneous, has bad table manners, good instincts, and he and all his kind have natural rhythm' (A. A. Stone 1999). Bruce Gottleib found Jar Jar to be a 'childlike sidekick with the unmistakably West Indian accent and enormous buttocks' and described him as 'likable, easygoing, and dumb as dirt'(Gottleib 1999). George Lucas was outraged by this response, arguing that there was no way that an orange amphibian could be a racist portrayal of African Americans (Wheat 2000). The subject became a heated one on internet discussion boards.

I do not intend to resolve this debate here, but I would note that an important aspect of the way in which Jar Jar is characterized is through his speech, as indeed Gottleib argues. An immediately notable feature of Jar Jar's speech is his intonation, which shows a much wider pitch range than the characters with whom Jar Jar interacts. This feature is suggestive of West Indian English. A salient phonological feature is the fact that Jar Jar shows evidence of TH-stopping, that is using the alveolar stops [t] and [d] for the dental fricatives /θ/ and /ð/. This is a commonly observed feature of many non-standard varieties of English, including West Indian English. In terms of vocabulary Jar Jar does not use any non-standard lexical items, but does use some quite Latinate words. Grammatically, one of the key features of Jar Jar's speech is his non-standard first person pronouns, which are puzzlingly inconsistent, as too is his use of auxiliary verbs. He also uses some stigmatized grammatical forms, such as the use of the double superlative. Overall, there is insufficient evidence to conclude that Jar Jar's speech is an attempt to represent the English of any particular social or ethnic group. Elements are present in his speech that can be identified as AAE or West Indian English, but they are used very inconsistently. Even allowing for the fact that, as Bucholtz notes, the representation of a particular language variety in popular culture can result in 'a stereotyped and highly simplified fiction', it is hard to decide exactly what is being stereotyped and simplified here. However, this does not make the representation a benign one. Jar Jar's non-standard English is part of the general depiction of him as a clueless and happy-go-lucky individual, who repeatedly puts the central (and invariably Standard English speaking) characters in danger through his actions, or occasionally rescues them in an equally haphazard manner. His variety of English draws on the varieties of several social and ethnic groups who often find themselves stereotyped in film. While the filmmakers may be able to claim that they did not intend to depict him as belonging to any specific group, the effect is to reinforce negative stereotypes of several groups, and indeed of non-standard English speakers in general.

Does stereotyping language variety = stereotyping character?

In many cases, the stereotyping of a language variety is an integral part of the stereotyping of the speakers of that variety. Bucholtz finds, for example, that when films represent white Hollywood AAE, they typically perpetuate 'both racist language ideologies associated with

AAE and essentialist racialized and gendered stereotypes of blackness and whiteness'(Bucholtz 2011: 259). More generally, it is possible to see that character stereotyping and linguistic stereotyping are often two parts of the same process: the stereotyped characters are (in Kozloff's words) presented as being 'silly, quaint or stupid' and this goes hand-in-hand with their language variety being played for laughs. Once filmmakers begin to rely upon a common stereotype in order to evoke a particular character, the end result is likely to be a stereotyped character, and once a stereotype is being evoked for a character, the temptation exists for filmmakers and writers to employ linguistic stereotyping in order to enhance the effect.

At the same time, however, it is worth considering the two processes – character stereotyping and linguistic stereotyping – separately and to bear in mind that they are not necessarily identical. It is possible, for example, to find an accurate linguistic portrayal that nevertheless presents a negatively stereotyped character, and Scarlett in *Four Weddings and a Funeral* is arguably a case in point. Her London English accent is a fairly accurate depiction of the variety and not of itself exaggerated, stylized or played for laughs. As such, it might be argued that her character is somewhat stereotyped and that her language variety is a part of that stereotyping, but that the language variety itself is not stereotyped. Whether the inverse is possible – a film in which a dialect is stereotyped but not the character who speaks it – is less certain. Certainly in ten years of thinking about this subject I have yet to come across a really good example. This may be because once the viewer has identified stereotypical features in the speech of a character, it becomes hard to think of that character as anything other than a stereotype.

Conclusion

In this chapter I have explored the topic of stereotyping in relation to film. I started from the basic definition that stereotyping occurs when a group of people are characterized as possessing a fixed set of characteristics on the basis of a single aspect of their identity. Taking *Four Weddings and a Funeral* as an example, I argued that dialect-speaking characters in films are often shown to be less serious and less intelligent than Standard English-speaking characters. However, I also argued that it is important to distinguish between the stereo-typing of a dialect itself (where a narrow range of features may be used to represent the dialect) and stereotyping of character (where the character is, in Kozloff's words, presented as 'silly, quaint or stupid'). While linguistic stereotyping and character stereotyping may often occur together, they represent different processes. I return to this issue of stereotyping in Chapter 6 in relation to literary dialect, and in the final chapter on authenticity where I consider the relationship between authenticity and stereotyping more carefully.

In the next chapter, Chapter 5, I turn my attention to literature, exploring how dialect is represented on the page.

Further reading

Michael Pickering's *Stereotyping* (2001) provides an excellent introduction to stereotyping and I particularly recommend Chapters 1 and 2 for those getting to grips with the topic. Rosina Lippi-Green's book *English with an Accent* (1997) has several interesting chapters, and Chapter 5 'Teaching Children to Discriminate' is particularly relevant to this chapter. There are a few excellent articles on film and stereotyping. Barbra Meek's article 'And the Injun goes "How!": Representations of American Indian English in white public space' (2006) offers a very thought-provoking exploration of representations of American Indian English. Park et al.'s article 'Naturalizing Racial Differences Through Comedy: Asian, Black, and White Views on Racial Stereotypes in *Rush Hour 2*' (2006) is not specifically about dialect, but it offers a nuanced account of audience responses to stereotype. Recent articles by Mary Bucholtz ('Race and the re-embodied voice in Hollywood film') and Mary Bucholtz and Quiana Lopez ('Performing blackness, forming whiteness: Linguistic minstrelsy in Hollywood film') draw on some quite advanced linguistic theory to analyse the role of language in white Hollywood performances of AAE (Bucholtz 2011; Bucholtz and Lopez 2011).

Exercises

Exercise 1

Watch the scene in *Dumbo* where the group of crows first find Dumbo asleep (it starts at 49 minutes). Think about the following questions:

1. Do some research to discover the distinguishing features of African American English (AAE). What features of AAE are represented in this scene? How consistently are they used?
2. How does the linguistic representation of the crows relate to other aspects of the scene – e.g. the appearance of the crows, the composition of shots, etc.?
3. You may find it helpful to do some background research into the film. For example, can you discover anything about the actors voicing these characters? Does it matter?
4. In your opinion, is stereotyping occurring in this scene?

Exercise 2

Watch the scene in the diner from *The Princess and the Frog* where Tiana's friends invite her to come dancing with them (it starts around 9 minutes). Think about the following questions:

1. What features of AAE are represented in this scene? How consistently are they used?
2. How does the linguistic representation of Tiana and her friends relate to other aspects of the scene – e.g. the appearance of the characters, the composition of shots, etc?
3. You may find it helpful to do some background research into the film, which was Disney's first film with an African American 'Princess' in the lead role. For example, can you discover anything about the actors voicing these characters? Does it matter?
4. What can you find out about the critical reception of the film?
5. In your opinion, is stereotyping occurring in this scene?

Exercise 3

Watch the scene in the diner from *The Princess and the Frog* where Ray tells the story of his love for Evangeline, and the group are attacked by frog hunters (it starts around 48 minutes 30 seconds). Think about the following questions:

1. Do some research to discover the distinguishing features of Louisiana English. What features of Louisiana are represented in this scene? How consistently are they used?

2. How does the linguistic representation of Ray relate to other aspects of his character – e.g. his appearance, his personality?
3. You may find it helpful to do some background research into this aspect of the film. For example, can you discover anything about the actor who voiced him?
4. How was this character received by audiences? What did people from New Orleans think of him?
5. In your opinion, is stereotyping occurring in this scene?

5

Analysing dialect in literature

The representation of dialects of English in literary texts is considerably better studied than the representation of dialects of English in film. This is for three main reasons. First, the language of literature as a whole is much better studied than the language of film because literature, unlike film, has always been perceived as a verbal rather than visual medium. Second, as I began to outline in Chapter 1, the significant practical challenges involved in representing the audible medium of speech via the visual medium of print means have ensured that it appears as an obvious object of study. Third, written representations of dialects from before the time of sound recording have often attracted the interest of dialectologists who wish to gather evidence for the historical development of dialects.

In this chapter I survey some of the technical considerations underlying the representation of dialect in literature, drawing on the existing literature about literary dialects in order to do so. This survey will fall into two parts: first I will consider *where* dialect occurs and then focus in more detail on *how* it is represented.

Where does dialect occur in fictional texts?

One theorist who did much to focus attention on the way in which different varieties of language appear in literature is Mikhail Bakhtin. His essay 'Discourse in the novel' (written in Russia in the 1930s) challenges the idea that the language of literature is single and unitary. Bakhtin points out that any national language is composed out of multiple different linguistic strata:

> At any given moment in its evolution, language is stratified not only into linguistic dialects in the strict sense of the word ... but

also – and for us this is the essential point – into languages that are socio-ideological: languages of social groups, 'professional' and 'generic' languages, languages of generations and so forth. From this point of view, literary language itself is only one of these heteroglot languages – and in its turn is also stratified into languages.

(Bakhtin 1981: 271–2)

According to Bakhtin, each of these language varieties is associated with a different social group and with a different ideological perspective. Bakhtin terms this multiplicity of language 'heteroglossia' and he argues that any language exists in a state of continual tension between the forces that promote unity of language (which he terms monologia) on the one hand, and the forces of heteroglossia on the other. The novel, he argues, is an inherently heteroglossic form because it is composed of multiple voices, including a narrative voice which adopts and incorporates different styles, as well as the reported speech of different characters. Despite Bakhtin's focus on the novel, heteroglossia is not the sole preserve of the novel: a good example of a heteroglossic poem is 'Them & [uz]' by Tony Harrison, which I discussed in Chapter 2.

For the purposes of this book, I am focusing specifically on regional and social language varieties and I will therefore not be exploring language varieties as broadly as Bakhtin proposes. Nevertheless, Bakhtin's central point, that much literary language is by its nature heteroglossic, provides an important starting point. In the next three subsections I explore the three key places where we find dialect represented in literary texts: direct speech, narrative voice, and free indirect speech. If you are unfamiliar with the terminology used to describe speech and thought presentation (direct speech, indirect speech, etc.) Mick Short's *Exploring the Language of Poems, Plays and Prose* provides a valuable guide (1996, particularly Chapter 10).

Direct speech

Perhaps the most canonical place to find dialect representation in literary texts is in direct speech, as can be seen in this passage from Charles Dickens' *Oliver Twist* (first published 1838):

The boy who addressed this inquiry to the young wayfarer was about his own age, but one of the queerest-looking boys that Oliver had ever seen. He was a snub-nosed, flat-browed, common-faced boy enough; and as dirty a juvenile as one would wish to see; but he had about him all the airs and manners of a man ...

'Hullo, my covey! What's the row?' said this strange young gentleman to Oliver.

'I am very hungry and tired,' replied Oliver, the tears standing in his eyes as he spoke. 'I have walked a long way. I have been walking these seven days.'

'Walking for sivin days!' said the young gentleman. 'Oh, I see. Beak's order, eh? But,' he added, noticing Oliver's look of surprise, 'I suppose you don't know what a beak is, my flash com-pan-ion?'

Oliver mildly replied, that he had always heard a bird's mouth described by the term in question.

'My eyes, how green!' exclaimed the young gentleman. 'Why, a beak's a madgst'rate; and when you walk a beak's order, it's not straightforerd, but always a going up, and nivir a coming down agin. Was you never on the mill?'

(Dickens 1966: 100–1)

When direct speech is used, the speech is typically signalled by the use of speech marks, and introduced by a reporting clause such as here with 'said the young gentleman' and 'exclaimed the young gentleman'. Within these speech marks, literary convention dictates that what is represented is reported verbatim as the person spoke. This means that he uses the first person pronoun 'I' to refer to himself, and the present tense to talk about current events ('Oh, I see', 'I suppose'). It also means – as I shall be exploring in more detail throughout this chapter – that an attempt may be made to capture something of the dialect with which the character speaks, as well as any personal oddities in their speech. This dialectal speech will often contrast sharply with the Standard English of the main narrative. In the passage above the speech of the 'young gentleman' (who proves to be the Artful Dodger) is marked as dialectal through non-standard spelling ('madgst'rate', 'sivin'), grammar ('Was you never') and vocabulary ('covey', 'beak', 'flash'). There is also some attempt to indicate his intonation through punctuation, such as the exclamation marks which indicate emphasis, the question marks which indicate a rising intonation, and the dashes in the word 'com-pan-ion' which presumably indicate that each syllable of the word is sounded out in full.

All of this can be contrasted to the way in which Oliver's speech is reported in this passage, which is given the form of indirect speech as the narrator summarizes what Oliver said, without giving any flavour of how he said it: 'Oliver mildly replied, that he had always heard a bird's mouth described by the term in question.' It might be imagined that Oliver said something like 'I always thought that a beak was a bird's mouth'. As reformulated by the narrator in the text, there is no indication of Oliver's exact phrasing (it is unlikely that any speaker, let alone a young beggar, would use 'the term in question' in conversation), and no hint is provided as to his intonation. The pronouns are third person and the tense has been back-shifted to align with the past tense of the narration as a whole, so that what Oliver actually said, 'I have always heard', becomes 'he had always heard'. In short, whereas the representation of the Artful Dodger's speech attempts to give an indication of how it sounds, Oliver's speech is summarized for content alone.

The overall effect of this use of dialect representation in direct speech is that the dialect speech is differentiated from the Standard English of the main narrative voice. This nearly always creates a sense of hierarchy: the dialect speech is 'other' and its peculiarities are highlighted, while the main narrative work is conducted in Standard English.

Narrative voice

Another common place to find dialect representation in literary texts is in the narrative voice. There is a long history in English Literature of narrators who use non-standard English, going back to at least Maria Edgeworth's *Castle Rackrent* (first published 1800), which is narrated by the 'illiterate old steward' Thady Quirk (Edgeworth 1992: 62). It is common in this kind of narration for the narrator to be a named character in the story who relates events of which they have personal knowledge. The effect is often highly oral, as if the narrator were speaking directly to the reader. Another example of a dialectal narrator can be seen in Thomas Hardy's short story, 'Absent-Mindedness in a Parish Choir', which is one of the series of interlinked short stories that make up the longer tale *A Few Crusted Characters*, each individual story being recounted by passengers on a carrier van. *A Few Crusted Characters* as a whole is framed by the voice of a third person narrator in Standard

English, who sets the scene and introduces the characters at the beginning, and draws the overall narrative to a conclusion at the end. However, each short tale is recounted by one of the passengers, giving the
piece echoes of Chaucer's *Canterbury Tales*. 'Absent-Mindedness in a
Parish Choir' is told by the master-thatcher and is about a band of
local musicians who have a very busy Christmas season, playing both
church events and parties across the social spectrum. Dialect markers
are scattered throughout his narration. For example:

> 'Twas so mortal cold that year that they could hardly sit in the
> gallery; for though the congregation down in the body of the church
> had a stove to keep off the frost, the players in the gallery had noth-
> ing at all. So Nicholas said at morning service, when 'twas freezing
> an inch an hour, 'please the Lord I won't stand this numbing weather
> no longer: this afternoon we'll have something in our insides to
> make us warm, if it cost a king's ransom.'
>
> (Hardy 1996: 507)

Hardy does not do much to indicate the dialect of the master-thatcher,
although there is the elision ''Twas' and the use of 'mortal' as an
intensifier. Perhaps more noticeable than these respellings and minor
instances of non-standard grammar, however, is his frequent use of
colourful similes and metaphors in phrases such as ''twas freezing
an inch an hour'. One effect of this dialectal narrator is that Nicholas
speaks in much the same way as the master-thatcher. There is no
immediate hierarchy implied between a Standard English narrator and
the dialect speaking characters.

Free indirect discourse

The final key situation in which dialect representation may occur is
when there is some blending between the speech or thought of a character and the narrative voice. This most commonly happens when
the character is a dialect speaker and the narrative voice is Standard
English, and the thoughts or speech of the character is conveyed in
the narrative through free indirect discourse. An example of this is
provided by Alan Sillitoe's novel *Saturday Night and Sunday Morning*
(1958), a novel which I will be exploring in greater detail in Chapter 7.
Saturday Night and Sunday Morning tells the story of Arthur, a young
man earning a good wage at a bicycle factory who drinks to excess

every Saturday night, and conducts an affair with a married woman. The story is related through a third person narrator, but much of it is told from the point of view or Arthur (in stylistic terms, it is focalized through Arthur). The main narrative voice is high register Standard English, which is clearly distinguished from the dialectal direct speech of the characters. However, passages such as this also regularly occur:

> The doors closed behind him. He hurried up the street, pushed his way through a gang of soldiers towards lights and main-road traffic, walking away from the obstinacy of two women who had no use for him. He cursed them in foul, well-polished language: they had come out for a night on the batter, he said to himself, and had got the shock of their lives when he walked into the Match and settled himself at their table. They had drunk his stout, and hadn't got guts enough to say he was not wanted. Not that he minded them drinking his stout. He expected it from Nottingham women who, he told himself, were cheeky-daft and thought so much of themselves that they would drink your ale whether they liked your company or not. Whores, all of them. Never again.
>
> (Sillitoe 1985: 168–9)

It is quite difficult to tell who is speaking here. Much of it is clearly written from the third person perspective of the external narrator, using the Standard English of the narrator: phrases such as 'the obstinacy of the two women' and 'foul, well-polished language' are markedly different from Arthur's normal speaking style. Furthermore, there are no speech marks here to indicate direct speech or direct thought, and the tense aligns with the narrator's perspective too. However, phrases such as 'a night on the batter', 'shock of their lives', 'hadn't got guts enough' and 'cheeky-daft' are much more dialectal and/or colloquial and appear to voice the thoughts of Arthur himself. It is also noticeable that at the end of this passage the sentences break up into incomplete fragments: 'Whores all of them. Never again.' The fact that these are Arthur's thoughts that are being represented is confirmed by the presence of clauses such as 'he said to himself' and 'he told himself'. This, then, is an example of free indirect discourse, where the thoughts of the character are blended with the narrative voice. There are no speech marks and the tense and the pronouns remain aligned to the narrative voice (past tense, third person pronouns) but features of the accent, intonation, vocabulary and grammar of the character may appear. Sylvia Adamson has argued that this is 'a technique which, by blurring the distinction between voices of character and narrator, has promoted a diffusion of non-Standard forms from dialogue to narrative' (Adamson 1998: 603). Equally, however, it can be argued that it is precisely the marked distinction between the narrator's Standard English and Arthur's Nottingham dialect that makes free indirect discourse such a valuable tool for Sillitoe: the appearance of dialect terms in the narration signals the transition to Arthur's internal thought processes.

Analysing language variety

As with the representation of different varieties of English in film, the representation of different varieties of English in literature is best approached through the three levels of linguistic analysis: sound, vocabulary and grammar. As an example text I will take an extract from Joseph Conrad's 1897 novel, *The Nigger of the 'Narcissus'*. This is a novel about a voyage of the ship the Narcissus from Bombay to London. On the voyage, the West Indian sailor James Wait falls ill, arousing the sympathy of some of the crew. In this scene from early on in the novel, the Londoner Donkin first speaks to James Wait:

'There's a blooming supper for a man,' he whispered bitterly. 'My dorg at 'ome wouldn't 'ave it. It's fit enouf for you an' me. 'Ere's a big ship's fo'c'sle ... Not a blooming scrap of meat in the kids. I've looked in all the lockers ... '

The nigger stared like a man addressed unexpectedly in a foreign language. Donkin changed his tone:- 'Giv' us a bit of 'baccy, mate,' he breathed out confidentially, 'I 'aven't 'ad smoke or chew for the last month. I am rampin' mad for it. Come on old man!'

'Don't be familiar,' said the nigger. Donkin started and sat down on a chest near by, out of sheer surprise. 'We haven't kept pigs together,' continued James Wait in a deep undertone. 'Here's your tobacco.'

(Conrad 1984: 23)

In what follows I shall pay most attention to the representation of sound, firstly because this is often the most significant feature of dialect representation in literary texts and secondly because the issues raised are very different from those raised by the representation of sound in film.

Sound

Semi-phonetic respelling

The most obvious aspect of dialect representation in this passage is the respelling of various words in an endeavour to communicate something about Donkin's accent to the reader. For example, the word 'dog' is respelled as 'dorg', and the word 'enough' is respelled as 'enouf'. A brief consideration of the effect of these respellings reveals that there are some problems with this endeavour, however. For example, the respelling of 'dog' to 'dorg' would at first glance seem to indicate that the word is to be pronounced with /r/ in the middle. However, this seems unlikely given that no variety of English would insert /r/ in this way. What therefore seems more likely is that the spelling 'dorg' is intended to indicate something about the vowel – possibly that instead of the RP pronunciation [dɒg] a longer and more closed [dɔːg] is intended. Such a pronunciation is likely to make sense to an RP speaker by analogy with words such as 'cord' and 'pork', where the 'or' spelling is equivalent to [ɔː]. However, this representation will be confusing to anyone with a rhotic accent, who is likely to try to insert /r/. In other words, the reader's ability to identify the intended pronunciation depends upon their own accent. Would it not have been possible for Conrad to have employed a more transparent respelling?

A cursory consideration of the current state of the English spelling system reveals the root of many of the problems that authors face when attempting to communicate the accents of their characters: modern English spelling is neither phonemic nor internally consistent. The reasons why English spelling has such a poor relationship to English pronunciation are primarily historical. The conventions of English spelling began to be laid down over a thousand years ago. Although these conventions did not become firmly fixed for many centuries, they were well enough established to ensure that English spelling did not keep pace with many of the considerable alterations in the sound system of English which took place between 1000AD and the present day. For example, the Great Vowel Shift, which occurred in the fourteenth century and significantly rearranged the vowel system in English, has not been matched by a concomitant rearrangement of the spelling system, so that for many speakers the pronunciation of words such as 'blood' and 'great' now bear little relationship to their spelling. Similarly, the loss of the unvoiced palatal fricative /ç/, has not been matched with a loss of the spelling 'gh' from words where it once existed, which is why words such as 'knight', 'light' and 'right' look so odd in modern English.

The problems have in some cases been exacerbated by later attempts to regularize the spelling system. For example, around the sixteenth century, the same 'gh' spelling found in 'light' was introduced into the word 'delight', presumably because it seemed wrong to have different spellings for 'light' and 'delight'. Etymologically, however, 'delight' never contained an unvoiced palatal fricative because the word was borrowed into English from French where it was spelled 'delit'. Similarly, also in the sixteenth century, people began to introduce a 'b' into the spelling of words like 'doubt' and 'debt' to show their Latin origins. For example, 'doubt' is derived originally from Latin *dubitare* (to hesitate, to doubt) even though the 'b' was never sounded in English and originally the word was spelled 'dut(e)' or 'doute'.

Even leaving aside these historically-created oddities of English spelling, there remains the fact that English has a single orthographical system which is used for a very diverse range of accents. As the difficulties that the respelling 'dorg' reveals, for example, many British English speakers do not pronounce /r/ in words such as 'cord' and 'pork' despite the fact that they will always spell the words with the 'r' present. Conversely, many speakers of Southern British English draw a distinction between the vowels in 'put' [ʊ] and 'putt' [ʌ] despite the fact that the spelling system, along with most speakers of Northern British English, recognizes no such distinction. What all this illustrates is that any attempt to regularize the spelling system of English would result in a system that was phonemic only for a minority of speakers.

For a literary author, then, any attempt to manipulate the spelling of a word in order to indicate a dialectal pronunciation is always going to be a very inexact art, and one that is liable to be interpreted in different ways by different readers. Paul Hull Bowdre Jr illustrates this point:

> It is true that the same nonstandard spelling may on occasion represent different pronunciations to different readers. For example, the spelling *haid* for *head* may appear to one reader to be intended to rhyme with *aid*, in which case it would be a substandard dialect form, perhaps intended to represent a pronunciation heard

in some parts of the South [America] but recognized in all regions as nonstandard. To another reader it may appear that *haid* is intended to rhyme with *said*.

(Bowdre Jr 1971: 179)

As Bowdre points out, it is difficult to decide what alternative pronunciation is intended, because words ending 'aid' have more than one pronunciation. In some cases, these kinds of problems may be resolved within the text by additional evidence in the form of, for example, direct commentary from a narrator in a novel or an obvious rhyme in a poem (haid/bade or haid/bed). Without such information, and unless the reader is already familiar with the variety in question, the reader has no way of deciding what *haid* indicates.

Overall, then, such respellings often appear to indicate a highly specific pronunciation, but the inexact nature of the English spelling system makes it difficult to be confident about what that pronunciation is. For the reader, it can feel rather like trying to do a logic puzzle with a number of equally valid, but mutually exclusive, answers. Of course, if the reader is already familiar with the dialect in question – if, in other words, the reader already has a good idea of what the answer to the puzzle is – then the respelling may prove quite effective at providing broad hints about the intended accent. For example, if the reader has grasped the fact that Donkin is a Cockney speaker, and if the reader is broadly familiar with the Cockney accent, it becomes much easier to make sense of many of the respellings (the 'dorg' spelling still looks a little odd, but might be ignored). Indeed, Roger Cole has argued that any attempt at indicating accent through orthographical manipulation will only work if writer and reader share an understanding of the variety being so represented:

there can be seen to exist an unstated 'communicative contract' between writer and audience which hold [*sic*] that both writer and reader 'know' their common language and 'know' that the orthographic system is simply a representation of the phonology (and other components) whose sound structure they 'know' anyway. Moreover, a writer, depending upon the language and culture, of course, probably assumes on the part of his reader a general familiarity with a number of spoken varieties of their common language, regardless of the variety actually used by either the writer or the reader in everyday speech ... The fact is that, unless this 'contract' holds, there is no real way, orthographical distortions, phonetic renderings, or anything else, for the author to represent the pronunciation of his characters. *Both standard and non-standard orthography succeed in representing the illusion of human speech only because the reader already knows what it sounds like.*

(Cole 1986: 6)

This argument suggests that respelling to indicate pronunciation is not just an inexact art, but an illusion that the writer and readers work together to maintain.

To this end, it is worth pointing out that while it is convenient to refer to all of these respelling practices as 'semi-phonetic respelling', in practice what we see varies considerably. Some respellings are reasonably phonetically transparent (for example, TH-fronting represented by replacing 'th' with 'f' as in 'fick' for 'thick' and 'fank you' for 'thank you'). Some make sense once the reader understands which particular sound is being evoked (as in 'dorg' for 'dog' or 'haid' for 'head'). But many are entirely conventional. Consider, for example, the use of 't' to indicate the glottal stop produced by definite article reduction which is found in many parts of Yorkshire and Lancashire ('there's trouble at t'mill') or the use of 'ch' to represent an unvoiced palatal fricative in Scottish dialects ('och, you don't want that'). These representations are liable to be opaque to anyone who is not already familiar with *both* the dialectal feature in question *and* the orthographic convention that is used to represent it.

It is instructive to consider a case where we do not have a conventionalized representation for a specific sound. Recently a friend was holding a party and wanted to give the instruction 'Dress: casual' on the invitation, but shorten the word 'casual' to just the first syllable in order to reinforce the casualness of the event. How, she asked me, should she spell this abbreviated word? The problem is that English does not have an orthographical convention to represent the sound [ʒ] because historically this sound has not been part of the English phonological repertoire. It has only been borrowed in because of a few French loanwords, including 'casual', 'treasure', 'measure', etc. As a result, obvious possible respellings are misleading: 'cas' would suggest an alveolar fricative [cas] while 'cash' would suggest an unvoiced postalveolar fricative [caʃ]. The best solution might be a new spelling 'cazh', which would capture the fact that the sound should be both voiced and postalveolar by analogy with the spelling 'sh' for an unvoiced postalveolar fricative. However, while this might be phono-logically satisfactory, the instruction 'Dress: cazh' is liable to confuse most guests. Orthographic conventions work because both reader and writer understand them. Writers who wish to devise new conventions must find some way of communicating them effectively to readers, and even then might find that readers (who are highly attuned to existing conventions) resist the new coinage.

Finally, it is worth noting how partial many semi-phonetic respellings are; they only work on the assumption that both reader and writer share the same accent. For example, we can return to the fact that most Southern British English speakers draw a distinction between the vowels in 'put' and 'putt' whereas Northern British English speakers do not. How should this be represented on the page? A South-ern British author who wishes to represent the fact that a Northern character says the words 'up' and 'bucket' in a way that differs from her own accent may be tempted to use spellings such as 'oop' and 'boocket'. For Northern British readers, however, such a respelling will lead them to produce long vowels [u:p] and [bu:kət]. For a Northern British author, it is not the single Northern 'u' that needs special repre-sentation, but rather the fact that Southern English speakers have two different ways of realizing 'u'. For a Northern British author, therefore, a better solution would be to represent Southern British characters as saying 'ap' and 'backet', in order to capture the fact that the vowels in these words are unexpectedly open and unrounded, and to leave Northern British accents with the standard spelling. Which option is chosen will depend on who the target audience is, because as Traugott and Pratt note:

> By convention ... when a writer uses normal English spellings in dialogue ... we infer that the pronunciation intended is the stan-dard of the audience for which the work is written, while special deviant spellings indicate the pronunciation of a dialect that is not the audience's standard.
>
> (Traugott and Pratt 1980: 338–9)

Hence, what a writer is attempting is to represent as being noticeably *different* from 'normal' for their audience. Given that, in Britain at least, Standard English and RP (based on the language of the South East) are considered to be 'normal', this means that most typically what dialect representation is doing is representing how the speech in question differs from Standard English. Hence in practice, even when the author is from the North, she is likely to use respellings that take RP as the default and to show how the accents of her characters differ from that norm.

Eye dialect

In addition to respellings which indicate something about the alternative pronunciations of the words in question, there are also words in the *'Narcissus'* passage where the respelling does not alter the pronunciation at all. This kind of respelling is often termed eye dialect because it is dialect to the eye but not the ear. That is, it gives the impression of being dialectal when the reader looks at it, but it does not convey any information about the pronunciation when the reader sounds it out. Examples of this in the *'Narcissus'* passage include 'Giv" and 'enouf'. In the case of 'Giv" the 'e' is not pronounced in any modern variety of English. Instead, the 'e' on the end of a word often indicates that the preceding vowel should be a diphthong, as in the case of 'mad' versus 'made' and 'bid' versus 'bide'. In the case of 'give', however, the preceding vowel is a monopthong, so it is difficult to see that the removing the 'e' indicates any change in pronunciation at all. Similarly, the respelling 'enouf' seems to suggest that the final vowel sound, represented by the spelling 'gh' in Standard English, is to be pronounced [f]. However, this is its modern universal pronunciation, so again the change does not impart any information about Donkin's accent. Indeed, Conrad could have taken this eye dialect respelling further by representing the word as 'enuff'.

What, it might be asked, is the purpose of such eye dialect? A straightforward answer is that they visually mark the speech of the individual in question as non-standard. Given the strong association between literacy and the standard language that was discussed in Chapter 2, these phonologically empty respellings give the impression that the character in question is uneducated. Of course, on reflection this does not make much logical sense: direct speech purports to transcribe how the character speaks not how they write, so the fact that the writer has chosen to use a non-standard spelling such as 'giv' or 'enouf' should not reflect on the educational level of the character whose speech is so represented. Nevertheless, as Adamson has noted, 'the effect of eye-dialect is always derogatory: the forms are read as

mis-spellings and the character whose speech they represent somehow acquires the social stigma attached to illiteracy'(Adamson 1998:
600).

Again, however, it is important to be aware that eye dialect might
more usefully be recognized as existing on a range. In some instances,
the accusation that it simply marks ignorance and illiteracy are completely justified. For example, in his essay on slave narratives Albert
H. Tricomi quotes a passage from Mattie Griffith's 1856 *Autobiography
of a Female Slave* and then analyses it :

> 'Oh, chile, when Masser Jones was done a-beatin' ob yer, dey all ob
> 'em tought you was dead; den Masser got orful skeard. He cussed
> and swore, and shook his fist in de oberseer's face, and sed he had
> kilt you, and dat he was gwine to law wid him 'bout de 'struction
> ob his property. Den Masser Jones he swar a mighty heap, and tell
> Masser he dar' him to go to law 'bout it. Den Miss Jane and Tilda
> kum out, and commenced cryin', and fell to 'busin' Masser Jones,
> kase Miss Jane say she want to go to de big town.'

> Not only is the dialect comprised of profuse word truncations and
> the substitutions of 'd' for 'th' and 'b' for 'v,' but the rendering is
> also full of 'eye dialect,' which is to say, visual devices to indicate
> a spoken dialect. In the quote above and throughout Griffith's *Auto-
> biography*, the dialogue is suffused with spelling substitutions that
> do not change at all the pronunciation of the words themselves. Far
> from even trying to approximate black speech, Griffith's eye dialect
> functions to mark the speaker, invidiously, as ignorant and of low
> class. Examples of such spellings are 'sed' for 'said,' 'kum' for 'come,'
> and 'kase' for 'case.'

> (Tricomi 2006: 622)

Tricomi is quite right that the instances of eye dialect he identifies
indicate nothing about pronunciation and serve to elide speech performance with illiteracy. There is no variety of English where the
replacement of 'c' with 'k' in the spelling indicates anything about
pronunciation, although it is the kind of spelling that children use
when first learning to write. However, a more complex case is presented in this speech from Dickens' *Great Expectations* (first published 1861), where Abel Magwitch reveals to Pip that he is his secret
benefactor:

'Yes, Pip, dear boy, I've made a gentleman on you! It's me wot has done it! I swore that time, sure as ever I earned a guinea, that guinea should go to you. I swore arterwards, sure as ever I spec'lated and got rich, you should get rich. I lived rough, that you should live smooth; I worked hard, that you should be above work. What odds, dear boy? Do I tell it, fur you to feel a obligation? Not a bit. I tell it, fur you to know as that there hunted dunghill dog wot you kep life in, got his head so high that he could make a gentleman,—and, Pip, you're him!'

(Dickens 2003: 319)

The respelling of 'what' as 'wot' at first glance appears to be another instance of eye dialect, and the fact that in his letter to Pip, Magwitch uses the phrase 'wot larx' further hints at the fact that Dickens is eliding spoken and written performance here. However, the case of 'wot' is more complicated. When the 'wot' spelling was first recorded (in 1829, according to the *Oxford English Dictionary*) it is likely that it did carry at least some phonological information for many readers. Historically, English distinguished between word-initial 'wh' [ʍ] (voiceless labialized velar approximant) and 'w' [w] (voiced labialized velar approximant) and some varieties of English continue to do so. For many Scottish and Irish English speakers, for example, the word 'witch' [witʃ] is pronounced differently from 'which'[ʍitʃ]. At the time Dickens was writing it is likely that for many speakers of English the spelling 'wot' would have carried phonological information, and this points to the fact that we need to be careful when labelling a respelling as 'eye dialect' that we do not mean that it is eye dialect for us now. Secondly, 'wot' quickly became so well associated with representations of Cockney and working-class English that its appearance on the page can in its own right alert readers that a Cockney voice is being attempted. When contemporary British readers encounter the spelling 'wot' they may find themselves performing the rest of the utterance in a broadly 'Cockney' voice, and adding in Cockney features which are not directly specified in the respelling. In the case of 'wot', for example, I have found that when students read a sentence with the word 'wot' in aloud, they will glottalize the word-final 't'. There is nothing in the respelling 'wot' that tells them to do this, but their general knowledge of what a Cockney accent sounds like is triggered by the presence of a conventionalized Cockney spelling. In other words, eye dialect may in some instances be doing phonological work after all, through its conventionalized associations.

Apostrophes

Apostrophes are used by authors to indicate that letters have been omitted on purpose rather than as a typographical error. At the same time, they cue the reader as to where they should re-insert the missing letter or letters. Examples of this from the *'Narcissus'* passage include 'I 'aven't 'ad smoke or chew' to indicate H-deletion, and 'rampin' mad' to indicate that the final consonant of 'ramping' has been pronounced as an alveolar nasal [n] rather than a velar nasal [ŋ].

As well as helping the reader to reconstruct the intended words, however, the apostrophes themselves serve to create a hierarchical relation between the dialect and the standard language, signalling that something is absent that should be present. One effect of this is that stigmatized features of low-prestige dialects get treated quite differently from the features of Standard English, and that non-standard speakers are therefore treated differently from the standard speaker. For example, it is conventional in British fiction to mark H-deletion in the speech of a Cockney character, as is the case with Donkin in *'Narcissus'*. However, R-deletion in non-rhotic varieties of English is unlikely to be marked because in Britain non-rhoticity is not a stigmatized feature. In the case of James Wait in *'Narcissus'*, for example, it appears that Wait speaks with an RP accent, and as such presumably does not pronounce the word final /r/ in 'together' or 'familiar'. Similarly, Cockney-speaking Donkin will also have a non-rhotic accent and so will not pronounce the word final /r/ in 'supper'. The two characters are treated equally and the lack of /r/ is not marked in either of their accents. Overall, however, the effect of only signalling stigmatized phonological features means that apostrophes are typically used to point up how non-standard speech deviates from a presumed norm, and therefore what is 'wrong' with the pronunciation of the speaker in question. Some writers, including James Joyce and Irvine Welsh, have preferred not to use apostrophes.

Allegro speech

In everyday conversation, speakers do not sound each word out fully and separately. Speech requires the rapid and continuous realignment of multiple different parts of the vocal tract (tongue, teeth, lips, oral cavity, nasal cavity). Adjacent sounds influence one another or become merged, consonant clusters are simplified, and unstressed vowels reduce or disappear. These rapid speech processes happen below the level of consciousness and present no barrier to communication. Indeed, it can be argued that it is only the existence of writing systems that makes us think in terms of individual 'words', and a speaker who articulates each word of a casual conversation fully and separately is likely to be perceived as speaking very oddly by listeners.

Dennis Preston has termed attempts to represent such processes in print 'allegro speech'. He notes that '[t]hey attempt to capture through the use of nonstandard spellings (some more traditional than others) the fact that the speech is casual, not carefully monitored, relaxed – perhaps slangy' (Preston 1985: 328). The contexts that Preston discusses are non-literary (linguistics, folklore, etc.) but it is a practice shared by literary texts. In novels, convention dictates that these rapid speech processes are ignored for speakers of Standard English. The exception to this rule arises with dialect speakers. As Ives has pointed out:

> Once an author has decided to represent the speech of a character in 'dialect,' he is likely to give a 'dialectal' spelling to all pronunciations he observes that do not conform to his notions of 'proper' English, which in such usages are likely to be influenced by conventional spelling. On the other hand, if he is not representing the speech of a character in 'dialect' – that is, if the character does not, in his opinion, speak 'dialect' – he is unlikely to represent such features in his conversation.
>
> (Ives 1971: 169)

This means that for dialectal characters, apostrophes and respellings are often used to indicate the elisions and contractions of ordinary speech. In the *'Narcissus'* passage, for example, Donkin is represented as saying 'you an' me'. The fact is that in real-life conversation 'you and me' will almost always be contracted by RP speakers as much as by Cockney speakers, because pronouncing the 'd' in the middle is unnecessary and inconvenient from a phonological point of view. However, literary tradition dictates that Standard English speakers have their words reported in full. This means that standard and non-standard speakers are again treated differently in the reporting of direct speech,

with the effect that non-standard speakers generally seem more care-
less about pronunciation than standard speakers. A good example of
this differential treatment can be seen in J.D. Salinger's *The Catcher in
the Rye* (first published in serial form 1945–6). In this scene the young
narrator, Holden Caulfield, has got into an argument over payment
with a pimp:

> 'I told you about ten times, I don't owe you a cent. I already gave her
> the five –'
>
> 'Cut the crap, now. Let's have it.'
>
> 'Why should I give her another five bucks?' I said. My voice was
> cracking all over the place. 'You're trying to chisel me.'
>
> Old Maurice unbuttoned his whole uniform coat. All he had on
> underneath was a phony shirt collar, but no shirt or anything. He
> had a big fat hairy stomach. 'Nobody's tryna chisel nobody,' he said.
> 'Let's have it, chief.'
>
> (Salinger 1994: 91)

Here the same phrase is rendered 'trying to chisel' when spoken by
Holden, but 'tryna chisel' when spoken by Old Maurice. In fact, it is
very unlikely that Holden would enunciate each word absolutely separately, particularly given that he is speaking to a pimp who is unlikely to
be impressed by an upmarket accent. Indeed, Holden's use of the slang
word 'chisel' suggests that he is adopting a low register speech style.
However, the visual difference between 'trying to chisel' and 'tryna
chisel' serves to emphasize the differences between the two characters, and to associate Old Maurice with being a slovenly speaker, thus
reinforcing the impression created by his 'phony shirt collar' and 'big
fat hairy stomach'.

Vocabulary

Donkin's speech in the *'Narcissus'* passage contains several words
that are unlikely to appear in formal written English. First, there are
slang vocabulary items such as 'blooming', 'rampin' mad', 'smoke' and
'chew'. None of these are specifically dialectal, but they do serve to
mark the fact that he is speaking in a colloquial register. Second, there
are specialized sailing vocabulary items including 'fo'c'sle' (which is the

forecastle, or sleeping area on a ship) and 'kids' (which are containers to eat out of). These sailing terms emphasize the specialized nature of the sailors' profession, but may well present comprehension problems to the reader (although, in the case of the *'Narcissus'* some of these words have already been introduced by other characters).

It is not, of course, essential that readers understand every single word in a text. In the phrase 'a blooming scrap of meat in the kids', for example, it is possible to glean that 'kids' must be something that could be expected to contain food, even if the precise meaning of the word is unknown. Nevertheless, deducing the import of unfamiliar vocabulary requires conscious effort on the part of the reader, and can be particularly daunting when combined with lots of respelling, not least because for each unfamiliar word the reader has to decide whether it is genuinely unknown or simply a respelling of a common word. Norman Blake has noted that writers are unlikely to respell dialectal words in order to indicate pronunciation, for example 'time' might be respelled as 'toim' but 'rile' will be allowed to stand because it would be too difficult for the reader to process both the respelling and the unfamiliar word (Blake 1981: 17). In some instances writers will make it easier for the reader by glossing an unknown word in the narrative, or using another character to provide an explanation. For example, in the passage from *'Narcissus'*, James Wait responds to Donkin's request for ''baccy' by saying 'Here's your tobacco', thus clarifying the request for any reader who has not managed to deduce the meaning of ''baccy'. Some writers may even provide a glossary, as Ken Saro-Wiwa does in his 1985 novel *Sozaboy*, although this has the effect of both requiring readers to flick to the back of the book each time they encounter an unfamiliar word (thus interrupting the narrative flow) and suggesting that the words in question are like a foreign language that require 'translation'. Overall, while a few unfamiliar vocabulary items can serve to convey a general impression of dialect speech or of a particular technical vocabulary, readers are likely to find the speech of a character who uses lots of non-standard items difficult to follow.

Grammar

Speech, as has already been discussed in Chapter 1, is inherently different from writing because it is normally produced spontaneously, and because spoken utterances are structured differently from written sentences. What readers are accustomed to think of as written direct speech is a literary construct that aims to capture some of the features of the spoken language, but which ignores many of the normal features of real speech. This means that characters who are represented as standard speakers will typically be given entirely standard written grammar, even though no real person actually speaks in this way. Dialectal speakers will also be tidied up, but some features of their grammar may be permitted to remain to indicate their deviance from the presumed norm. In particular, writers tend rely on stereotypical grammatical features to indicate dialect grammar, particularly those condemned by prescriptive grammarians, such as the use of double negatives or a lack of concordance between verb and noun. In the case of Donkin, for example, he uses the plural pronoun 'us' instead of 'me' when he asks Wait to 'Giv' us a bit of 'baccy, mate', and he omits the determiner in the sentence 'I 'aven't 'ad smoke or chew.' Overall, however, the representation of non-standard grammatical features is much less significant in Donkin's speech than phonology or vocabulary, and this is common to many other authors.

Discussion of *The Nigger of the 'Narcissus'*

Given that Wait is from the West Indies, he might be expected to speak with a variety of English with some West Indian English features. This certainly appears to be what Donkin anticipates, and it is perhaps why Donkin assumes that his familiar tone and colloquial Cockney speech will be acceptable to Wait. However, when Wait replies to Donkin's request for tobacco there is no marking of non-standard English in Wait's speech and he uses a high register vocabulary and formal phrasing. In some ways, this decision by Conrad challenges the standard language ideology: if Conrad had attempted to represent a West Indian accent, whatever he did would have been in danger of creating an impression of illiteracy and inarticulacy in the minds of readers. However, the problem is that because Wait does not speak with a West Indian accent, the reader is left to assume that he speaks with an RP accent, and so no hint of his cultural identity or personal history is communicated. Wait emerges in *'Narcissus'* as an interesting character, but not a very strongly delineated one. The question of what options writers have in depicting characters who, in real life, would be dialect speakers is one I take up further in the next chapter.

Conclusion

In this chapter I explored first *where* dialect occurs in literary texts (direct speech, narrative, free indirect speech) and then *how* it is represented. I focused in particular on how writers use techniques including semi-phonetic respellings, eye dialect and apostrophes in order to indicate something about the accent of the character. I argued that such techniques draw heavily upon tradition; to a great extent dialect representation in literature is effective because readers are already familiar with both the dialect itself and the conventions by which it is represented. In the next chapter, Chapter 6, I explore how readers respond to dialect representation, arguing both that readers dislike long stretches of dialect representation, and that the conventionalized nature of these representations encourages readers to interpret dialect-speaking characters as stereotypes.

Further reading

Norman Blake's *Non-standard Language in English Literature* is still an important survey of dialect across the history of English Literature (1981). Traugott and Pratt's 'Chapter 8: Varieties of English: Regional, Social, and Ethnic' in their *Linguistics for Students of Literature* (1980) offers an excellent overview of some of the key issues, focusing in particular on US literature. Norman Page's chapter 'Speech and Character: Dialect' in his *Speech in the English Novel* (1988) also offers a good survey, focusing in particular on British literature. Raymond Chapman's chapters on 'Standard and non-standard speech' and 'Dialect' in his *Forms of Speech in Victorian Fiction* (1994) discusses dialect representation in British fiction of the nineteenth century. Sylvia Adamson offers some valuable perspectives on the literary uses of dialect in her chapter 'Literary Language' in the *Cambridge History of the English Language Volume IV* (1998).

Exercises

Exercise 1

'Sir, you're just the man I wanted to see. I'm going to Joe's house tonight, and if you come too I know you will be made very welcome.

You will get plenty of beer to drink, and some beef and Yorkshire pudding to eat.'

1. Rewrite the above extract as dialect, for example Yorkshire English, Cockney, New York, African American English. You might choose a dialect with which you have some personal familiarity, or one that you know from reading and television. You can change the spelling, vocabulary and grammar as you see fit. You could also choose the food type to fit with your chosen dialect.
2. Now imagine another character responding to this speech and write a couple of sentences of what they say. Think about the language variety you choose for the respondent, and what effect this has upon the piece
3. Reflect on how easy or difficult you found this task. How did you decide which dialect to represent? Which features did you choose to represent the dialect and why did you choose them? Who are the people whose voices you have represented here?

Exercise 2

1. Examine the two extracts below, which both contain a representation of Yorkshire English. List all the features which represent dialect (respelling, apostrophes, grammar, vocabulary, etc.).
2. Which text has the greater density of non-standard features? (You could calculate this by counting 'standard' and 'non-standard' forms and working out a ratio or percentage.)
3. Why do you think each author has represented dialect in this way? Who is the intended readership for each text do you think?
4. Do you think that either of these texts evoke any particular stereotypes of Yorkshire people?

Text 1: extract from Second from Last in the Sack Race *by David Nobbs*

A burst of molten light came from the open-hearth furnaces of the great steelworks of Crapp, Hawser and Kettlewell, which lay on the other side of the main road, dwarfing the dingy back-to-back terraces, and a dun-coloured Thurmarsh Corporation tram clanked noisily down the main road.

'Bugger off,' said the parrot.

Ezra examined the bird sadly. It had been a bad buy. Henderson had assured Ada that it was a master of Yorkshire dialect, and would amaze her visitors with comments like 'Where there's muck, there's brass,' ''Ee, he's a right laddie-lass. He's neither nowt nor summat.' and 'Don't thee tha me; tha thee them that tha's thee.' Ada had spent long hours rehearsing it. All it ever said was 'Bugger off.' Admittedly, it said it in a south Yorkshire accent, but that was scant consolation to its disappointed owner . . .

Cousin Hilda popped her head round the door.

'She's started,' she said.

'Aye, I've heard,' said Ezra.

'Bugger off,' said the parrot.

Cousin Hilda sniffed. Her nose looked as if it disapproved of her mouth, and her mouth looked as if it disapproved of her nose, and probably they both did, since Cousin Hilda was known to disapprove of orifices of every kind.

'I don't blame t' parrot,' she said, 'It doesn't know owt different. I blame Henderson. That sort of thing comes from t' top. Look at Germany. Pet shop? Sodom and Gomorrah more like. Every animal from that shop's the same. Foul-mouthed.'

'They can't all talk,' protested Ezra, 'Fair dos, our Hilda. Tha's not suggesting Archie Halliday's goldfish swears, is tha?'

(Nobbs 1983: 9–10)

Text 2: extract from 'T' Big Drum' by Tom Hague

T' band 'ad 'ad a reight 'ard day,
When they'd ter wait at t' 'Crahn an' Thistle'.
They tuk advantidge on t' dilay
Ter goo an' wet ther wissle.

Nah Bill an' Tom tuk too much on,
An' ne'er 'eerd t' driver shaht 'em.
Nob'dy missed 'em in all t' throng
An't t' cooach went off beaht 'em.

Tommy Clegg 'e played t' big drum,
Bill Earnshaw, t' clarinet.

Tom strapped on t' drum an' said 'cum on!
We've three miles' walkin' yet!'

When they got ter top on t' brow,
They stopped ter rest on t' wall.
Tom unstrapped drum an' set it dahn
An' it began ter roll.

'Ey up!' cried Tom 'Mi drum! Cum on!
It's steeper ner Ah thowt.
Don't stan' like a gret pot dog,
Tha gret big gormless nowt!'

(Hague 1976: 8)

6

Stereotyping and dialect in literature

In Chapter 4 I examined one of the problems that can occur when dialect is represented in film, which is that characterization through dialect can easily slide into stereotyping. In this chapter I will explore what happens when dialect is represented in literature, and I argue that in this case the problems are more acute because readers are inherently resistant to the representation of dialect on the page. I then survey some different approaches that authors have taken in order to try to counteract negative response from readers to dialect speaking characters.

The problem of 'reader resistance'

A key problem for any writer who wishes to represent a character who speaks with a non-standard dialect of English is that readers tend to dislike such representations. Michael Toolan has termed this dislike as 'reader resistance' and he notes that it will be provoked by 'rendered speech that departs to any appreciable degree from standard colloquial speech' (Toolan 1992: 34). One reason for this negative reaction is that, as I began to explore in Chapter 2, there is a close cultural association between Standard English and literacy. This means that when dialect is represented in print through the techniques described in the previous chapter (semi-phonetic respellings, non-standard grammar and regional vocabulary items, etc.) many readers will respond negatively to the 'bad English' so presented. Another reason is that dialect representation on the page, particularly through respelling, requires additional effort from the reader. As Toolan notes, readers often engage with passages of dialect representation 'in a spirit of enforced labour' (Toolan 1992: 34). As a result, reading speeds decrease, and in some instances important plot information may be lost if the dialect is not interpreted correctly, or if it is skipped over in irritation.

The issue of how readers respond to representations of dialects has been explored in relation to non-literary texts by sociolinguists, with a view to understanding how practices of transcription among ethnolinguists, oral historians and folklorists can shape the attitudes of researchers and audiences towards the data so presented (see, for example, Macaulay 1991; Preston 1982; Preston 1985; Preston 2000). Alexandra Jaffe and Shana Walton conducted a study to examine these attitudes, developing a methodology which they describe as 'combining features of matched guise tests with sociolinguistic interviewing and oral performance'(Jaffe and Walton 2000: 561). This involved presenting their participants with a sequence of texts, at least one of which was part of a transcript of an oral history interview written in non-standard orthography in order to represent the Mississippi English accent of the original speaker. Three different versions of the same transcripts were used, and different participants were given different versions: *Standard* (with the informant's non-standard lexical tenses regularized and conventional spelling employed), *Light* (with the informant's non-standard lexical tenses left in place, some features of casual speech represented and some eye dialect introduced) and *Heavy* (which used a phonetic spelling system to reflect the informant's accent as accurately as possible) (Jaffe and Walton 2000: 564–5). Participants were asked to read the texts aloud and their performances were recorded. After each reading, the participants were asked to describe the person they imagined while reading the text. Their performances were also compared to the way in which the participants read a short passage from a history textbook, as well as to the participants' more casual speech. This methodology allowed Jaffe and Walton to gain a detailed insight into the social meanings that their participants ascribed to the non-standard orthographies they encountered in the passages.

What they found was that respondents were quick to make all kinds of assumptions about a speaker's background and personality based on a lightly marked orthographical representation of non-standard features in their speech: respondents 'took for granted that orthography could authentically represent social voices and identities' (Jaffe and Walton 2000: 582). Respondents reported imagining 'a scrawny, young, hay-chewing person' or 'someone who's not very educated...I almost picture a redneck' (Jaffe and Walton 2000: 580–1).

This, Jaffe and Walton argue, demonstrates that orthography is intrinsically tied up with the standard language ideology in written texts:

> Our readers' performances and comments also illustrate the ideological power of orthography. Orthography stands for linguistic form, for regularity, for authority, for systematicity. For these reasons, it plays a major role in positioning the language it represents vis-à-vis 'the standard:' both specific standard languages, and the very idea of 'a standard'.
>
> (Jaffe and Walton 2000: 582)

Jaffe and Walton's work was on non-literary texts, but their findings chime with Adamson's observation that 'the effect of eye-dialect is always derogatory: the forms are read as mis-spellings and the character whose speech they represent somehow acquires the social stigma attached to illiteracy' (Adamson 1998: 600). Jaffe and Walton continue:

> the use of non-standard orthographies to represent features of non-standard speech runs the risk of delegitimizing the 'non-standard' code's claim to be a language (to be 'like' the 'standard'). Our research suggests that it is almost impossible to avoid stigma in the non-standard orthographic representation of others' low-status speech varieties. *Light* orthography cues voice, but it does so by using stereotyped forms whose meanings are inescapably linked to their use in texts whose aim is to denigrate the speakers being represented. *Heavy* orthographies require too much investment and decoding to allow voice to come through; few readers are able or prepared to sustain the work of attending closely to spelling as a vehicle for voice.
>
> (Jaffe and Walton 2000: 582–3)

In other words, Jaffe and Walton found that there is a trade-off. A light representation of dialect which relies on a few well-established conventions successfully cues voice, but in relying upon such conventions it particularly encourages negative judgements. However, a more detailed representation that does not trade upon stereotyped features may deter readers because it requires too much work to decode.

Literary implications of reader resistance

Reader resistance to dialect representation has a number of practical implications for the way that dialect speech is employed by writers.

First, it can mean that writers are deliberately inconsistent about their application of dialect representation. It is, for example, common to find that non-standard speaking characters are represented using a lot of dialectal features to begin with. Once the basic principle of their dialect has been established, the density with which it is marked diminishes. This is apparent in a novel like *Saturday Night and Sunday Morning* where early dialogue by Arthur is densely marked through respelling, grammar and vocabulary, but the respellings in particular are much reduced in later speech.

Second, it can mean that a major character who might logically be expected to speak a non-standard variety by reasons of birth and upbringing will nevertheless be represented as a standard speaker. The canonical case in point here is perhaps Charles Dickens' *Oliver Twist*, which I quoted from in Chapter 5. Given that Oliver has been brought up in circumstances of extreme hardship, it is unclear why he speaks Standard English while the similarly disadvantaged Artful Dodger is represented as speaking a strongly marked London dialect. The explanation for this is that Oliver is a major central, and that, as Page, Chapman and Ferguson all note, Victorian conventions demanded that major characters speak Standard English lest they prove too difficult to read and too unsympathetic to Victorian audiences (Ferguson 1998: 2–3; Chapman 1994: 221; Page 1988, 2: 103). However, the fact that central characters were, and still are, so frequently represented as speaking Standard English means that it tends to only be more peripheral figures that are represented as dialect speakers, and this in turn means that the reader never becomes accustomed to reading extensive passages of dialect.

Third, and following on from this, dialect speaking characters will often be treated with less respect than characters who speak Standard English. As Toolan notes, 'That strong sense, for most readers (themselves conforming or aspiring to national standards in their own speaking and writing) in turn means there is an inbuilt bias against treating dialect-speaking characters as worthy of the most serious respect' (Toolan 1992: 29–46, 34). This may result in the dialect characters receiving less space on the page, being represented as less intelligent, or having their dialect played for laughs. As Norman Blake has observed:

> When, in a literary work, a character speaks in a non-standard way he will immediately be contrasted to those characters who use the standard. To those who speak the standard, the way in which others speak may be regarded as comic because it may sound to them as though such people are mangling the language in an attempt to speak in a standard manner. Those writers interested in comedy will increase the number of misunderstandings that can arise from this use of two languages. Thus a Welshman might be allowed to say *pig* for 'big'. Non-standard language will therefore often signal comedy, because the serious matters will be handled by the major characters. If those matters need some comic relief, minor characters will be produced to provide it. Otherwise non-standard language will indicate class.
>
> (Blake 1981: 13)

Blake's perspective here is historical. Nevertheless, his observation still holds true in many novels written today.

The challenge for writers

The difficulties for a writer who wishes to represent dialect are brought into focus by this review of T. S. Eliot's *A Choice of Kipling's Verse* (1945) by George Orwell. Orwell offers the following critique of Rudyard Kipling's representation of dialect:

> If one examines his best and most representative work, his soldier poems, especially *Barrack-Room Ballads*, one notices that what more than anything else spoils them is an underlying air of patronage. Kipling idealizes the army officer, especially the junior officer, and that to an idiotic extent, but the private soldier, though lovable and romantic, has to be a comic. He is always made to speak in a sort of stylized Cockney, not very broad but with all the aitches and final 'g's' carefully omitted. Very often the result is as embarrassing as the humorous recitation at a church social. And this accounts for the curious fact that one can often improve Kipling's poems, make them less facetious and less blatant, by simply going through them

and transplanting them from Cockney into standard speech. This is especially true of his refrains, which often have a truly lyrical quality. Two examples will do (one is about a funeral and the other about a wedding):

> So it's knock out your pipes and follow me!
> And it's finish up your swipes and follow me!
> Oh, hark to the big drum calling,
> Follow me — follow me home!

and again:

> Cheer for the Sergeant's wedding —
> Give them one cheer more!
> Grey gun-horses in the lando,
> And a rogue is married to a whore!

Here I have restored the aitches, etc. Kipling ought to have known better. He ought to have seen that the two closing lines of the first of these stanzas are very beautiful lines, and that ought to have overridden [*sic*] his impulse to make fun of a working-man's accent. In the ancient ballads the lord and the peasant speak the same language. This is impossible to Kipling, who is looking down a distorting class-perspective, and by a piece of poetic justice one of his best lines is spoiled — for 'follow me 'ome' is much uglier than 'follow me home'.

(Orwell 1954: 129–30)

Orwell is responding to one of the issues raised by Jaffe and Walton: that when a writer chooses to represent a character as speaking in a non-standard variety, that non-standard variety immediately stands in contrast to the standard and will frequently be understood to be comic. Orwell takes it for granted that Kipling is making fun of the private soldier through his orthographic manipulation of the lines, and he ascribes this to Kipling's 'distorting class-perspective'. Kipling would have done much better, Orwell proposes, to have presented the lines without the respellings.

It might be questioned, however, whether Orwell's own attitude is entirely egalitarian. For a start, it can be noted that Orwell's views are closely aligned with the standard language ideology: he finds the lines 'beautiful' when written in Standard English, but 'much uglier' when an attempt is made to represent the Cockney accent. He does not examine his use of these aesthetic terms, or question his own assumption that any such attempt at representing Cockney speech is automatically comic and patronizing. He also indulges in something of a rhetorical sleight-of-hand in appealing to a golden age of the past when 'the lord and the peasant speak the same language'. As I briefly discussed in Chapter 2, this age existed before the rise of a centralized, literate society and before the codification of Standard English. Hence, the fact that the lord and peasant speak the same language should not be read as indicating that the middle ages were untroubled by social distinctions, but rather that social distinctions were not yet seen as inherently tied up with the varieties of English they speak. This means that making the officer and private soldier speak the same language in the twentieth century carries very different social and artistic meanings from making the lord and the peasant speak the same language in the middle ages. In particular, in the modern era making all characters speak the same language regardless of their social background is in danger both of bleaching out the identity of the non-standard speaker, and of reinforcing the standard language ideology by insisting that it is the only variety that can be taken seriously. Orwell does not attempt to address the question of how an author might attempt to give a flavour of the private soldier's voice without triggering negative reactions on the part of the reader.

A different version of the same basic problem can be seen with Mark Twain's *The Adventures of Huckleberry Finn*. In an explanatory note at the start of the text, Twain writes that he has taken considerable effort to delineate the dialects he represents accurately, and that he has drawn on his own local knowledge of these dialects in order to do so:

> In this book a number of dialects are used, to wit: the Missouri Negro dialect; the extremest form of the backwoods South-Western dialect; the ordinary 'Pike-County' dialect; and four modified varieties of this last. The shadings have not been done in a haphazard fashion, or by guess-work; but painstakingly, and with the trustworthy guidance and support of personal familiarity with these several forms of speech.
>
> (Twain 1985, 'Explanatory')

This certainly sounds like an author who is attempting linguistic accuracy, and on this basis it might seem difficult to accuse Twain of the kind of 'stylized' representation of which Orwell accuses Kipling. A short extract of Twain's dialect representation is as follows:

Pretty soon Jim says:

'Say – who is you? Whar is you? Dog my cats ef I didn' hear sumf'n.
Well, I knows what I's gwyne to do. I's gwyne to set down here and
listen tell I hears it agin.'

(Twain 1985: 5)

It might be noted here that Twain is attempting to represent something
about Jim's language at all linguistic levels (for example, semi-phonetic
respelling 'going to' as 'gwyne to', non-standard grammar 'I knows', colloquial phrase 'Dog my cats'). It might also be noted that all of these
manipulations of the standard do appear to be trying to communicate something about the variety in question: there is no eye dialect
in this passage. Despite Twain's efforts, however, his representation of
Jim has been condemned by some critics. For example, Toni Morrison
finds Twain is guilty of 'over-the-top minstrelization of Jim' and writes
that 'Jim's portrait seems unaccountably excessive and glaring in its
contradictions like an ill-made clown suit that cannot hide the real
man within' (Morrison 2005: 282–3). Morrison is here responding to
the overall depiction of Jim rather than just his dialect, and she specifically acknowledges that 'Twain's black characters were most certainly
based on real people' (Morrison 2005: 283), but nevertheless it is clear
that she finds the character of Jim as a whole to be stereotyped and
unconvincing. In turn, some linguists have attempted to defend Twain
on the basis of that he did achieve a high degree of linguistic accuracy
(Carkeet 1979; Fishkin 1994). Lisa Minnick, for example, in a study of
Twain's dialect representation that utilizes computer analysis, writes:

But where is the evidence that Twain actually uses the depiction of
his speech to disparage Jim? I contend that it is not in the text of the
novel nor in the articles produced by critics of Twain's version of
AAVE. What I suspect is more likely is that such critics find evidence
that Jim is portrayed negatively or stereotypically, evidence which
has nothing to do with the actual linguistic features Jim uses. The
view may be that if Jim is stereotyped, then so is his speech.

(Minnick 2001: 119–20)

This returns us to the discussion of stereotyping that I introduced in
Chapter 4. There I argued that it is necessary to distinguish between
character stereotyping and linguistic stereotyping, character stereotyping being the representation of a character as 'silly, quaint, or

stupid' based solely upon their membership of a particular social or ethnic group, and linguistic stereotyping being the inaccurate rendering of a particular dialect based upon a small number of linguistic features. As I argued in Chapter 4, linguistic stereotyping frequently goes hand-in-hand with character stereotyping: when no effort is made at an authentic realization of a particular dialect or sociolect, it is common to find that the character who speaks that variety is also represented in a two-dimensional way, and that features of their speech are treated as humorous. Nevertheless, these two aspects of stereotyping can function separately. In the case of *Huckleberry Finn*, as Minnick argues, we have a text where the author attempts linguistic authenticity, but nevertheless some readers still perceive that author as engaging in character stereotyping. There are at least two possible factors that may account for this: first, although Twain himself may have been anti-slavery he was nevertheless the product of a slave-owning society and his depiction of Jim is shaped by the attitudes of his time. Secondly, and more importantly from the point of view of the current chapter, there is the fact that readers often perceive *any* attempt at dialect representation in writing as stereotyping.

What these findings suggest is that from some perspectives it does not really matter whether or not Kipling was intending to make fun of his private soldiers through his stylized representation of their Cockney speech, or whether Mark Twain succeeded in accurately rendering the different dialects he set out to depict: the problem is that the potential always exists that the reader will interpret any such attempt at dialect representation as negative. This presents a serious artistic problem for authors: how can the voice of a character be represented in a way that indicates something about the character's speech patterns, but without immediately triggering the response that the speaker so represented is being denigrated?

Contextual factors

There are two important contextual factors that can affect how readers respond to any given representation of dialect: identity of the intended audience, and the identity of the writer.

Graham Shorrocks has proposed that there are two broad categories of dialect representation in literature. He draws the difference on the basis of the extent of dialect representation, and its intended audience.

One category is dialect literature, which Shorrocks defines as 'aimed essentially, though not exclusively, at a non-standard-dialect-speaking readership'(Shorrocks 1996: 386). The primary audience will thus be closely familiar with, and probably speakers of, the dialect in question. Dialect literature is most typically written in 'a non-standard dialect', and it commonly takes the form of poetry and ballads, although it does also occur in prose (1996: 386). The other category is literary dialect. That is, 'the representation of non-standard speech in literature that is otherwise written in Standard English ... and aimed at a general audience' (1996: 386). Most of the examples that I am drawing on for this book are from works aimed at national or international audiences and thus should be considered literary dialect, although a few might be considered examples of dialect literature.

In practice, the boundary between dialect literature and literary dialect can be a rather permeable one. There are for, example, texts that have found an audience beyond that they were originally intended for, as in the case of Cumberland poet Josiah Relph (Relph 1747), while collected volumes often contain poems written entirely in dialect alongside poems written primarily in Standard English with just a small amount of dialect, as in the case of Tom Hague (Hague 1976). As such, the categories of 'dialect literature' versus 'literary dialect' should be not considered as rigidly absolute. They do, however, provide a useful way of thinking about the relationship between dialect representation and intended readerships. In the case of dialect literature, much of the pleasure for the readership lies in encountering their own dialect in print, and a significant number of different dialect features may be employed with a high degree of frequency. The representation is often rich and affectionate, and several critics have argued that its primary function is to reinforce regional identity (see for example Beal 2000; Wales 2006; Taavitsainen and Melchers 1999), although Hermeston makes the case for a more nuanced and historicized understanding of the functions of dialect literature, including satire (Hermeston 2011). In the case of literary dialect, the author is more concerned with making the work accessible to a national audience not personally familiar with the dialect in question. As such the dialect representation may be limited both in terms of the range of dialect features represented and the frequency with which they occur.

The second contextual factor to be aware of is whether or not the writer themselves is considered to be an authentic speaker of the variety in question. Where an author can make no claim to be an authentic speaker of the dialect they are trying to represent, questions of stereotyping are particularly likely to arise. This is one of the problems with Mark Twain's representation of Jim. As an American of European origin, Mark Twain may be able to claim 'personal familiarity' with the 'Missouri Negro dialect' but he can hardly claim to speak it himself. As such, his attempts at representing this dialect are always going to be that of the outsider and therefore susceptible to criticism. By the same token, Rudyard Kipling would be much less susceptible to Orwell's assumption that he is 'looking down a distorting class-perspective' if he were himself a private soldier from London.

When an author can claim to be an authentic speaker of the variety some of these difficulties are reduced. However, in order to have succeeded in having something published a writer will by definition have had to learn to write and, as I discussed in Chapter 2, this means that they will have had extensive education in Standard English. As a result, whatever variety of English they speak at home, by the time they get published they have been extensively exposed to the standard language ideology, and are likely to be bidialectal with Standard English. This can result in a somewhat mixed attitude towards the variety they are trying to represent. Thomas Hardy, an author I shall discuss further in Chapter 10, may have championed the Dorset dialect from a philological point of view, but was nevertheless concerned to make the point that the dialect was not spoken in his childhood home. Tony Harrison, as I discussed in Chapter 2, shows a keen awareness in his poetry of the irony that, although he is attempting to examine and challenge linguistic prejudices, he is doing so by publishing in forms and places that are inaccessible to the people he is writing about. In each of these cases the fact that the writer in question comes from the area they are trying to represent means that it is less likely that they will be accused of linguistic stereotyping. Nevertheless, they still face the same problems as non-local authors in terms of how to represent the dialect in question without triggering a negative response in the audience.

Solving the problem?

In the remainder of this chapter I will explore some of the different strategies that writers have adopted to deal with this underlying problem.

Possible solutions 1: use *Standard English*

One possible option, as Orwell suggests, is to represent the character as speaking Standard English. This is something that Joseph Conrad chooses to do with the character of James Wait in *The Nigger of the 'Narcissus'*, as I discussed in Chapter 5. As I noted there, the problem is that such a representation can have the effect of 'bleaching out' the identity of the character. A slight variation on this approach is to represent a character as speaking Standard English when logically he or she would be speaking a non-standard variety, but then find a way to alert the reader to the fact that the character's accent should not be assumed to be RP. For example, in Ian Rankin's 'Rebus' series of crime thrillers, the central character, John Rebus, is a Scottish police officer. Nevertheless, Rankin does not engage in orthographic manipulation to represent Rebus's speech, and there are very few dialectal vocabulary items or grammatical structures to signal to the reader that Rebus speaks anything other than Standard English with an RP accent. Occasionally, however, Rankin signals to the reader that Rebus's speech has a Scottish accent. In the novel *Tooth and Nail* Rebus travels to London to work with the CID. He is greeted by Chief Inspector Laine:

> 'So,' said Chief Inspector Laine, 'you're here to help us with our little problem?'
>
> 'Well,' said Rebus, 'I'm not sure what I can do, sir, but rest assured I'll do what I can.'
>
> There was a pause, then Laine smiled but said nothing. The truth hit Rebus like lightning splitting a tree: *they couldn't understand him*! They were standing there smiling at him, but they couldn't understand his accent. Rebus cleared his throat and tried again.
>
> 'Whatever I can do to help sir.'
>
> Laine smiled again. 'Excellent, Inspector, excellent.'
>
> (Rankin 1998, 19–20)

Here, Rankin employs free indirect thought '*they couldn't understand him!*' to communicate Rebus's shock realization that his accent is impenetrable to the people he is speaking to. This serves to point up the fact that, although Rebus's speech is represented in Standard English with standard spelling, the reader should nevertheless infer a

Scottish accent for the character. In some ways this is quite an effective solution to the problem: the character's accent is pointed out to the reader but no attempt at orthographic representation needs be made. It can also be defended on the basis that no one has an accent in their own head, and that someone like Rebus would habitually use Standard English and standard spelling in writing but would speak with a Scottish accent. However, the problem is that readers do tend to assume that speech represented in Standard English is spoken with an RP accent (or possibly with an accent close to the reader's own). The effect of the reminder that Rebus has a Scottish accent is likely to be quite temporary.

Possible solutions 2: write the whole text in non-standard

Another possible solution to the problem of trying to represent a dialect in a literary text is to write the whole text in the dialect. In novels, this means that the story is typically told by a first-person narrator who does not themselves use Standard English. One advantage of such an approach, which I have already discussed briefly with reference to Hardy's short story 'Absent-mindedness in a Parish Choir', is that it diminishes the contrast between the narrative voice and the direct speech of the characters. A second advantage is that, in the course of a whole novel, it forces the reader to become accustomed to the representation of non-standard language. When the direct speech of a minor character is represented as non-standard in the middle of a novel written in Standard English, that representation is always new and unfamiliar to the reader in comparison to Standard English, and it is therefore not surprising that it results in 'reader resistance', as the reader has to slow down in order to work out the orthographical manipulations and think carefully about the unfamiliar vocabulary. However, if an entire novel is written in dialect, then readers often find that, although they may struggle with the first few pages, they quickly become familiar with the new orthographical conventions and vocabulary items and that they are then able to read at normal speeds. In other words, although the preference for reading texts written in Standard English is typically inculcated through many years of education and experience, readers are actually quite quick to adapt to a new set of conventions. Notable novels written primarily in a non-standard include Ken Saro-Wiwa's *Sozaboy* (first published 1985) and James Kelman's *How Late It Was, How Late* (first published 1994). Such novels continue to be much rarer than novels written in Standard English, however, and the additional initial effort required may deter potential readers, which in turn deters publishers from taking them on. While *How Late It Was, How Late* achieved considerable critical acclaim and won the Booker Prize in 1994, it also provoked considerable controversy, with one of the panel of judges, Rabbi Julia Neuberger, declaring it a disgrace.

Possible solutions 3: avoid representing the character's speech at all

A third solution to the problem of representing non-standard English in literary texts is to simply avoid representing the speech of non-standard characters at all. This approach has been discussed in detail by Michael Toolan in relation to the white South African writers Nadine Gordimer and J. M. Coetzee. In the case of South Africa, with its recent history of apartheid, the ideological challenges of trying to represent black South African speech when you are a white South African writer are particularly intense. Toolan finds that one of Gordimer and Coetzee's solutions is to avoid representing the speech of their inner city black African characters altogether, relying instead upon indirect speech and description. In some instances, for example Coetzee's novel *The Life and Times of Michael K*, it may be that the black African character is literally unable to speak (in the case of Michael K, as the result of an unspecified birth defect) thus rendering the character's silence both symbolic and highly visible. As Toolan discusses, this kind of approach avoids some of the major ideological problems of representing black speech:

> Intent on avoiding perpetuating the insult of appropriation, not wishing to be seen attempting to confer legitimacy or worth on speech (since they reject, as another version of ideological domination, the very idea of 'conferring legitimacy') these authors have maintained a kind of problematic silence with regard to the voices of ordinary black people.
>
> (Toolan 1992: 42)

Gordimer and Coetzee avoid 'the insult of appropriation' (that is, speaking on behalf of black Africans) and being seen 'to confer legitimacy' (that is, trying to represent black African speech in a way that makes it appear a valid form of speech, but which can come across as simply patronizing). Nevertheless, as Toolan concludes, this solution is itself problematic. As he discusses, characters who do not have direct speech 'remain at a distance, noticeably bereft of, or attenuated in, voice, excluded from the conventional illusion of self-expression' (Toolan 1992: 31). Not representing the speech of black African characters may avoid some ideological problems, but it also results in silent black African characters.

Possible solutions 4: challenge the standard language ideology

There are many different ways that writers have found to challenge the linguistic status quo, with greater and lesser degrees of success. For example, in his novel *Something Leather* Alasdair Gray challenges the convention whereby speakers of RP are represented with Standard English, while speakers of other dialects are represented through modifications to Standard English:

> 'I apologize!' says the headmistress, flinging her arms up in a gesture of surrender, 'I promise not to suggest that again. I will eventually destroy your father's record because you beg me to and then you can begin to speak the language of Shakespia and Docta Johnson. But Harriet is a lot lonelia than you, Linda, and *she* neva giggles at how you speak. *She* never giggles at anything. If you made friends with ha you would be helping ha, and yawself, and (I confess it) me! I am a selfish businesswoman, Linda. Mine is not a good school, it is a bad school if the cousin of a queen and the daughta of a famous singa are both lonely little gels hia.'

> (Gray 1991: 31)

Gray uses semi-phonetic respelling to indicate that the headmistress speaks with a non-rhotic accent, and that some of her vowels are distinctively RP (not in particular 'ha' for 'her' and 'hia' for 'here'). In the acknowledgements at the end of the novel, Gray writes:

> The device of putting the English Queen's dialect into phonetic speech is taken from James Kelman's unpublished story, *Cogmentum*. I have not done it to mock the diction which perhaps a twentieth of the British islanders employ with skill and confidence, but because I enjoy its weird music.

> (Gray 1991: 252)

Although Gray here claims only personal enjoyment as the moti-
vating factor behind his respelling, the terms in which he does so
make a series of political points. For example, rather than using
the conventional phrase 'the Queen's English' he instead calls it 'the
English Queen's dialect', implying both that she has no jurisdiction
over Scotland, and also that she speaks only one among many dialects.
By the same token, referring to RP's 'weird music' Gray emphasizes the
strangeness of the accent, rather than taking it as the default accent
from which all other accents differ.

Another approach is taken by David Dabydeen. Dabydeen is from
a relatively poor background in Guyana, and he earned a scholarship
for his education, eventually moving to England to attend Cambridge
University. In 1984 he published a set of poems, *Slave Song*, based on
the traditional Guyanese folk songs he had heard growing up. These
poems are presented first in Guyanese Creole in the main body of the
text. Then, at the back of book, each poem is translated into Standard
English and there is a short interpretative commentary upon the poem.

The poem 'The Servant's Song' tells the story of a white woman who
loses her ring. She harasses her servants to look for it, until one of them,
Peter, who has been brain damaged since a childhood accident, tells
his fellow servants that a dream told him to look up a duck's anus. Sure
enough, the ring is there and it is retrieved, washed and given back to
their mistress. She puts it on and kisses it, much to the entertainment
of the servants who do not tell her where it has been. Here is a short
extract from the middle of the poem:

> Till Peta, chupit in e ead since e bin young baai when e fall dung
> coconut tree –
> Man chase am, hooman scaan am, call dem husband 'Peta' when
> dem a cuss –
> Dis maaad – rass, maga – baai seh,
> 'Leh we go look in duck-battie, me get mind da ring deh-deh
> All night me studyation dis ting an me know e deh-deh.'
>   (Dabydeen 1984: 24)

There is considerable respelling to indicate alternative pronunciations
of words, and that these are generally consistent throughout the text;
for example there is TH-stopping in words such as 'dem' and 'ting'.
Syntactically, pronouns do not appear to inflect for case ('Leh **we** go
look') and verbs do not appear to inflect for tense ('when e **fall** dung

coconut tree'). There are also quite a lot of non-standard vocabulary items (although sometimes the respelling makes it difficult to determine if it is an unfamiliar word or if it simply looks unfamiliar), for example 'maaad-rass', 'maga-baaie' and 'scaan'. Overall, Dabydeen is representing quite a basilectal variety of Guyanese English, and it is one that speakers of Standard English are likely to struggle with. This is, of course, an immediate challenge to the reader familiar with Standard English because the convention of dialect representation is that whatever is done to represent non-standard English, it will not be too challenging to a reader.

In the case of *Slave Song*, translations are provided at the back of the collection to ensure that the reader is not left completely baffled. The translation provided for above lines is:

> Till Peter, stupid in his head since he was a young boy when he fell down a coconut-tree/ Men shoo him away, women are scorned of him, call their husband 'Peter' when they are cursing / This mad-arsed, emaciated boy says / 'Let's go look up duck's backside, my mind tells me that the ring is there / All night I thought and dreamt upon this thing and I just know it's there'
>
> (Dabydeen 1984: 51)

This is a fairly direct translation, although not a very tonally successful one. For example, the alliterative 'maaad – rass, maga – baaie' becomes 'mad-arsed, emaciated boy', with the colloquial phrasing of the first part standing in clumsy contrast to the Latinate 'emaciated' of the second. The 'duck-battie' that Peter talks about becomes 'duck's backside', which is a reasonable colloquial translation but it is unclear why 'duck-botty' would not have been better. Peter's speech as a whole sounds more logical but less interesting when rendered in Standard English; note in particular the replacement of the word 'study-ation' (studying? thinking about?) which becomes the more prosaic 'dream'.

A commentary is provided alongside the translation to help the reader interpret the poems. In the case of 'The Servant's Song' the commentary opens:

> *The Servant's Song* is an example of Guyanese peasant humour, simple and bawdy in a Chaucerian way but more crude. Vulgarity

is as natural as a cow-pat, as indicated above. However, on a serious level, the poem does reveal some of the characteristics of village life. For instance Peter, the village idiot – he fell from a coconut-tree when he was young and damaged his brain, a not uncommon village accident – who is the saviour of the moment.

(Dabydeen 1984: 50)

The register of this commentary is formal academic English. There is an attempt at placing these poems within the tradition of English literature by comparing them to Chaucer while acknowledging that they are 'more crude' (although this is a dubious claim given that Chaucer's *The Miller's Tale*, for example, concludes with Absalom kissing Alison's 'naked arse'). The commentary also claims that the poems are interesting for the anthropological insights they provide, suggesting that the poem 'does reveal some of the characteristics of village life' including the somewhat implausible-sounding claim that receiving brain damage in a fall from a coconut tree is a 'not uncommon village accident'.

There is thus a layering of different discourses around the central poems. One viewpoint might be that it is all rather patronizing: Dabydeen presents poems that do little to accommodate the Standard English reader, but this is then undercut by the condescending tones of the translation and commentary. An alternative reading is that Dabydeen is well aware of the shortcomings of the translation and commentary (indeed, he wrote them himself). They are deliberately allowed to appear stiff and unconvincing in comparison with the language of the poem. Indeed, in the introduction to the volume Dabydeen notes of one poem that '[t]he English fails where the Creole succeeds, particularly in the impossible translation of "dodo" as "sleep" ' (1984: 14). Hence the effect of the translations and commentary is not to patronize the original version, but to point to the inadequacy of Standard English. This is only possible, of course, because Dabydeen is of Guyanese origin, and is bidialectal in Guyanese English and academic Standard English.

Conclusion

In this chapter I have explored some of the reasons why 'reader resistance' to dialect representation occurs, and I have considered what implications it has for how dialect is handled in literary texts.

I have then explored some of the different ways in which authors have attempted to circumvent reader resistance, concluding that it is perhaps impossible to represent a character who uses dialect without opening up the potential for readers to judge the character stereotypically. In other words, the written nature of literature ensures that the problems of stereotyping that occur in film (which I discussed in Chapter 4) are if anything compounded in literature.

In the next chapter, Chapter 7, I compare the representation of dialect in literature and film in more detail, focusing on two novels which have been adapted into film: *Saturday Night and Sunday Morning* (Karel Reisz 1960) and *Howards End* (James Ivory 1992).

Further reading

Michael Toolan's article 'The Significations of Representing Dialect in Writing' (1992) is an important statement of the key issues. Dennis Preston's various articles on the subject of dialect representation are not specifically related to literature, but nevertheless engage with many of the issues I discuss here (Preston 1982; Preston 1985; Preston 2000). Jaffe and Walton's article 'The voices people read: Orthography and the representation of non-standard speech' (2000) is an important investigation of how real readers respond to written dialect representation. Genie Giaimo makes the case that one particular novel upends stereotypes through its representation of African American English in 'Talking Back through "Talking Black" ' (2010).

Exercises

Exercise 1

The Neon Court is a 2011 Urban Fantasy novel by Kate Griffin. In the extract below Matthew Swift, a Standard English speaker, is meeting the leader of the tribe, Toxik, whose speech is marked as non-standard. Read the extract, and think about the following questions:

- Griffin has created Toxik's speech using a range of linguistic features. What features can you identify and where do they originate?
- What is the effect of this mix?
- Think about the content of what Toxik says – how does it fit with the way that he speaks?

- Taken as a whole, do you think this representation challenges or reinforces stereotypes?

'Sorry u got beat up.'

'I shrugged, and even that hurt. 'I get that reaction'.

'Bein tribe – its not jus bout respec, u kno? its not jus bout strength or honor or dat. its bout not bein the other guy.'

'The other guy . . . ?'

'Its bout the whole world scream @ u, b dis way, walk dis way, talk dis way. u not talkin this way, u not walkin this way, u not lookin, u not speakin, u not bein wat we want u 2 be? den u rnt 1 of us. u r asbo kid, u r hoodie, u r da problem. kids wiv knives, kids wiv guns, kids wiv drink, kids wiv babies, kids dat make da old ladies run in2 da corner an say he didnt lok nice he didnt speak proper he must b out 2 get me, u kno? bcaus u r different, u dont do wat dey expect. n dey gotta b right. someone gotta b right bout something, otherwise dis world is shit, i mean real shit. ders gotta b absolutes, ders gotta be rules else y shuld der b good n bad, right n wrong n true n lie? dese r jus da thins made up by da time we liv in. 1 day right n wrong n good n bad will change agen, like theyve changed b4, n change agen n agen until 2moro isnt anythin we can name 2day, n all da futur looks back on da big old ere n now n says 'u lived evil – u all lived so evil.'

'That's a lot of big philosophy for a guy who lives in a shed.'

He shrugged. 'I red philosophy uni.'

(Griffin 2011: 179–180)

Exercise 2

Read the Jaffe and Walton article 'The voices people read: Orthography and the representation of non-standard speech' (2000). Based upon Jaffe and Walton's work, devise an experiment to test reader's responses to the literary representation of dialect. Think about:

- What is it about readers' responses to dialect representation that you are investigating?

- Which text(s) will you use as a basis for your study, and how will you need to rewrite them?
- Who will you ask to participate in the experiment?
- How will you conduct the experiment?
- What results do you expect to find?
- Can you identify any problems or limitations you might expect your study to have?

Exercise 3

Go back to the dialect representation you created in Chapter 5 Exercise 1. Do you think it stereotypes the speakers? Can you rewrite the passage to differentiate between a representation that challenges stereotypes and one that reinforces stereotypes? What features have you changed? How successful do you think the representation that challenges stereotypes is?

7

Comparing film and literature

In this chapter I draw the two halves of the book together by considering what happens when novels are taken as the source material for films. I seek to identify the differences in the way that dialect is handled in the two art forms. A comparison of this type can throw light onto the function and treatment of dialect in the two forms, offering insights into what is and is not possible, what works and what does not work in the spoken medium of film as against the written medium of literature.

I will be focusing on two pairs of novel to film adaptations: *Saturday Night and Sunday Morning* (novel by Alan Sillitoe 1958, film by directed Karel Reisz 1960) and *Howards End* (novel by E. M. Forster 1910, film directed by James Ivory 1992). I have already discussed an excerpt from the 1958 novel *Saturday Night and Sunday Morning* in Chapter 5, and I have undertaken an extended exploration of the role of dialect in some scenes from the 1992 Merchant Ivory film *Howards End* in Chapter 3. This chapter builds upon both these analyses, moving from the novel to the film in the case of *Saturday Night and Sunday Morning* and in the opposite direction, from the film back to novel, in the case of *Howards End*. As I will discuss, these two novel–film pairs offer rather different examples of the process of adaptation and this has direct implications for the way in which dialect is treated. The film for *Saturday Night and Sunday Morning* was produced very quickly after the novel's publication, and the screenplay was written by the author himself, Alan Sillitoe. By contrast, over 80 years elapsed between the publication of the novel *Howards End* and the film based upon it. As such the author had no involvement in the production of the film, and what was at the time of publication a contemporary novel had become a period piece by the time the film was made.

Following recent work in film adaptation, I take it as a basic principle that a film adaptation of a novel should not be judged simply on its faithfulness to the source text, but as a work of art in its own right. I further note that the study of the film adaptation of novels is a complex and growing field and I do not attempt to do justice to the films of novels as a whole in what follows: my focus is on what happens to the dialect representation.

Saturday Night and Sunday Morning

The novel *Saturday Night and Sunday Morning* by Alan Sillitoe was first published in 1958. It tells the story of Arthur, a young man earning a good wage at a bicycle factory who drinks to excess every Saturday night, and conducts an affair with Brenda, the wife of one of his colleagues, as well as Brenda's sister Winnie, who is married to a soldier. When Brenda becomes pregnant an abortion is induced at home, and when Winnie's husband catches up with him, Arthur receives a beating. Towards the end of the novel it appears that Arthur is beginning to settle down and he makes plans to marry Doreen, a young woman he has been seeing off and on during his other affairs.

As Sillitoe notes in a preface to the 1979 edition, '[t]he novel was turned down by four publishers. I thought I would make £200 from it at most' (Sillitoe 1985: 5). Unexpectedly it proved to be a bestseller, with the gritty plot, Northern setting, and flawed protagonist Arthur chiming with an emerging taste for novels, plays and films with social realist settings and 'angry young man' antiheroes. Other notable instances in this genre include the 1956 play by John Osbourne *Look Back in Anger* and the 1957 novel by John Braine *Room at the Top*, both of which were made into successful films in 1959. In order to capitalize on this box office trend for 'kitchen sink' films, plans were quickly made to bring *Saturday Night and Sunday Morning* to the screen. Owing to financial constraints on the production, Sillitoe was hired to write the screenplay of his novel. Sillitoe's deft handling of his source material, the pre-publicity afforded to the film by the novel, and the casting of up-and-coming young actor Albert Finney (himself from a Northern working-class background), all helped to ensure the commercial and critical success of the film, and it was nominated for six BAFTA Film Awards and won three, including Best British Film. It is today considered to be a classic of the 'British New Wave'.

In the transition from novel to film, some changes were made to the basic outlines of the plot, not least to keep the censor at bay. For example, in the film Arthur does not also have an affair with Winnie, and the attempted home abortion is unsuccessful (Brenda has a miscarriage later on instead). From the point of view of this chapter, however, what is more significant is how the Nottingham English of the novel is handled in the transition to film. As I discussed in Chapter 5, the novel is told in the third person and primarily focalized through the character of Arthur. The third person narrative voice is Standard English and the direct speech is represented as Nottingham English, with Arthur's speech being particularly densely marked. As such, there are many passages where there is a strong contrast between the variety of English used by the novel's narrator and that of the main character. However, as I discussed in Chapter 5, there are also numerous passages in the novel of free indirect discourse when the voice of the narrator and the voice of Arthur become blended, typically when the narrator is relating Arthur's thought processes. What happens to these different voices in the transition to film?

One element that transfers from film to novel relatively straightforwardly is the direct speech of Arthur and other characters. The following is from the scene in which Arthur meets Doreen for the first time. Arthur is standing at the bar and he strikes up a conversation with her when she orders drinks. She takes the order to her table, has a loud interchange with her mother, and then returns to continue talking to Arthur. Here is the scene in the novel:

'Is your mother deaf?' he asked when she came back, offering a cigarette.

'Yes, she is. And when people hear me shouting at her in the street they think I'm a pan-mouth. No duck, I don't smoke, thanks.'

He laughed and asked her name.

'Doreen. A rotten name ain't it?' She pushed out her tongue, healthy, spade-shaped, and drew it back into its warm retreat.

'What's wrong wi' it? Doreen's all right. My name's Arthur. Neither on 'em's up to much, but it ain't our fault, is it?'

'Well, I can think of better names than mine, I can tell yer.'

He drew the last drop of black-and-tan from his jar. 'Nobody's satisfied wi' what they've got, if you ask me. There'd be summat wrong with the world if they was. Where do you work then?'

'Me? Harris's, the hairnet factory. All right, I will have a fag. I'd better not let mam see me though, or she'll get on to me. I've worked there four years now, since I left school.'

I thought so, he said to himself. Nineteen.

(Sillitoe 1985: 174–5)

The primary means by which accent is represented in the direct speech in this passage is by the omission of 'th' in 'wi'' and ''em' and the secondary reduction of 'isn't' to 'ain't'. There is only one semi-phonetic respelling, 'yer', that indicates anything about vowel sounds, and this only indicates that the vowel is reduced. Overall, there is little here that is likely to slow the reader down in terms of deciphering respellings. However, it also means that there is little to help the reader who is unfamiliar with the Nottingham dialect acquire any understanding of how it might sound. In part this is because this excerpt comes from around halfway through the novel, when Arthur's style of speech has already been well-established for the reader. There is a greater density of semi-phonetic spellings earlier in the novel, but by the midway point Sillitoe is simply reminding readers that Arthur speaks with an accent, rather than attempting a more detailed representation of that accent. There is rather more in terms of dialectal vocabulary, particularly with 'pan-mouth', 'duck', 'summat', 'fag', 'mam'. These are unlikely to present problems to a British reader because most of these words are regularly used in representations of dialect speech in British literature. Only one word, 'pan-mouth', is less familiar, and the meaning of this can be easily deduced from context. Finally, there is some non-standard grammar, notably the non-standard preposition 'on' in 'Neither on 'em's up to much', an absent preposition in 'I've worked there four years' and non-standard concordance in 'if they was'. These grammatical features are not specific to Nottingham and serve to give a general sense of dialectal speech rather than particular geographical location. Overall, the direct speech in the extract gives a strong sense of being dialect speech, but there is little that specifically ties it to Nottingham.

Another notable aspect of the scene is that there is little difference between the speech of Arthur and Doreen. Although there is perhaps more detail in the depiction of Arthur's speech, particularly in the 'nobody's satisfied' speech, Doreen uses dialectal vocabulary such as 'pan-mouth' and 'duck', her speech is marked for the conventional contractions 'I'm', 'she'll' and 'don't', her accent is signalled with the one respelling 'yer' and her grammar features the non-standard 'I've worked there four years'. It is thus made clear from the outset that there is nothing about the romance between Doreen and Arthur that crosses socioeconomic classes. Indeed, the novel as a whole presents a homogeneous set of characters in terms of class, education and regional origin.

Finally, it is worth noting the strong contrast that exists between the characters' speech and the narrative voice. This contrast is particularly marked when the narrator reports Doreen's speech and then describes how she sticks her tongue out: "'Doreen. A rotten name ain't it?" She pushed out her tongue, healthy, spade-shaped, and drew it back into its warm retreat.' While Doreen is shown to be quick-witted and verbally dextrous in sparring with Arthur, the contrast between narrative and direct speech does underline the fact that she does not have the same level of education as the narrator.

The same scene in the 1960 film, which starts at 18 minutes 40 seconds. The scene is filmed with a shot/reverse shot sequence, creating the impression that the audience is seeing the characters alternatively from the other's perspective. When Arthur offers Doreen a cigarette, his hand and cigarette packet briefly appear at the bottom of the screen, suggesting that the camera's viewpoint at this point is closely aligned with his own. The style of filming places the spectator in an omniscient position, able to witness both sides of the conversation. It is a well-established cinematic technique, one that tends to feel very 'natural' because the audience is so accustomed to seeing it.

The dialogue replicates much of the scene in the novel, although in truncated form. To state the obvious, novels are generally much longer than film scripts. Whereas a typical novel is around 80,000–120,000 words in length, a typical film script is just 20,000–30,000 words. The comparison is not a direct one because novels contain more background description and narrative discussion than films, but a film will always contain fewer individual scenes than the novel on which it is based, and those scenes will be of shorter duration in terms of words uttered. In the case of this scene from *Saturday Night and Sunday Morning* both Arthur's observation that no one is ever satisfied and Doreen's fears that her mother will see her smoking have been cut. In the process some of the dialect words ('pan-mouth' and 'summat') have also been cut, although enough remain ('fag' and 'mam') to indicate that there is no consistent attempt to remove this vocabulary.

What is noticeable in the transition to film is that whereas the novel does not specify much about Doreen or Arthur's accents, the film cannot avoid doing so. One instance of this is that while the novel does not mark H-deletion for any of its characters (so Doreen says 'Harris's, the hairnet factory') the film clearly and repeatedly depicts H-deletion (Doreen deletes /h/ in both 'Harris' and 'hairnet'). It is interesting to speculate upon why Sillitoe chose not to represent H-deletion in the novel, despite the fact that it is an integral part of the Nottingham dialect. I would suggest two reasons for this. First, in Britain H-deletion has a strong cultural association with illiteracy and inarticulacy. In the written form, it is highly visible, so Sillitoe may have avoided this feature because he wishes the reader to understand that his characters, while dialectal, are neither unintelligent or inarticulate. Second, as I discussed in Chapter 4, some features become enregistered to certain dialects over time. H-deletion is a feature that historically has been particularly associated with London English, and even though it is now widespread across the British Isles, the association with London English remains. Sillitoe may therefore have felt that representing H-deletion on the page would cue his readers to reading with the wrong accent. In the film, the fact that the H-deletion is heard rather than written lessens its impact, and furthermore it occurs in a context where there are multiple other phonological features that mark the dialect as Northern English. For example, when Doreen says 'I don't **smoke**' she uses the long vowel [smɔ:k] rather than the diphthong [sməʊk], and when Arthur says 'the engineering **trade**' he uses the long vowel [tre:d] rather than diphthong [treɪd]. Sillitoe has made no attempt to represent these vowel sounds in the novel, but they emerge naturally in the film. As such, the H-deletion forms one aspect of the dialect representation, rather than standing alone as a potential marker of inarticulacy and a London identity.

Long before an actor opens his or her mouth on screen, decisions will have been taken by those involved in the filmmaking process about the kind of accent they will use for the role. In the case of *Saturday Night and Sunday Morning*, both actors are Lancastrian by birth and upbringing (Albert Finney is from Salford, Shirley Anne Field is from Bolton). As such they are authentically 'Northern English', which was a significant departure from standard filmmaking practice at the time, which tended to either ignore the North or use Southern actors imitating Northern accents. Nevertheless their accents are not authentic for the Nottingham area and some of their vowel sounds in particular are more typical of Lancashire than Nottinghamshire. Whether this matters to the audience is likely to depend on how familiar the viewer is with the Nottingham accent: most viewers are unlikely to notice or care, but for viewers from Nottingham, it may provide a distracting reminder that these are actors, not real people. This is a topic which I shall return to in Chapter 11.

Scenes in the novel that consist primarily of direct speech can be transferred to screen relatively straightforwardly, but scenes which made extensive use of free indirect discourse presented more of a challenge. Consider, for example:

> But Arthur's gaiety lapsed by the tennis courts, and both became sad, as if they had taken on a happiness that could not be sustained. Brenda walked with head slightly bent, starting when she stepped on a patch of ice. Arthur thought again about Jack, this time with a feeling of irritation that he should be so weak as to allow his wife to go off with other men. It was funny how often you felt guilty at taking weak men's wives; with strong men's you have too much to fear, he reasoned.
>
> Did Jack know? he wondered. Of course he did. Of course he did not. Yet if he doesn't know by now he will never know. He must know: no man is that batchy. He must have been told. Arthur had no positive reason for thinking that he knew, yet relied on the accuracy of his total 'weighings-up' from meetings with Jack and the reports of Brenda. But you could never be sure. Not that it would matter either way, as long as Jack didn't object to it. There wasn't much he could do about it: he would never make a divorce. It would cost too much, one way or another. And no woman is worth making a divorce over.
>
> (Sillitoe 1985: 60)

What is represented here is Arthur's thought processes as he tries to decide whether or not Jack knows about the affair his wife is having. There are some reporting clauses ('Arthur thought again', 'he reasoned' and 'he wondered') that indicate that Arthur's thoughts are being related; the sentences become short and contradictory ('Of course he did. Of course he did not.'); and some of the vocabulary becomes dialectal ('no man could be that batchy'). Through this free indirect thought the reader gets the impression of listening in to Arthur's thought processes.

Film, of course, has no easy way of representing thought, so Arthur's internal debate has to be externalized. In the case of this passage it is achieved through a scene in which Arthur and Brenda discuss whether or not Jack knows of their affair. The two of them emerge from some woods rearranging their clothes, and then stroll towards the club. The entire conversation is shot in a single long tracking shot, the camera dollying with them so that they are consistently in midshot as they seriously debate the issue. The scene starts at 29 minutes 10 seconds. In this version of the scene, the dialogue makes clear that Arthur is fully convinced that Jack does not know about the affair, and Brenda is the one who thinks that he might know. Elsewhere the film makes use of scenes where Arthur is fishing with his cousin, Bert, in order to create scenes that correlate with free indirect thought passages from the novel. The leisurely pace of fishing provides a pretext for Arthur to hold forth at slightly more length and with rather more forthrightness than might seem natural in other contexts, and it is in this context that he delivers perhaps the most famous line from the film 'All I want is a good time. Everything else is propaganda.' Nevertheless, the result of this transition to film is that the extended interior monologues and explorations of Arthur's mental state, presented in the novel through a combination of the narrator's Standard English and Arthur's own turn of phrase, are lost. As such Arthur's interior life is inevitably less fully represented than in the novel, and he emerges as a less thoughtful and reflective character. At the same time, the film benefits from the fact that Arthur is embodied onscreen in the person of Albert Finney, allowing the audience to infer information about his character from his actions, expressions and general demeanour in a way that is not possible in print. For example, Arthur's expression in the bar room scene as he waits for Doreen to return is a study in hopeful – if somewhat predatory – anticipation.

Overall, then, there are significant continuities in terms of dialect representation in the two versions of *Saturday Night and Sunday Morning*. In both novel and film, all the characters speak Nottingham English which means that Arthur lives, works and moves among characters who speak as he does. As such, his own social and regional identity never becomes a matter for conscious comment by him or anyone around him in either form. However, the shift from film to novel also creates some significant differences. For example, while literature can only hint at what accents might sound like, film must commit to portraying a specific accent every time a character opens his or her mouth. Also, while the characters may all speak Nottingham English, in the novel Standard English narration surrounds this direct speech, which provides a continual contrast with the dialectal characters. At the same time, however, the novel makes frequent use of free indirect discourse in order to weave the Standard English of the narrator together with Arthur's dialect. While this depends for its effectiveness on the distinction between Arthur's mode of speech and the narrator's written English, it does enable extended explorations of Arthur's consciousness in a way that is impossible in film. As I stated at the outset, it is not necessary to conclude that one medium is 'better' than the other at handling dialect, or to judge one art form as providing a more accurate and authentic account of the dialect speaking characters it represents. In the case of *Saturday Night and Sunday Morning* there are both gains and losses in the transition to film.

Howards End

The second literary adaptation I will consider is *Howards End*. This provides a useful point of comparison because, unlike *Saturday Night and Sunday Morning* which is firmly positioned within a single social milieu, the question of social identity and the interaction and potential slippage between classes is a central topic in *Howards End*, and one that is often signalled through language. As I shall argue, in both book and novel there is much greater awareness of the social meanings of language, although differences between literature and film mean that these issues are handled in different ways in the two versions of the story.

As I noted in Chapter 3, both the film and the novel of *Howards End* follow the lives of the two Schlegel sisters, Helen and Margaret, as their lives intersect with Leonard Bast, a clerk teetering of the edge of poverty, and the wealthy Wilcox family. The novel was published in 1910 by E. M. Forster, a writer who had already established his literary reputation with three previous novels: *Where Angels Fear to Tread* (1905), *The Longest Journey* (1907) and *A Room with a View* (1908). The 1992 film of the novel was produced by the Merchant Ivory film company, which was founded by director James Ivory and producer Ismail Merchant in the 1960s. Over the course of 44 years this company produced more than 50 films, including two earlier Forster adaptations, *A Room with a View* (1985) and *Maurice* (1987). *Howards End* proved to be one of their most successful films both commercially and critically, making around 70 million dollars in the course of its theatrical run in the US (not an enormous amount by blockbuster standards, but impressive for a small-budget literary adaptation) as well as being nominated for nine Oscars. The film is a richly detailed period piece, displaying the high production values that are a trademark of Merchant Ivory films. The cast features many notable actors of the British stage and screen, including Vanessa Redgrave, Emma Thompson, Anthony Hopkins and Prunella Scales.

At times, the film clearly directly takes its cue from the novel in terms of the representation of speech. For example, in terms of their language variety, one of the chief ways in which both Margaret and Helen Schlegel are characterized is through their rapid and plentiful speech. This is emphasized right from the start of the novel when Helen, reporting in a letter to Margaret on how much she is enjoying her stay with the Wilcoxes, asks her sister 'Meg shall we ever learn to talk less?' This line is directly borrowed from the novel into the film. Indeed, rather like Charles's tendency to speak hesitantly and indirectly in *Four Weddings and a Funeral*, in the film the breathless rapidity of Margaret and Helen's speech makes their RP accents seem less cold and distancing than they may otherwise do.

At the same time, however, their loquaciousness can be intimidating in and of itself. In the film, for example, when Leonard calls at the Schlegels' house in order to recover his umbrella he utters fewer than 40 words, most of which are used at the start of the encounter to explain the reason for his call, and at the end to make his escape. During the same period Helen and Margaret between them use over 250 words, introducing a number of different topics and making repeated offers of tea in an effort to get their visitor to stay. The effect is that they completely unnerve Leonard, who retreats hastily from their house.

A parallel scene occurs in the novel, where first Margaret and then Helen talk non-stop until Leonard flees. However, the novel can do what the film cannot so easily do, which is to give us direct access into what Leonard thinks of Margaret's speech:

> Her speeches fluttered away from the young man like birds. If only he could talk like this, he would have caught the world. Oh to acquire culture! Oh, to pronounce foreign names correctly! Oh, to be well informed, discoursing at ease on every subject that a lady started! But it would take one years. With an hour at lunch and a few shattered hours in the evening, how was it possible to

catch up with leisured women, who had been reading steadily from childhood?

(Forster 1973: 37).

As with *Saturday Night and Sunday Morning*, free indirect discourse is used so that the voice of the narrator merges with the character's thoughts ('Oh to acquire culture!'). Here, however, the point is not a blending between Standard English and dialect. Indeed, Leonard appears to think in a register not that distinct from that of the narrator, apparently employing words such as 'discoursing' and 'leisured' as well as the formal third person pronoun 'one'. What the free indirect thought does offer is an insight into how Leonard responds to the educated, culturally knowledgeable speech that he hears. What Leonard thinks here might be termed metalanguage or 'talk about talk' (or more precisely perhaps in this instance, 'thought about talk'). And the point is that while there is nothing overtly dialectal about either Leonard's speech or thought in this introductory scene, he is acutely aware that he lacks cultural capital in other ways and thus that by some measures his speech falls short of Margaret's. This is not something that film can explicitly state in the same way.

In other scenes, the difference in media between film and novel has necessitated some specific alterations in the way that the characters speak. In Chapter 3 I explored the scene between Jacky and Leonard when Leonard gets home from his first encounter with the Schlegels. I found that the scene showed a difference between Jacky and Leonard through their contrasting accents, with Jacky having a much more marked London accent than Leonard. Looking for the same scene in the novel, we find this:

'What ho!' said Leonard, greeting that apparition with much spirit, and helping it off with its boa.

Jacky, in husky tones, replied, 'What ho!'

'Been out?' he asked. The question sounds superfluous, but it cannot have been really, for the lady answered, 'No,' adding, 'Oh, I am so tired.'

'You tired?'

'Eh?'

'I'm tired,' said he, hanging the boa up.

'Oh, Len, I am so tired.'

'I've been to that classical concert I told you about,' said Leonard.

'What's that?'

'I came back as soon as it was over.'

'Any one been round to our place?' asked Jacky.

'Not that I've seen. I met Mr Cunningham outside, and we passed a few remarks.'

'What, not Mr Cunningham?'

'Yes.'

'Oh, you mean Mr Cunningham.'

'Yes. Mr Cunningham.'

'I've been out to tea at a lady friend's.'

Her secret being at last given to the world, and the name of the lady-friend being even adumbrated, Jacky made no further experiments in the difficult and tiring art of conversation. She never had been a great talker. Even in her photographic days she had relied upon her smile and her figure to attract and now that she was

On the shelf,

On the shelf,

Boys, boys, I'm on the shelf,

She was not likely to find her tongue. Occasional bursts of song (of which the above is an example) still issued from her lips, but the spoken word was rare.

(Forster 1973: 48–9)

It is noticeable that, contrary to the explicit statement made by the narrator in this scene, Jacky *is* shown to be a great talker in the film. In the comparable scene in the film, she chatters away to him about what she was thinking while he was absent. Much of Jacky's dialogue in this film scene, as well as the telling moment where Leonard corrects her double negative, has been freshly written for the film by the scriptwriter, Ruth Prawer Jhabvala. One of the reasons for this change is that in a novel the omniscient narrator can provide background explanations about characters' speech and motivations, as Forster does above when he offers the metalinguistic explanation 'She never had been a great talker.' In films it would be difficult to provide such explanations without resorting to clumsy devices such as a voiceover or explication by another character (for example, Leonard could tell Helen that 'Jacky does not talk very much because in her youth she relied upon her looks rather than her tongue'). Instead, the filmmakers have found an alternative way to illustrate the main point of the scene, which is that, despite the fact that Leonard has taken responsibility for Jacky, she is not in tune with his social and cultural aspirations. This has been done by giving Jacky and Leonard contrasting varieties of English, and also by depicting Jacky as a chatterbox while Leonard is quiet and reserved.

In fact, in the novel very little is done orthographically to indicate the accent of either Jacky or Leonard. In the scene above, for example, the fact that they greet each other with the phrase 'What ho!' sounds colloquial, although one might expect a couple to greet each other in a familiar way. Similarly, there is a hint of non-standard grammar when Leonard asks Jacky 'You tired?' instead of 'Are you tired?' but this is the kind of contraction that often occurs in casual conversation and does not necessarily denote dialect, even if it is more likely to be represented in the speech of characters further down the social spectrum. Later in this scene in the novel, as in the film, Jacky questions Leonard about whether he loves her:

'You do love me?'

'Jacky, you know that I do. How can you ask such questions?'

'But you do love me, Len, don't you?'

'Of course I do.'

A pause. The other remark was still due.

'Len—'

'Well? What is it?'

'Len, you will make it all right?'

'I can't have you ask me that again,' said the boy, flaring up into a sudden passion. 'I've promised to marry you when I'm of age, and that's enough. My word's my word. I've promised to marry you as soon as ever I'm twenty-one, and I can't keep on being worried. I've worries enough. It isn't likely I'd throw you over, let alone my word, when I've spent all this money. Besides, I'm an Englishman, and I never go back on my word. Jacky, do be reasonable. Of course I'll marry you. Only do stop badgering me.'

(Forster 1973: 50)

Again, there is some colloquial phrasing with 'worries enough', 'throw you over' and 'badgering me'. However, there is nothing in the presentation of these lines to indicate that Jacky and Leonard speak at all differently from each other, or that either speaks with a London English accent.

It is instructive to turn to the scene where Jacky visits the Schlegels in order to try and find Leonard. In the novel, this scene is not shown directly, but is instead recounted by Helen (who was the only one at home) to Tibby and Margaret:

'Annie opens the door like a fool, and shows a female straight in on me, with my mouth open. Then we began – very civilly. 'I want my husband, what I have reason to believe is here.' No – how unjust one is. She said 'whom', not 'what'. She got it perfectly. So I said, 'Name, please?' and she said, 'Lan, Miss, and there we were.'

'Lan?'

'Lan or Len. We were not nice about our vowels. Lanoline.'

(Forster 1973: 111)

What is interesting about this scene is that Helen reports that she hears Jacky's pronunciation of 'Len' as 'Lan'. This raised vowel suggests that Jacky does indeed speak with a noticeable London accent. However, at no other point in the direct speech of the novel does Forster make use of semi-phonetic respellings in order to indicate this to the reader: Jacky says 'But you do love me, Len, don't you?' not 'But you do love me, Lan, don't you?' This then is a conscious choice on Forster's part, pre-sumably made because he wished to avoid the effect that representing Jacky's accent on the page would have triggered for the reader. Jacky is a 'fallen woman' who has latched onto Leonard and is financially, socially and culturally dragging him down. Yet the novel is not unsym-pathetic towards her, showing that she has ended up in this position because she was left alone in the world at a young age. Forster per-haps felt that presenting her as speaking in a marked London dialect would have made his readers more quick to judge her as uneducated and thriftless, rather than seeing her as a victim of circumstance.

The question remains, however, as to why Forster nevertheless included Helen's commentary upon Jacky's language variety. Was it simply to alert the readers that Jacky does have a marked accent? If so, the effect is quite subtle. More significantly, what the scene does is to illustrate that Helen, despite her professed concerns for the lower orders, is nevertheless rather thoughtless in her approach to them. From Helen's perspective, Jacky's visit provides the oppor-tunity for a comic turn. First she draws on a stereotype of London speech in order to report that Jacky used a non-standard relative clause marker 'I want my husband, what I have reason to believe is here.'

Then she corrects herself, but nevertheless goes on to use her mishearing of 'Len' to create the joke name of 'Mrs Lanoline' for Jacky. Her lack of empathy for Jacky's position is further underscored by her use of the socially distancing term 'female' to describe Jacky to her siblings.

By contrast, in the film Jacky's visit is shown directly, and Margaret and Tibby are present along with Helen. Helen and Tibby are inclined to see the funny side of the encounter (for example, they joke about having 'corrupted a married man by giving him tea!') but Jacky maintains her dignity and leaves them looking uncomfortable for having mocked her. None of the Schlegels pass comment upon Jacky's English. This change may have occurred simply because it makes much more sense in the visual medium of film to portray Jacky's visit directly rather than have it related verbally by Helen. However, another factor may have been that, owing to the passage of 80 years and changing social attitudes, Helen's commentary upon Jacky's speech would seem even more jarringly snobbish to modern filmgoers than it would have done to Edwardian readers.

Finally, I will consider the key scene in which Leonard returns to the Schlegels in order to apologize for his wife's embarrassing visit, and begins to converse with the Schlegels on equal terms about literature. Here is the scene in the novel:

'But was the dawn wonderful?' asked Helen.

With unforgettable sincerity he replied, 'No.' The word flew again like a pebble from the sling. Down toppled all that had seemed ignoble or literary in his talk, down toppled tiresome R. L. S. and the 'love of the earth' and his silk top-hat. In the presence of these women Leonard had arrived, and he spoke with a flow, an exultation, that he had seldom known.

'The dawn was only gray, it was nothing to mention—'

'Just a gray evening turned upside down. I know.'

'—and I was too tired to lift up my head to look at it, and so cold too. I'm glad I did it, and yet at the time it bored me more than I can say. And besides—you can believe me or not as you choose—I was very hungry. That dinner at Wimbledon—I meant it to last me all night like other dinners. I never thought that walking would make such a difference. Why, when you're walking you want, as it were, a breakfast and luncheon and tea during the night as well, and I'd nothing but a packet of Woodbines. Lord, I did feel bad! Looking back, it wasn't what you may call enjoyment. It was more a case of sticking to it. I did stick. I—I was determined. Oh, hang it all! what's the good—I mean, the good of living in a room for ever? There one goes on day after day, same old game, same up and down to town, until you forget there is any other game. You ought to see once in a way what's going on outside, if it's only nothing particular after all.'

(Forster 1973: 117–18)

This contains another instance of metalanguage. The novelist is able to cue the reader to the shift in Leonard's linguistic behaviour at this point by writing of his 'unforgettable sincerity' and stating explicitly that 'he spoke with a flow, an exultation, that he had seldom known'. The comparable scene in the film is unable to offer such overt narrative comment, although the fact that the next scene shows Leonard sitting down and talking animatedly to the Schlegels shapes a similar understanding of the way in which Leonard has broken through the social barriers and found his own eloquence at this point. In terms of how he speaks, there is a slight shift in register in both versions. In the novel, Leonard begins to use more colloquial phrasing than he has previously employed in the presence of the Schlegels including 'Lord!', 'sticking to it', 'same old game' and 'hang it all'. In the film, it is Leonard's accent that shifts as he starts to H-delete and T-glottalize more frequently. This difference perhaps reflects the fact that the representation of accent through respelling on the page is often associated with illiteracy and as such it would not have been an appropriate way to convey Leonard's new-found eloquence. In film, shifts in accent can be shown without raising such associations.

In summary then, issues of class and language variety are central to both the novel and film version of *Howards End*, but the change in medium means that dialect is handled rather differently in each. In the novel, Forster makes no attempt to represent the accent of Leonard or Jacky on the page, even though there are indications that they do speak with marked London accents. In the film, accent is used as an important indicator of social distinction, with Jacky speaking in a strongly marked London accent and Leonard in a mildly marked one, which becomes stronger at moments of emotion or connection. Indeed, I would suggest that the filmmakers have made a virtue out of a necessity: because it is impossible to avoid giving characters an accent in film, they have used the contrasting accents of the Schlegels, Jacky and Leonard to provide background information about the characters and map their shifting relationships.

Conclusion

In Chapters 5 and 6 I discussed the difficulties that writers face in attempting to represent dialect in print. This chapter has illustrated the point that, while writers have to choose which dialect features to represent on the page, filmmakers are able to represent dialect more fully and flexibly. However, I also demonstrated that writers have some significant advantages. First, as I showed in *Saturday Night and Sunday Morning*, writers are able to combine dialect representation with free indirect speech in order to provide an insight into the thoughts and feelings of characters in a way that can be difficult to replicate in film. Second, as I showed in *Howards End*, narrators in literature can make metalinguistic comments that shape the way in which readers understand and respond to the speech of characters in a way that simply isn't possible in film, and that this can be particularly useful when writers wish to indicate that a character changes speech style. In the next chapter, Chapter 8, I consider this concept of 'metalanguage' further, exploring where it appears in films and literature and what function it fulfils.

Further reading

Brian McFarlane's *Novel to Film: An Introduction to the Theory of Adaptation* (1996) offers a readable introduction to adaptation. The Oxford University Press journal *Adaptation*, which launched in 2008, is well worth dipping into to get a sense of current work in the field.

Exercises

Exercise 1

In Chapter 5 I looked at the dialect representation in a short extract from Charles Dickens' *Oliver Twist*. Read the whole of Chapter 8 where that extract appears and think about the following:

- How are the voices of the characters represented on the page?
- What is the effect of this representation?
- To what extent and in what ways is language important in this chapter?

- If you had been advising a director on how to create a movie scene out of this chapter, what are the key messages you would have wanted to convey?
- What would be the challenges of creating this scene in film?
- What advice would you have provided to the director in terms of casting for the voices of the actors?

Now watch the relevant section of David Lean's *Oliver Twist* (Lean 1948). The scene starts at 32 minutes and runs to around 36 minutes. Think about the following:

- How does the scene compare to your ideas for it?
- In particular, how is Oliver's entry into the criminal underworld depicted? Consider all aspects of filmmaking in the scene.
- How is dialect handled in the scene?
- How do Oliver and the Artful Dodger's accents work in relation to one another?
- How does this compare to the novel?
- Alec Guinness's portrayal of Fagin was felt by many critics to be a negative Jewish stereotype. What role does language play in constructing that stereotype? How does the film version of Fagin relate to the book version of Shylock?

Exercise 2

This exercise compares the opening of Zadie Smith's *White Teeth* (2001) to the Channel 4 television adaptation (2002). Note: I have tried to stick to films for the purposes of this book, but *White Teeth* is such an interesting example of contemporary adaptation that I have used it for this exercise. Television is similar to film for the purposes of studying dialect representation, although there are some different production and reception issues (e.g. the serial nature of much television).

Focus in particular on the scene where Archie first meets Clara at a party, which occurs on p. 24 of the book and at 33 minutes 30 seconds in the first episode in the television series. It is, however, useful to contextualize this scene within the whole of the two chapters of the novel and the first episode of the television series (there is some significant reorganization and extension of scenes from the book in order to make Archie and Clara's story take up a whole television episode).

Think about:

- How are the voices of Clara and Archie represented on the page?
- What is the effect of the representation?
- Whose viewpoint and perceptions are being reported? You might think in particular about the metalinguistic comment about Clara's 'lilting Caribbean accent'.
- How are the voices of Clara and Archie represented on screen?
- What is the effect of the representation?
- Can you identify any significant differences in the handling of dialect in the two versions? What effects do these differences have?

8

Metalanguage

In the previous chapter I noted that E. M. Forster makes use of the fact that in literature it is possible for a narrator to comment directly upon a character's use of language, and so guide the reader's understanding and interpretation of what is presented on the page. The narrator of *Howards End* does this, for example, in order to explain that Jacky does not speak very much. I also noted that it is possible to find characters thinking and talking about each other's language, as Leonard does when he thinks about Margaret's cultured speech, or as Helen does when she mocks Mrs Bast for saying 'Lan' rather than 'Len'. I termed such overt commentary upon language metalanguage.

In this chapter I explore the concept of metalanguage further. I begin by considering some of the functions of metalanguage that have been identified by linguists investigating 'real world' language. I then look at the range of different places in which metalanguage can be found in literary texts, and the purposes to which it is put. To exemplify the way in which metalanguage can work in conjunction with dialect representation I undertake a case study of the short story 'The Son's Veto' by Thomas Hardy. In conclusion I return to the issue of film, and argue that although metalanguage is less frequent in film dialogue, it does nevertheless occur and can fulfil significant functions.

What is metalanguage?

Metalanguage is 'talk about talk'. It is what happens when language is not just the *means* of communication, but also the *topic* of communication. The whole of linguistics is a form of metalanguage, in that linguists use language to analyse and discuss the sounds, structure and meanings of language. This book you are currently reading is an extended exercise in metalanguage, as I am using language to write about one particular feature of language in literary texts. However, metalanguage is not confined to academic institutions, and it is not the preserve of academics. Non-linguists are engaging in metalanguage when they make comments such as 'Janine always talks so quickly I can hardly understand her!' or 'He's got such a lovely, deep voice'. They are also engaging in metalanguage when they express beliefs about language, such as 'Young people today don't talk properly' or 'People who use slang are just being lazy'. These kinds of beliefs are often described by linguists as 'folk linguistics', and they may have little basis in fact from the point of view of academic linguists. Nevertheless, they can be highly significant because of the way in which they shape people's understanding of the world.

Jaworski, Coupland and Galasiński note that a frequent purpose of metalanguage in natural speech is to shape the way in which a given utterance is understood by the audience:

> Metalanguage, in the sense of direct or indirect quotation of previous utterances, or commentary on language performance, style, or rhetorical function, can therefore be a resource for strategic communication. In doing metalinguistic commentary, for example 'What I was trying to say was . . . ', we can influence and negotiate how an utterance is or should have been heard, or try to modify the values attributed to it.
>
> (Jaworski et al. 2004: 3–4)

As we saw in Chapter 7, writers can make use of metalanguage to 'influence and negotiate' how readers respond to the language of a text. E. M. Forster, for example, comments that Jacky 'never had been a great talker', thus explaining to us why she falls silent at a particular point in the text and also providing the opportunity to describe her history a little. In a similarly descriptive vein, writers can also make use of metalanguage to define words, describe speech styles and explain why dialect is being represented in a particular way. Metalanguage can thus be a very useful tool for writers because it can guide the reader to interpret how characters speak. It is particularly valuable given all the practical limitations on dialect representation on the page that have been discussed in previous chapters.

However, there is often much more to the use of metalanguage than the description of how a particular utterance is to be understood. Jaworski, Coupland and Galasiński argue that metalanguage is often a crucial component to the social 'work' that language does:

Metalinguistic representations may enter public consciousness and come to constitute structured understandings, perhaps even 'common sense' understandings – of how language works, what it is usually like, what certain ways of speaking connote and imply, what they *ought* to be like. That is, metalanguage can work at an ideological level, and influence people's actions and priorities in a wide range of ways, some clearly visible and others much less so.

(Jaworski et al. 2004: 3)

As an example of the way in which metalanguage can work at an ideological level, it is worth revisiting the topic of Chapter 2, where we saw that there is a widespread belief that Standard English is inherently superior, and that speakers of other varieties are less intelligent and less well educated. When such beliefs are articulated, they can become a means of policing social boundaries, as is evident in this letter in a local paper, cited by the Milroys:

For many years I have been disgusted with the bad grammar used by school-leavers and teachers too sometimes, but recently on the lunchtime news, when a secretary, who had just started work with a firm, was interviewed her first words were: 'I looked up and seen two men' etc. It's unbelievable to think, with so many young people out of work, that she could get such a job, but perhaps 'I seen' and 'I done' etc. is the usual grammar nowadays for office staff and business training colleges.

(Letter in local paper, cited by Milroy and Milroy 1999: 38)

Here, the writer has observed someone on the television using a non-standard grammatical form, and decided that she therefore should not be employed as a secretary. There are lots of assumptions being made to underpin this pronouncement: that 'I seen' and 'I done' are not just different but that they are 'bad grammar'; that someone who uses such forms in speech will not be able to write Standard English; that someone who speaks like this does not deserve certain kinds of jobs; that this one instance is suggestive of a national decline in standards. Jaworski et al. write that:

it is in the interplay between usage and social evaluation that much of the social 'work' of language – including pressures towards social integrations and division, and the policing of social boundaries generally – is done.

(Jaworski et al. 2004: 3)

In social terms, then, it is the interaction between *how language is* and *how language is judged* that is significant. In the case of this letter, the metalanguage creates a potentially confrontational interpersonal dynamic between the secretary who was interviewed about a robbery and the letter writer who passes judgement on her. Imagine, for example, what might ensue if the letter writer had instead made these comments directly to the secretary, rather than through the medium of print! Jaworski, Coupland and Galasiński note that through metalanguage 'We can mark out personal or group identities, display expertise, claim incompetence, and do many other sorts of "personal identification work" or "social relationship work" ' (Jaworski et al. 2004: 4). It is perhaps unsurprising, then, that many writers and filmmakers have exploited metalanguage in order to dramatize relationships between characters or to explore wider themes of identity and division.

From this perspective, the whole of Tony Harrison's poem 'Them & [uz]', which I discussed in Chapter 2, can be seen as an extended exercise in character-based metalanguage. Right from the start of the poem the narrator is remembering the metalanguage of his teacher:

> 4 words only of *mi 'art aches* and ... 'Mine's broken,
> you barbarian, T.W.!' *He* was nicely spoken.
> *from* 'Them & [uz]' by Tony Harrison

(Harrison 2006: 122)

When the teacher pronounces that the schoolboy is a 'barbarian', he is doing social work by drawing boundaries around who is permitted to talk and who is not, who is permitted to play the full range of Shakespearean characters, and who is restricted to the 'drunken Porter in Macbeth'. This world view – which the schoolboy appears to have internalized at least to some extent – creates a social chasm between the 'nicely spoken' schoolteacher and his pupil, who is by implication 'poorly spoken'. In retrospective response, the narrator interpolates his own commentary. For example:

> 'Poetry's the speech of kings. You're one of those
> Shakespeare gives the comic bits to: prose!

All poetry (even Cockney Keats?) you see
's been dubbed by [ʌs] into RP,
Received Pronunciation, please believe [ʌs]
your speech is in the hands of the Receivers.'
from 'Them & [uz]' by Tony Harrison

(Harrison 2006: 122)

Again, the schoolteacher is drawing boundaries between, on the one hand, poetry, serious subjects, kings and RP speakers, and on the other hand, prose, 'comic bits', ordinary people and dialect speakers. This time the narrator disrupts these categories by inserting his own metalanguage, noting in brackets that the author of the poem, John Keats, was himself a 'Cockney' and later commenting that 'Wordsworth's *matter/water* are full rhymes'. This interplay between the schoolteacher's remembered metalanguage and the poet's own resistant metalanguage creates a dramatic situation and a striking poem.

Where does metalanguage occur in literary texts?

In this section I explore four primary areas in which metalanguage occurs in literary texts: paratexts, third person narration, first person narration, and character speech and thought. Very broadly speaking, in paratexts and third person narration metalanguage tends to be presented as descriptive and authoritative because it originates from the implied author of the text or from an omniscient third person narrator. The focus is thus on the language and speakers so described. In first person narration and character speech and thought, metalanguage is often more overtly doing 'social relationship work' because such comments originate from a specific character. As such, the focus tends to be more on what such comments tell us about the character who made them.

Metalanguage and paratext

The first place to look for metalanguage about dialect is in the paratexts that often accompany literary texts. Paratexts are all those parts of a book outside the 'text proper' which, as Gerard Genette points out, serve variously to convey information, suggest interpretations or offer advice to the reader as he or she encounters the main body of the text (Genette 1997: 11–12). Paratexts include prefaces, dedications, footnotes, glossaries, indexes, and so forth. While they are by no means restricted to commenting upon the language of the text, they not infrequently have a metalinguistic element. We have already encountered one metalinguistic paratext in Chapter 6: Mark Twain's 'explanatory note' for *Huckleberry Finn* in which he explains that he represents seven different local varieties in the novel, and insists that these were drawn 'painstakingly, and with the trustworthy guidance and support of personal familiarity'. This paratext is doing important textual work in terms of directing the reader to read the dialect representation as both detailed and authentic.

An even more famous paratext is William Wordsworth's *Preface to the Lyrical Ballads* (1800) in which he sets out to explain what is different about his poetic diction in *Lyrical Ballads* compared to prevailing tastes in poetry. In a recent article, Alex Broadhead explores the *Preface* alongside two footnotes that Wordsworth also added to *Lyrical Ballads* in 1800. These footnotes offer glosses to the words *clipping*, *gill* and *force*, highlighting these words as being distinct from Standard English and belonging to specific regional areas. However, as Broadhead notes, there are many other regional words in *Lyrical Ballads* which Wordsworth could potentially have footnoted but chose not to. Broadhead argues that Wordsworth 'used footnotes selectively to draw attention to the way in which all aspects of his authorial identity…were bound up with the places and people he represented' (Broadhead 2010: 260). Broadhead's article thus offers a detailed case study of the way in which writers can use paratexts to direct readers towards particular ways of reading their representation of dialect.

Genette notes that '[b]y definition, something is not a paratext unless the author or one of his associates accepts responsibility for it' (1997: 9), these associates including editors and publishers. As such, we tend to assume that most metalinguistic pronouncements made in these paratexts do aim to be descriptive of the texts to which they are attached. We may disagree over whether Twain genuinely did include seven different local varieties in *Huckleberry Finn*, and we may debate the extent to which Wordsworth's poems really adhered to the practices he described in his Preface, but in both instances readers are likely to accept that the paratexts primarily aim to *describe* the language of the main text. In a few instances, however, paratexts are used more playfully, as I noted in Chapter 6 in relation to Alasdair Gray and David Dabydeen. There I discussed the fact that, although in his 'Acknowledgements' to *Something Leather*, Gray claims that he put RP into 'phonetic speech' only for his own pleasure, nevertheless the terms in which he states this claim make a number of political points about the status of RP (calling it 'the English Queen's dialect', for example). In *Slave Song* Dabydeen draws attention to the way in which paratexts such as translations and commentaries put frames of interpretation around the language of literary texts, and he reminds us that even in apparently neutral scholarly discourse the function of metalanguage is often to draw boundaries between, for example, the 'simple and bawdy' language of the peasant and the language of the educated commentator. These examples reveal that while in most cases paratexts may appear to be authoritative and descriptive, and while they will often provide valuable information about what the author intended, they are nevertheless interventions into the way in which audiences read and respond to the text, and as such they are never entirely neutral.

Metalanguage and third person narration

Another common place to find metalanguage is in third person narration. Again, this metalanguage often appears to be primarily descriptive as it has the authority of the omniscient narrator. When, for example, E. M. Forster explains that Jacky 'never had been a great talker' this comment is doing important narrative work in terms of directing the reader as to how to interpret the speech and dialect representation. As readers, we are not invited to reflect upon why the narrator is making such comments or to consider whether or not the narrator's description is accurate.

The opening sentence of Angela Carter's novel *Nights at the Circus* offers a wonderful example of how a third person metalinguistic comment can accompany dialect representation in order to point the reader towards a particular understanding of a character:

'Lor' love you sir!' Fevvers sang out in a voice that clanged like dustbin lids. 'As to my place of birth, why, I first saw light of day right here in smoky old London, didn't I! Not billed the 'Cockney Venus', for nothing, sir, though you could just as well 'ave called me 'Helen of the High Wire', due to the unusual circumstances in

which I came ashore – for I never docked via what you might call
the *normal channels* sir, oh, dear me, no; but, just like Helen of Troy,
was *hatched*.'

(Carter 1985: 7)

The dialect here is marked orthographically by the omission of
the final consonant in 'Lor" and the H-deletion in ''ave' (although
H-deletion does not occur in the more formal phrase 'Helen of the
Hire Wire'), as well as the non-standard negation of 'I never docked'
and the frequent deployment of discourse markers such as 'Lor'
love you' and 'why'. These all add up to a conventional, if lightly
marked, representation of London English. However, the third person narrator offers metalinguistic commentary about how Fevvers
speaks, telling us that she 'sang out in a voice that clanged like
dustbin lids'. The metaphor 'like dustbin lids' reinforces an association between non-standard English and class (clanging dustbin lids
are common) but the exuberance of the metaphor and the fact that
Fevvers 'sang out' indicates that there is something energetic and
unapologetic about her. This first impression is fully borne out by
the ensuing description of a larger-than-life character who purports
to have been hatched from an egg and who has wings as well as
arms. But if you try reading this first sentence of the novel excluding this metalinguistic reporting clause ('Lor' love you sir! As to my
place of birth, why, I first saw daylight …') it has quite a different
effect. Instead of seeming energetic and unapologetic, the speaker may
seem garrulous and uneducated. The short third person metalinguistic
comment thus directs the reader to interpret the dialect representation in a particular way, working in conjunction with the semi-
phonetic respellings and other features to create the impression of a
character.

That writers are often very conscious of the way in which
metalinguistic comments can guide reader response is evidenced by
processes of revision. Patricia Ingham has explored the revisions that
Thomas Hardy made to the dialect representation in his novel *Tess of
the D'Urbervilles* between its initial publication in serial form in the
Graphic in 1891, the multiple book editions that followed, up to the
Wessex Novels edition of 1912. She finds that as well as revising the
level of detail in the dialect representation, and altering which characters speak dialect when, Hardy also changed some of the commentary
about dialect in the novel:

In the serial and first and second editions he writes:

> Mrs. Durbeyfield still habitually spoke the dialect; her daughter... used it only when excited by joy, surprise, or grief. (ch. 3)

... But in the fifth edition (1892) Hardy explicitly abandons his intended 'poetic' use by changing the passage quoted above to read as it still did in 1912:

> her daughter... spoke two languages; the dialect at home, more or less; ordinary English abroad and to persons of quality.
>
> (Ingham 1970: 359)

Ingham argues that his change signals that Hardy had reverted to 'an uncritical acceptance of dialect as a social indicator' (Ingham 1970: 359). Susan L. Ferguson offers an alternative interpretation, arguing that it is evidence that Hardy abandoned his initial project 'of identifying dialect speech with emotionality and the historical past' and that he revised the novel to project the idea that 'various styles of speaking can persist, that dialect as well as standard vocabulary can be learned' (Ferguson 1998: 15). This is a marked shift in perspective and, as Ferguson demonstrates, one that has significant repercussions for the handling of dialect throughout the novel.

Metalanguage and first person narration

In first person narration, metalanguage is attributed to a specific speaker who is not an omniscient commentator on the events of the novel but frequently an active participant. In such cases the point of the metalanguage is not that it is an objective description of the speech of other characters, but that it offers an insight into the mind of the describer. For example, in Chapter 1 I considered a passage from the novel *Small Island* where the first person narrator Hortense encounters an Englishwoman looking for her new nanny. The passage includes the following metalinguistic comment as Hortense reflects on the Englishwoman's speech:

> I thought I must try saying sugar with those vowels that make the word go on for ever. Very English. Sugaaaar.

This passage obviously provides a description of the Englishwoman's long vowels, but the Englishwoman is a very minor character and she does not reappear in the novel. Instead, the point of this comment, as I discussed in Chapter 1, is to illuminate the character of Hortense as someone very anxious to fit into the new community in which she finds herself.

Another example of the way in which first person metalinguistic comments can reveal more about the narrator than the character so described is provided in Zoe Heller's novel *Notes on a Scandal*. In the novel, an older teacher, Barbara Covett, relates the fallout from an affair between her younger colleague, Sheba Hart, and a schoolboy. Barbara narrates her first meetings with Sheba as follows:

> Early on, we made a few tentative approaches to one another. Somewhere in the second week, Sheba greeted me in the corridor. (She used 'Hello', I was pleased to note, as opposed to the awful, mid-Atlantic 'Hiya' that so many of the staff favour.) And another time, walking from the arts centre after an assembly, we shared some brief, rueful comments about the choral performance that had just taken place.
>
> (Heller 2003: 18)

Without Barbara's metalinguistic comment in parentheses it is unlikely that readers would give much thought to the fact that Sheba says 'Hello' rather than 'Hiya', and further it is unlikely that many readers would care as much as Barbara does about the distinction and what it might convey. Hence this parenthetical comment reveals more about Barbara's rather fussy and judgemental approach to language and her new colleague than it does Sheba herself.

First person narrators rarely recognize that their perceptions are subjective. An exception to this rule is provided by Rob Fleming in Nick Hornby's *High Fidelity*. At the start of the novel Rob looks back on his romantic history, and remembers his ex-girlfriend Charlie, who broke up with him, as an ideal woman:

> Even her name seemed to me dramatic and different and exotic, because up until then I had lived in a world where girls had girls' names, and not very interesting ones at that. She talked a lot, so that you didn't have those terrible, strained silences that seemed to characterize most of my sixth-form dates, and when she talked she said remarkably interesting things – about her course, about my course, about music, about films and books and politics.
>
> (Hornby 1995: 23)

Here Rob presents Charlie's 'interesting' speech as part of her overall perfection. But when in the course of the novel he makes contact with her again, he finds that his perceptions have shifted:

> It doesn't help that Charlie talks bollocks all night; she doesn't listen to anyone, she tries too hard to go off at obtuse angles, she puts on all sorts of unrecognizable and inappropriate accents. I would like to say that these are all new mannerisms, but they're not; they were there before, years ago. The not listening I once mistook for strength of character, the obtuseness I once misread as mystery, the accents I saw as glamour and drama. How had I managed to edit all this out in the intervening years?
>
> (Hornby 1995: 160)

Rob has become more analytical of Charlie's language, including her habit of putting on 'all sorts of unrecognizable and inappropriate accents'. He now perceives that far from saying 'interesting things' she really 'talks bollocks'. Again, this does not tell us anything particularly interesting about Charlie, who is a minor character in the novel. Rather, this shift in metalanguage marks the fact that, despite himself, Rob has grown up and is no longer as easily impressed as he used to be.

Character speech and thought

Finally, metalanguage also commonly occurs in the speech and thought of characters as they pass judgement upon each other's language. It is perhaps most evident in direct speech and thought, but can also be traced in free indirect discourse, indirect discourse, and also passages of focalization where access is provided to the perspective of a particular character. Metalanguage that is attributed to characters almost always serves to tell us about the characters themselves, their attitudes and beliefs. It can provide an insight into the kind of social work the speaker is trying to do, e.g. draw boundaries, and it can suggest how the speaker orientates themselves to the broader community. For example, as I discussed in Chapter 7, Leonard Bast's metalinguistic free indirect thought about Margaret's speech ('Oh, to pronounce foreign names correctly!') offers an immediate insight into his yearning to 'improve' himself, while Helen Schlegel's jokes about Jacky's pronunciation ('Lan or Len. We were not nice about our vowels. Lanoline') hint at the fact that, despite her professed political sympathies, she is rather thoughtless in her dealings with the poor.

J. K. Rowling's *Harry Potter and the Order of the Phoenix* offers an example of the complex relationship that can exist between dialect representation and character metalanguage. In Chapter XX Hagrid, the groundskeeper, who has taken over teaching classes in 'Magical Creatures' at Hogwarts school, is visited by a schools inspector, Professor Umbridge.

> '*Hem, hem.*'
>
> 'Oh, hello!' Hagrid said, smiling, having located the source of the noise.
>
> 'You received the note I sent to your cabin this morning?' said Umbridge, in the same loud, slow voice she had used with him earlier, as though she were addressing somebody both foreign and very slow. 'Telling you that I would be inspecting your lessons?'
>
> 'Oh, yeah,' said Hagrid brightly 'Glad yeh found the place all righ'! Well, as you can see – or, I dunno – can you? We're doin' Thestrals today –'
>
> 'I'm sorry?' said Professor Umbridge loudly, cupping her hand around her ear and frowning. 'What did you say?'
>
> Hagrid looked a little confused.
>
> 'Er – *Thestrals*!' he said loudly. 'Big – er – winged horses, yeh know!'
>
> He flapped his gigantic arms hopefully. Professor Umbridge raised her eyebrows at him and muttered as she made a note on her clipboard: '*Has ... to ... resort ... to ... crude ... sign ... language.*'
>
> (Rowling 2004: 395)

Hagrid's speech is only lightly marked as non-standard and colloquial, and the scene makes it clear that he can be easily understood. However, Umbridge pretends not to be able to understand him, which is in itself a powerful metalinguistic statement. This prompts Hagrid to repeat himself in simplified form with gestures, which Umbridge chooses to interpret as 'has to resort to crude sign language'. The implications of Umbridge's metalanguage are clear: Hagrid is unable to communicate effectively with his class and therefore cannot be a good teacher. The scene echoes the *Sparks* case discussed by Lippi-Green, which I mentioned in Chapter 2, where a school librarian was dismissed because of her supposed 'language problem' (Lippi-Green 1994: 179). Later in the scene Umbridge pursues the issue further by asking Pansy Parkinson, a student who is unsympathetic to Hagrid, 'Do you find ... that you are able to understand Professor Hagrid when he talks?' Pansy responds 'No ... because ... well ... it sounds ... like grunting a lot of the time.' Umbridge and Pansy are using language as a pretext for discrimination against Hagrid.

Towards the end of the scene, Hermione offers her own metalinguistic account to her friends Harry and Ron, explaining why Umbridge's actions make her angry: 'You see what she's up to? It's her thing about half-breeds all over again – she's trying to make out Hagrid's some kind of dimwitted troll, just because he had a giantess for a mother'. In other words, Hermione believes that Umbridge's discrimination is based upon Hagrid's identity as a half-human half-giant.

What is interesting about these metalinguistic interchanges is that up until this point in the novel series Rowling herself can be accused of relying on linguistic stereotypes in her depiction of Hagrid. Hagrid is a sympathetic character, but not a very bright one and he repeatedly endangers the children in his care by exposing them to dangerous creatures. His speech is not marked for any specific regional dialect, but displays a range of general low prestige features (e.g. alveolar nasal [ŋ] realized as [n] in 'doin'', T-glottalization in 'righ'') and is marked for allegro speech ('dunno'). Furthermore, he uses these features despite the fact that he has been at Hogwarts since middle childhood, on which basis it could be anticipated that he would be able to speak the Standard English used by Dumbledore and the other teachers. The reader might therefore be led to conclude that there is indeed a biological basis for his speech style, particularly given that his half-brother, who is a full giant, is entirely inarticulate. In this scene Rowling appears to be attempting to distance her novels from such an interpretation. She allows Umbridge and Pansy Parkinson to articulate a discriminatory account of Hagrid's speech, so that Hermione can offer a counter-analysis of their metalanguage, defending Hagrid against the accusation that his speech proves him to be a 'dimwitted troll'. The scene thus stands as testimony to the fact that metalinguistic commentary, wherever it originates in a text, is often doing very complicated 'social work' in order to guide the reader's interpretation of dialect representation.

Case study: Thomas Hardy's 'The Son's Veto'

Thomas Hardy's short story 'The Son's Veto' offers an example of the way in which metalanguage can ensure that language variety is a key concern in a text, even if that language variety is not represented in much detail on the page. 'The Son's Veto' tells a story about the subtle but impassable barriers that existed between the social classes at the time Hardy was writing. It focuses on a parlourmaid, Sophy, who works for a widowed clergyman, Mr Twycott. When, owing to an injury she sustains while working for him, Sophy is forced resign from her position, Mr Twycott asks her to marry him. This cross-class marriage breaches the social codes of the time. As the narrator puts it, 'Mr Twycott knew perfectly well that he had committed social suicide by this step' (Hardy 1996: 378). He therefore moves with his new wife to London where no one will know of her previous station in life, and where they will be under less scrutiny by their neighbours than in the country. In doing so, however, he isolates her from all her previous acquaintances and makes it difficult for her to form new friendships. The couple have a son, Randolph, who is given the best possible education, but this teaches him to be ashamed of his socially inferior mother. After the death of her husband, Sophy renews her acquaintance with Sam, a grocer who courted her before her marriage. However, her son cannot bear the social embarrassment that he believes his mother marrying a grocer will entail, and he makes her promise not to do so without his consent. Sophy is therefore condemned to live out her life with little sense of purpose and no meaningful social interaction, as the narrator says, she 'might have led an idyllic life with her faithful fruiterer and greengrocer' (Hardy 1996: 385).

One way in which the social nuances of Sophy's situation are enacted in the story is through the issue of language variety. However, there is really very little dialect represented in the novel. Consider, for example, the following interchange between Sophy and Sam before she marries Mr Twycott:

> He walked beside her towards her mother's. Presently his arm stole round her waist. She gently removed it; but he placed it there again, and she yielded the point. 'You see, dear Sophy, you don't know that you'll stay on; you may want a home; and I shall be ready to offer one someday, though I may not be ready just yet.'

> 'Why, Sam, how can you be so fast! I've never even said I liked 'ee; and it is all your own doing, coming after me!'

> (Hardy 1996: 376)

An important feature which distinguishes the direct speech of these characters from the language used by the narrator is allegro speech: 'don't', 'you'll' and 'I've'. It seems likely that these elisions are intended to mark these two speakers out as mildly colloquial speakers in comparison with other speakers in the story. Certainly Mr Twycott and Randolph are not represented as using such elisions (even though in real life all speakers use elision). Sophy does use one feature which suggests that her variety marks her out as coming from a rural background: 'I've never even said I liked 'ee', where ''ee' is an abbreviated version of either 'thee' or 'ye', which in either case is a non-standard pronoun. However, she only uses ''ee' at moments of emotional warmth; most of the time she uses the standard form 'you'.

Despite the fact that there is very little direct dialect representation in the story, metalanguage originating both from the character of her son and from the narrator is used to illustrate the way in which language variety marks out social distance. A key moment occurs early in the story when the narrator reports the conversation she has with her son, Randolph, while leaving the recital:

> In conversing with her on their way home the boy who walked at her elbow said that he hoped his father had not missed them.
>
> 'He have been so comfortable these last few hours that I am sure he cannot have missed us,' she replied.
>
> '*Has*, dear mother – not *have!*' exclaimed the public-schoolboy, with an impatient fastidiousness that was almost harsh. 'Surely you know that by this time!'
>
> His mother hastily adopted the correction, and did not resent his making it, or retaliate, as she might well have done by bidding him to wipe that crumby mouth of his, whose condition had been caused by surreptitious attempts to eat a piece of cake without taking it out of the pocket wherein it lay concealed. After this the pretty woman and the boy went on in silence.
>
> That question of grammar bore upon her history, and she fell into reverie, of a somewhat sad kind to all appearance. It might have been assumed that she was wondering if she had done wisely shaping her life as she had shaped it, to bring out such a result as this.

(Hardy 1996: 375)

What is going on here is an interplay between dialect representation, character-based metalanguage, and omniscient third person narrator metalanguage. The narrative voice, in which the majority of the story is told, is Standard English and the register is formal, making frequent use of Latinate words such as 'conversing', 'fastidiousness' and 'surreptitious'. When the narrative switches to direct speech to report Sophy's response to her son's comment, her use of the non-standard grammatical form 'He have been' immediately marks her out as a non-standard speaker. Of course, 'He have been' is a very minor infringement of the 'rules' of Standard English, and nothing else in the sentence conveys any information about her dialect or accent. Indeed, the sentence also contains the Latinate word 'comfortable', as well as grammatical subordination; Sophy does not sound either uneducated or inarticulate. Nevertheless, this one grammatical solecism draws the metalinguistic ire of her son: '*Has*, dear mother – not *have*!'. As with much character-based metalanguage, the effect does more to characterize the son as rude and impatient than to characterize his mother as socially deficient. This impression is reinforced by the third person narrative voice which in turn offers a metalinguistic commentary on the son, observing that he spoke 'with an impatient fastidiousness that was almost harsh'. Furthermore, the narrator hints that the son is employing double standards: while he takes her to task for her socially shaming grammar, he himself is presenting a less than well-groomed appearance on account of illicit cake crumbs.

The social barriers that Sophy's lightly marked dialect present are further commented upon by the narrator: 'she still held confused ideas on the use of "was" and "were", which did not beget a respect for her among the few acquaintances she made' (Hardy 1996: 378). The narrator also describes the social distance that Randolph's education puts between him and his mother:

Somehow, her boy, with his aristocratic school-knowledge, his grammars, and his aversions, was losing those wide infantine sympathies, extending as far as the sun and moon themselves, with which he, like other children, had been born, and which his mother, a child of nature herself, had loved in him; he was reducing their compass to a population of a few thousand wealthy and titled people, the mere veneer of a thousand million or so of others who did not interest him at all. He drifted further and further away from her.

(Hardy 1996: 379)

Again, it is through commentary upon Randolph's language – 'his grammars' – that Hardy highlights the social distance that is emerging between son and mother. Randolph's acquisition of a class-based education (which would include the knowledge of Latin and Greek grammar alongside English) is portrayed as directly linked to his growing lack of sympathy and interest in those who do not share this education. When Sophy tells her son of her plans to marry, and of the rank of her intended husband, her son bursts out into 'passionate tears' and once these have passed he says to her: 'I am ashamed of you! It will ruin me! A miserable boor! a churl! a clown! It will degrade me in the eyes of all the gentlemen of England!' (Hardy 1996: 385). By this point in the narrative the reader has seen enough of Sam to know that he is far from being any of these things. Randolph's outburst of short phrases (only his second stretch of direct speech in the story) marks him out as childish and self-serving by contrast with the more considered and considerate Sam.

This short story thus dramatizes the way in which education and language work together to keep the class system in place. As I have suggested, however, it is striking how little Hardy does to mark Sophy and Sam as dialect speakers in their direct speech. For a story that is about the ways in which language works to make class barriers impenetrable, the actual linguistic differences between characters are kept to a bare minimum. It is, I think, possible to read this in two ways. On the one hand we can argue that Hardy's point is precisely that the linguistic differences that serve to keep Sophy from integrating with her new social station are small (has/have, was/were), and the hypersensitivity of both her son and neighbours to Sophy's lapses is absurd. Neither Sophy nor Sam are presented as being difficult to understand – it is simply that they were not trained when young in the 'correct' use of these socially significant linguistic markers. As such, Hardy's decision not to represent the dialect of these characters more fully can be understood as making a subtle political point which challenges readers to consider their own prejudices. On the other hand, it might be noted that Hardy works hard throughout the story to secure the sympathy of the reader for Sam and Sophy. One of the ways in which he does this is by emphasizing the hard-heartedness of Sophy's son. Randolph is repeatedly portrayed in an unflattering light, from the initial exchange with his mother when he corrects her grammar, to the childishness of his outburst when she tells him of her potential marriage, to the final lines of the story when he glowers at a tearful

Sam as the funeral procession passes. Another way that he ensures that readers respond to the story sympathetically is by marking the dialect speech of Sam and Sophy as lightly as possible, and shaping the reader's understanding of their dialect through metalanguage rather than direct representation. In other words, the story analyses the relationship between language variety and social judgement, but is at the same time careful not to offend too far against Standard English.

Metalanguage in film?

Metalanguage in film is less frequent and less overt than in literary texts, primarily because there is less opportunity for it to occur. Whereas in texts metalanguage can occur in paratext, third person narrative, first person narrative or character speech and thought, in films it is restricted to character speech. This does not mean that film is limited as a whole compared to literature because the kind of 'work' that metalanguage can fulfil in literature – marking out identities, signalling relationships, identifying incompetence – can all be done through other semiotic systems in film, including costume, body language, editing and so forth. Such semiotic systems are not properly termed metalinguistic, but rather run parallel to (and intersect with) the linguistic systems.

Having said this, metalanguage can and does occur in film dialogue where it performs important social and interpersonal work, very much as it does in direct speech in novels. We have already encountered one brief example in the 1992 film of *Howards End* when Len corrects Jacky's grammar:

LEONARD: Let go Jacky. Every time I'm five minutes late you see me lying dead in the road crushed and killed in a gruesome accident.

JACKY: Well, people do get killed in accidents and don't come home no more.

LEONARD: Any more, Jacky. I told you I was going to a lecture on music and meaning. I lost my umbrella. It's all right I got it back.

(Ivory 1992)

As I noted in Chapter 3, the fact that Leonard corrects Jacky's grammar signals both his own fretting over social niceties, and the gap that exists between the couple in terms of their social aspirations. It functions in a similar way to the correction that Randolph makes in 'The Son's Veto'.

A more extensive instance of metalanguage occurs in the play *Educating Rita* by Willy Russell, which was first performed on stage in 1980 and was then made into a successful film starring Michael Caine and Julie Walters (Gilbert 1983). Rita, a hairdresser, studies for a degree in English Literature under the tutelage of Frank, an alcoholic lecturer. Initially, Frank finds Rita to be a breath of fresh air compared to his normal students and takes delight in introducing her to new ideas and new writers. However, when Rita moves in with a new flatmate, Trish, Frank is horrified at the way in which Rita starts to adopt Trish's theatrical RP accent. For reasons of copyright I have quoted from the play script rather than the film below. There are a few minor differences between the two, although the overall dynamic is the same in each. In the film, the scene starts at 1 hour 5 minutes 30 seconds:

Rita	(*in a peculiar voice*): Hallo, Frank.
Frank	(*without looking up*) Hallo, Rita. You're late.
Rita	I know, Frank, I'm terribly sorry. It was unavoidable.
Frank	(*looking up*) Was it really? What's wrong with your voice?
Rita	Nothing is wrong with it, Frank. I have merely decided to talk properly. As Trish says there is not a lot of point in discussing beautiful literature in an ugly voice.
Frank	You haven't got an ugly voice; at least you *didn't* have. Talk properly.
Rita	I am talking properly.

(Russell 2007: 63)

Rita intends her adoption of Trish's speaking style as a joke. Frank, however, takes it seriously, demanding to know why she is speaking in that way. Rita responds in character, providing a counter-argument which describes her own accent as 'ugly'. Frank takes this response seriously too and leaps to the defence of her accent, before Rita finally relents and starts using her normal speech style again. The scene thus plays out the emerging tensions in their relationship through this metalinguistic debate. Frank is becoming aware that through her education Rita is losing her uncultivated spontaneity and 'authentic' voice, and is becoming more like an ordinary undergraduate. From Rita's point of view this is entirely what she has set out to do through her studies, and Frank's concerns are an irritation. They both use metalanguage to do the 'social work' of debating what Rita's new educated identity will be.

Conclusion

In this chapter I have argued that it is important to watch for moments in film and literature where dialect is explicitly discussed or commented upon. At such moments, authors and narrators guide readers towards specific interpretations of dialect representation, and characters undertake the social work of policing the boundaries of class and identity. In literature metalanguage can occur in a range of different parts of the text (paratext, third person narration, first person narration, character speech and thoughts). In film metalanguage is confined to character speech, but nevertheless it can be important, identifying moments of character development, or underlining thematic concerns.

In the next chapter, Chapter 9, I consider what happens when speakers shift between speech styles. I identify three primary types of style-shifting in film and literature and I discuss their functions.

Further reading

The 'Introduction' to Genette's *Paratexts* (1997) is not focused specifically on language but it does offer a useful way in to thinking about paratextual materials. Jaworski, Coupland and Galasiński's introductory essay to their edited volume *Metalanguage* (2004) is short but valuable, and the volume itself contains some interesting articles. Alex Broadhead's article on footnotes and *Lyrical Ballads* offers an excellent example of the value of paying close attention to the details of dialect presentation and metalanguage.

Exercises

Exercise 1

The following extract from *Lady Chatterley's Lover* occurs early in the novel. Lady Connie Chatterley has previously talked to the gamekeeper

Mellors about the possibility of having a key to the hut so that she can use it to sit in. Mellors was uncooperative, leaving Connie annoyed. This time she is sitting outside the hut when he arrives. Read through the passage and think about the following issues:

- What instances of metalanguage can you identity?
- How does the metalanguage relate to the dialect representation in direct speech?
- What effect does the metalanguage have in terms of providing insight into characters?

A wet brown dog came running and did not bark, lifting a wet feather of a tail. The man followed – in a wet black oilskin jacket, like a chauffeur, and face flushed a little. She felt him recoil in his quick walk, when he saw her. She stood up, in the handbreadth of dryness under the rustic porch. He saluted without speaking, coming slowly near. She began to withdraw.

'I'm just going,' she said.

'Was yer waitin' to get in?' he asked, looking at the hut, not at her.

'No, I only sat a few minutes in the shelter,' she said, with quiet dignity.

He looked at her. She looked cold.

'Sir Clifford 'adn't got no other key then?' he asked.

'No, but it doesn't matter. I can sit perfectly dry under this porch. Good afternoon!'

She hated the excess of vernacular in his speech.

He watched her closely, as she was moving away. Then he hitched up his jacket, and put his hand in his breeches pocket, taking out the key of the hut.

''Appen yer'd better 'ave this key, an' Ah mun fend for t' bods some other road.'

She looked at him.

'What do you mean?' she asked.

'I mean as 'appen Ah can find anuther pleece as'll du for rearin' th' pheasants. If yer want ter be 'ere, yo'll non want me messin' abaht a' t' time.'

She looked at him, getting his meaning through the fog of the dialect.

'Why don't you speak ordinary English?' she said coldly.

'Me! – I thowt it *wor*' ordinary.'

She was silent for a few moments, in anger.

'So if yer want t' key, yer'd better ta'e it. Or 'appen Ah'd better gi'e 't yer termorrer, an' clear all t' stuff aht fust. Would that du for yer?'

She became more angry.

'I didn't want your key,' she said. 'I don't want you to clear anything out at all. I don't in the least want to turn you out of your hut, thank you! I only wanted to be able to sit here sometimes – like today. But I can sit perfectly well under the porch. So please say no more about it.'

He looked at her again, with his wicked blue eyes.

'Why,' he began, in the broad, slow dialect, 'your ladyship's as welcome as Christmas ter th' hut an' th' key an' iverythink as is. On'y this time O' th' year the's bods ter set, an' Ah've got ter be potterin' abaht a good bit, seein' after 'em, an' a'! Winter time I ned 'ardly come nigh t' pleece. But what wi' spring, an' Sir Clifford wantin' ter start t' pheasants —— An' your ladyship 'ud not want *me* tinkerin' around an' about when she was here, a' t' time —-'

She listened with a dim kind of amazement.

'Why should I mind your being here?' she asked.

He looked at her curiously.

'T' nuisance on me!' he said briefly, but significantly. And she flushed.

'Very well!' she said finally. 'I won't trouble you. But I don't think I should have minded at all sitting and seeing you look after the birds. I should have liked it. But since you think it interferes with you, I won't disturb you, don't be afraid. You are Sir Clifford's keeper, not mine.'

The phrase sounded queer – she didn't know why. But she let it pass.

'Nay, your ladyship. It's your ladyship's own 'ut. It's as your ladyship likes an' pleases, every time. You can turn me off at a wik's notice. It wor only –'

'Only what?' she said, baffled.

He pushed back his hat in an odd comic way.

'On'y as 'appen yo'd like th' pleece ter yersen, when yer did come, an' not me messin' abaht.'

'But why?' she said, angry. 'Aren't you a civilised human being? Do you think I ought to be afraid of you? Why should I take any notice of you, and your being here or not? Why is it important?'

He looked at her, all his face glimmering with wicked laughter.

'It's not, your ladyship. Not in the very least,' he said.

(Lawrence 2006: 94–6)

Exercise 2

The Longman edition of Ken Saro-Wiwa's novel *Sozaboy* is prefaced by two paratexts: a five-page 'Introduction' by William Boyd and a one-page 'Author's Note' by Saro-Wiwa himself. Read through the excerpts below, and think about the following:

- What claims are being made about the language of the novel in these paratexts?
- How is the language being positioned in relationship to Nigerian English, Standard English and literary language?
- What political claims are being made about the language of the novel?
- What does Saro-Wiwa mean by 'rotten English' and are there any potential dangers in using this term?
- To what extent do you think we have to accept and agree with the terms that Saro-Wiwa and Boyd use?
- How do the two metalinguistic descriptions of the language compare?

N.B. for an example of the language of *Sozaboy*, see Chapter 9 where I discuss an extract in relation to style-shifting.

> Sozaboy's language is what I call 'rotten English', a mixture of Nigerian pidgin English, broken English and occasional flashes of good, even idiomatic English. This language is disordered and disorderly. Born of a mediocre education and severely limited opportunities, it borrows words, patterns and images freely from the mother-tongue and finds expression in a very limited English vocabulary. To its speakers, it has the advantage of having no rules and no syntax. It thrives on lawlessness, and is part of the dislocated and discordant society in which Sozaboy must live, move and have not his being.

(From 'Author's Note', Saro-Wiwa 1998)

It is also vivid with a language of uncommon idiosyncrasy and character. Saro-Wiwa subtitles the novel as 'A Novel in Rotten English'. Rotten English, as he explains, is a blend of pidgin English (the lingua franca of the West-African ex-colonies), corrupted English and 'occasional flashes of good, even idiomatic English'. In other words, the language of the novel is a unique literary construct. No one in Nigeria actually speaks or writes like this but the style functions in the novel extraordinarily well. Sozaboy's narration is at times raunchily funny as well as lyrical and moving, and as the terror of his predicament steadily manifests itself, the small but colourful vocabulary of his idiolect paradoxically manages to capture all the numbing ghastliness of war far more effectively than a more expansive eloquence. It helps to hear the rhythms of a Nigerian accent in your ear as you read, but even if that cannot be reproduced, the cadences of the prose take over after a few lines or so and this remarkable tone of voice holds the reader's attention absolutely.

(From 'Introduction' by William Boyd, Saro-Wiwa 1998)

9

Style-shifting

In Chapter 1 I noted that, while the way in which someone speaks is to a large extent determined by their social and regional background, the particular context within which he or she speaks and the purpose of the speech will also influence the language variety used. When a speaker changes style in response to a particular situation, this is style-shifting. In his book *Style: Language Variation and Identity* (2007) Nikolas Coupland argues that:

> We need to understand how people *use* or *enact* or *perform* social styles for a range of symbolic purposes. Social styles (including dialect styles) are a resource for people to make many different sorts of personal and interpersonal meaning.
>
> (Coupland 2007: 3)

In earlier chapters I have already explored a number of scenes in which style-shifting takes place, including an excerpt from the novel *Small Island* in which Hortense attempts to style-shift in response to the Englishwoman, and a scene from the 1992 film *Howards End* where Leonard style-shifts when he gets upset. In this chapter I look at the topic more closely, exploring what sociolinguists have to say about style-shifting and identifying some of the ways in which style-shifting is used by writers and filmmakers. I conclude the chapter with an in-depth case study of a single scene from the film *East is East* which shows multiple and varied instances of style-shifting.

Note: I have throughout this chapter preferred the term 'style-shifting' to 'code-switching' as style-shifting refers to an alternation between styles of speech within a single language, whereas code-switching often refers to switching between languages. Some work on the fictional uses of this phenomena (see for example Shuy 1975;

Omole 1987; Hess 1996) use the term code-switching, particularly where the text studied includes both style-shifting and code-switching.

The question of how style-shifting is to be accounted for in 'real world' conversation has been the subject of much debate within sociolinguistics. Indeed, as indicated by my careful scare quotes, the whole question of 'real world' conversation is problematic, and one I will be considering further in the final two chapters. In the past, linguists have often drawn a clear distinction between 'real world' or 'natural' conversation, and that found in 'fictional' or 'artificial' contexts (including literature, film, advertising, plays, etc.). More recently, however, sociolinguists including Coupland have argued that such a distinction is difficult to maintain in practice, and that ordinary everyday conversations may have highly performative aspects. I will continue to refer to 'real world' speech as distinct from literary or filmic speech, but I will continue to use the scare quotes to indicate that the term 'real world' is not in itself unproblematic.

In what follows I draw upon the sociolinguistic literature in order to discuss the patterns of style-shifting found in literary texts and films. My focus, I should note, is on style-shifting as it occurs within the speech of individual characters, and I do not here attempt to analyse entire films and texts in terms of style-shifting (even though, from a Bakhtinian perspective, such approaches are entirely valid). When analysing the style-shifting of characters it is important to bear in mind some of differences between 'real world' speech and the speech that occurs in film and literature. When a person style-shifts in 'real life' sociolinguists tend to ask questions about the underlying reasons for the shift, and these necessarily revolve around the speaker. Did the style-shift occur in response to an interlocutor? Was it a change in context or topic that caused the speaker to style-shift? Was the speaker referencing or projecting a particular identity? However, when a character style-shifts in a fictional film or text we need to ask questions that focus on what the author or filmmakers were trying to communicate and what the reader or audience understood from the style-shift. Did the style-shift occur because the author wished to reveal something about the relationship between the characters? Were the filmmakers trying to show something about the emotional state of the character? Does the shift in the character's speech style signal a significant development for the character? As I discussed in Chapter 3, Sarah Kozloff has argued that film dialogue 'has been purposely designed for the viewers to overhear' in order to enable them to comprehend the onscreen action (Kozloff 2000: 15). This is as true of style-shifting as it is true of dialogue more generally in both film and literature. One result of this is that while sociolinguists may have rejected a particular explanation for style-shifting as not fitting the observed data, it may remain a valid explanation for what occurs in film and literature. This is particularly the case if it is an explanation that has some popular currency, and it accounts for the fact that we can find many representations of style-shifting in film and literature that occurred long before sociolinguistics started to analyse the phenomenon. In short, I am drawing on sociolinguistic frameworks as a way of thinking about patterns of style-shifting that can be observed in literary texts. However, those patterns can be quite different from those that the sociolinguists were attempting to explain.

A further point to bear in mind is that, as has been discussed in earlier chapters, there are some significant differences in the way in which film and literature handle style-shifting. In literature the representation of dialect is necessarily impressionistic and frequently inconsistent. A character's speech may be densely marked as dialectal at the beginning of a text or chapter, but the density often reduces once the character has been established in order to make it easier for the reader to process. What this means is that it can be difficult for a writer to signal style-shifting through dialect representation alone. Unless a style-shift is very marked, readers may not identify that a change has taken place, and even if they do, they may struggle to decide whether it was intentional or simply the result of inconsistent representation. Writers therefore often employ metalinguistic commentary in order to draw attention to the style-shift and interpret it for the reader. In film the fact that the dialogue is being recorded directly as sound means that style-shifts can occur more naturalistically, as occurs in the scene between Leonard and Jacky in the film of *Howards End*. Of course, the question remains as to whether the audience will be aware of the shift. In the scene from *Howards End* it is unlikely that any viewer will be specifically aware of the style shift that takes place in Leonard's speech, even though it does form a part of the general performance of this scene. Where filmmakers want to specifically draw attention to a style-shift they can show reaction shots or use commentary from other characters to draw attention to it and offer an interpretation of it to the reader. As we saw in Chapter 8, for example, this happens in *Educating Rita*:

Frank   (*looking up*) Was it really? What's wrong with your voice?

Rita   Nothing is wrong with it, Frank. I have merely decided
         to talk properly. As Trish says there is not a lot of point
         in discussing beautiful literature in an ugly voice.

Frank   You haven't got an ugly voice; at least you *didn't* have.
         Talk properly.

Rita   I am talking properly.

(Russell 2007: 63)

Rita's style-shift is very marked here, so it is unlikely that the audience
would miss it, but they may not immediately understand why it occurs.
However, attention is drawn to it by Frank's metalinguistic comment,
and the ensuing discussion about the meaning and implications of
Rita's style-shift cues the audience to its significance.

In the next three sections I discuss three types of style-shifting that
occur in film and literature: emotional style-shifts; interpersonal style-
shifts and transformative style-shifts. Approaching the topic in this way
opens up the range of functions that style-shifting fulfils in film and
literature. However, this categorization is not absolute: there is some
overlap between the three categories and there are some style-shifts
that do not fit neatly into any of the categories. For example, towards
the end of *Educating Rita* there is a scene (at around 1 hour 10 minutes) during which the two characters briefly adopt other accents: Rita
mimics Tiger's RP 'slumming it' and Frank mimics Rita's Liverpudlian
'dead honest'. These instances of playful performance of other accents
are dramatically interesting, but they cannot be easily categorized
with the tripartite framework presented here. In order to avoid an
overly long and taxonomic chapter, I have focused on offering a framework for thinking about some of the most frequently encountered and
dramatically interesting types of style-shifting in film and literature.
I am confident, however, that this framework can be extended by the
consideration of other types of style-shifting.

Emotional style-shifting

Emotional style-shifting occurs when a character is surprised, upset
or otherwise disturbed from their normal emotional state. In his early
sociolinguistic studies, William Labov posited that speakers operate
along a scale of formality, and he designed tests that elicited speech

from his informants in a range of settings, from the very 'careful' speech of reading word lists, to the 'casual' speech of unstructured conversation. He found that as readers paid more attention to their speech, so the number of dialect markers in their speech dropped. Conversely, as I noted in Chapter 3, when people were asked to describe situations in which they felt that their lives had been in danger, they became so wrapped up in the story that they became less aware of their own speaking style, and so became less formal (Labov 1966). Since its publication there has been debate among sociolinguists as to whether this 'attention-to-speech' model accounts for all aspects of style-shifting, but the basic idea that underpins it remains a staple feature of literature and film: characters become more dialectal when under pressure. We have already encountered an example of this when Leonard Bast shifts style when he becomes upset about how his family have cut him off on account of his relationship with Jacky in the scene from the film of *Howards End* discussed in Chapter 3.

A good literary example of this occurs in Harper Lee's 1960 novel *To Kill a Mockingbird*. The narrator, Scout, recounts how her family's African American housekeeper, Calpurnia, style-shifts when angry:

> She was furious, and when she was furious Calpurnia's grammar became erratic. When in tranquillity, her grammar was as good as anybody's in Maycomb. Atticus said Calpurnia had more education than most coloured folks.

> When she squinted down at me the tiny lines around her eyes deepened. 'There's some folks who don't eat like us,' she whispered fiercely, 'but you ain't called on to contradict 'em at the table when they don't. That boy's yo' comp'ny and if he wants to eat up the table-cloth you let him, you hear?'

> (Lee 2010: 27)

In this example it is particularly important that the style-shifting is commented upon metalinguistically by the first person narrator because readers might otherwise miss the shift. Calpurnia speaks with a marked dialect at all times. For example, later in the same chapter she says 'I missed you today... The house got so lonesome 'long about two o'clock I had to turn on the radio' (Lee 2010: 32). While the level of detail in the dialect representation is certainly higher when she loses her temper, the difference is not so marked that a reader would automatically identify it as a style-shift. Lee has thus combined dialect representation with narrative metalanguage to guide the reader's understanding. The result is a scene in which the African American housekeeper chastises her European American charges for their lack of manners using African American Vernacular English. The point, perhaps, is that human decency is not the preserve of Standard English speakers, and that Calpurnia's angry style-shifting here authenticates her sincerity. Overall, Calpurnia's ability to use different dialects marks her out as an interesting and complex character.

A more recent example occurs in Zadie Smith's 2001 novel *White Teeth* which traces the connections and friendships between two multicultural families in London (this novel was also used as a basis for an exercise in Chapter 7). Early in the novel, Clara, who has recently arrived in Britain from the West Indies, meets and marries an Englishman, Archie. As a metalinguistic narrative comment notes, Clara consciously sets out to lose her Caribbean accent: "'Now, isn't that strange, Archie?" said Clara, filling in all her consonants. She was already some way to losing her accent and she liked to work on it at every opportunity' (2001: 56). However, when she is surprised her old accent returns. For example, in this scene she is beginning a tentative friendship with Alsana, the wife of Archie's closest friend:

'Those shoes look truly comfortable,' said Clara.

'Yes. Yes. I do a lot of walking, you see. And with this –' She patted her stomach.

'You're pregnant?' said Clara surprised. 'Pickney, you so small me kyant even see it.'

Clara blushed the moment she had spoken; she always dropped into the vernacular when she was excited or pleased about something. Alsana just smiled pleasantly, unsure what she had said.

(Smith 2001: 65–6)

The style-shift is signalled by the introduction of the dialect vocabulary 'Pickney', the absence of a copula in 'you so small', the use of the pronoun 'me' instead of 'I' in 'me kyant' and the semi-phonetic respelling of 'can't' as 'kyant'. The shift is quite obvious, but here too the narrator provides a metalinguistic explanation for why Clara suddenly shifts her style so dramatically.

A key feature of such scenes is that they are based on the premise that characters will display their 'real' speech styles when they come under emotional pressure. As such, they represent moments in the text or film where the reader is able to identify the 'authentic' character beneath whatever facade is being put on.

Interpersonal style-shifting

As I have already noted in my discussions of a number of scenes, characters often alter their speech style depending upon who they are talking about. One useful framework for discussing the style-shifting that occurs when speakers attempt to modify their language in response to the language of others is Accommodation Theory (see Giles and Smith 1979 for a full account). A frequently observed process is that of convergence, whereby speakers alter their speech style so that it becomes like that of the person they are addressing, as Hortense wishes to do with the Englishwoman in the scene from *Small Island* that I have already discussed. Allan Bell's 'Audience Design' provides another way of thinking about how speakers modify their speech to suit their perceived audience (see Bell 1984).

An example of this can be seen in Ken Saro-Wiwa's novel *Sozaboy*, which was first published in 1985. *Sozaboy* tells the story of the Nigerian civil war of 1967–70 from the perspective of a young man caught up in the middle of it. Mene, the narrator who is also the eponymous 'sozaboy' or 'soldierboy', has not received any education beyond primary level and as such he is unable to speak Standard English, although he would very much like to. He makes a friend, Bullet, who as an only child of wealthy parents has received a much better education and is therefore able to access a more acrolectal language variety. This means, however, that Mene is often unable to understand what Bullet says:

'Oh yes. That man is the enemy,' Bullet replied. 'Look, Sozaboy, we are in war front o.k. And in the war front there are all sorts of people. Drunkards, thieves, idiots, wise men, foolish men. There is only one thing which binds them all. Death. And everyday they live, they are cheating death. That man came to celebrate the fact.'

'Bullet,' I said, 'I beg you, no make too much grammar for me. I beg you. Try talk the one that I will understand. No vex because I ask you this simple question.'

'No, I no dey vex,' Bullet replied after some time. 'I no dey vex. What I am saying is that all of us who are here can die any time. Any time. So while we live, we must drink. Because, as you know, man must wak.'

(Saro-Wiwa 1998: 94–5)

Mene explicitly asks Bullet to style-shift so as to make his thoughts comprehensible and after a little thought, Bullet does so. Bullet's ability to switch between the basilectal Nigerian English spoken by the ordinary soldiers and the acrolectal Nigerian English spoken by the officers is a central part of his characterization, and Saro-Wiwa draws attention to it here. Of course, in real life speakers often accommodate without being aware that they are doing so and without anyone commenting upon it. In films which elicit particularly naturalistic performances (such as the films of Ken Loach) linguistic accommodation may occur spontaneously and pass without mention. However, in literature and films where issues of identity, power and prestige are particularly salient, writers and filmmakers will often find ways to highlight interpersonal style-shifts, as in this scene.

As well as convergence, it is also possible to find situations in which speakers adopt a strategy of linguistic divergence from their addressee. An oft-cited sociolinguistic experiment involved interviewing Welsh learners of the Welsh language. During the interview, the participants 'overheard' the RP-speaking interviewer making negative remarks about the Welsh language. Unsurprisingly, participants who felt strongly invested in their learning of Welsh responded by diverging from the speech style of the interviewer, and increasing the dialectal Welsh elements of their speech (Bourhis and Giles 1977) . On this occasion, the speakers shifted the variety they used in order to increase the social and cultural distance between themselves and their audience.

An example of this kind of behaviour in fiction can be seen in Richard Jeffries' *Amaryllis at the Fair*, which was first published in 1886, long before anyone thought to put a label on this kind of linguistic behaviour. Amaryllis's father, Iden, is by birth a gentleman, but he works as a farmer, much to the irritation of his wife. One dinnertime he talks about the variety of potato he has just been planting:

'Forty-folds,' he repeated; 'they comes forty to one. It be an amazing theng how thengs do that; forty grows for one. Thaay may be an old-fashioned potato; you won't find many of thaay, not true forty-folds. Mine comes true, 'cause I saves um every year a' purpose.' ...

'Farty-folds – '

'Farty-folds!' said Mrs Iden, imitating his provincial pronunciation with extreme disgust in her tone.

'Aw, yes, too,' said Iden. 'Varty-volds be ould potatoes, and thur bean't none as can beat um.'

The more she showed her irritation at his speech or ways, the more he accentuated both language and manner.

(Jeffries 1939: 210–11)

The fact that Iden repeats the same basic phrase three times draws attention to the style-shift and allows readers to compare the different versions. Furthermore, the third person narrator explains the gradual increase in dialectal features and explains that this is a deliberate strategy of linguistic divergence: the more his wife is irritated by his adoption of rural dialect, the more he increases its presence in his speech. The comment thus both explains the dialect representation, and provides a telling insight into the relationship between the couple.

Such scenes often point to the underlying power dynamics in a conversation, as an insecure and uncertain character will converge towards the language variety of a more powerful character, or a manipulative character will converge towards the language of a character they wish to persuade. At the same time, a character will diverge away from the language of a character that he or she wishes to annoy or disassociate themselves from.

Transformative style-shifting

The final type of style-shifting I wish to discuss I term 'transformative shifting'. This describes a situation where someone, by shifting to a new language variety, brings about a change in their circumstance. Crucially, the language variety should not be one that anyone in the scene is currently using (this keeps it distinct from interpersonal style-shifting). A useful sociolinguistic model for thinking about transformative shifting is Robert Le Page and Andrée Tabouret-Keller's *Acts of Identity* framework (Le Page and Tabouret-Keller 1985). These two sociolinguists studied conversations and storytelling among Creole speakers in London. Their central argument was that 'the individual creates for himself the patterns of his linguistic behaviour so as to resemble those of the group or groups with which from time to time he wishes to be identified' (Le Page and Tabouret-Keller 1985: 181). What is noticeable about Le Page and Tabouret-Keller's formulation is that, although it has some significant points of commonality with accommodation theory, it does not require either that speakers are 'natural' members of the group they wish to identify with, or that they are in active communication with someone from that group. Rather, the speaker can project an identity by referencing some of the linguistic features of a target group which is geographically, socially or culturally distant from the current conversation. The speaker's ability to project this identity may be limited by a number of factors, including their ability to accurately identify the target language variety and their ability to modify their speech in line with the target.

Several researchers have drawn on the Acts of Identity framework in order to examine why and how British singers have so often adopted 'American' features when performing pop songs (Trudgill 1983; Simpson 1999; Beal 2009). Trudgill explains, for example: 'it is appropriate to sound like an American when performing what is predominantly an American activity; and one attempts to model one's singing style on that of those who do it best and who one admires most' (Trudgill 1983: 144). I am here proposing a similar function for style-shifting in film and literature, as characters attempt to adopt a new language variety in order to bolster their social standing in some way. Style-shifts of this type thus offer writers and filmmakers the opportunity to demonstrate dramatic shifts in character and situation through speech.

An excellent example of transformative style-shifting can be seen at the end of the 2009 film *Sex & Drugs & Rock & Roll* (Whitecross 2010) which tells the story of popstar Ian Dury. Born into a middle class family, Dury contracted polio as a young boy which left him crippled. As an adult he formed numerous bands before finding chart success in his 30s. His songs, which included 'Hit me with your rhythm stick' and 'Reasons to be cheerful, part 3', were strongly influenced by the Cockney music hall tradition and he performed them in a fake London English ('mockney') accent. The film tells the story of Dury's rise to success and his driven, often self-destructive behaviour. Interwoven with this is the story of his childhood, and in particular the time he spent in a home for disabled boys where he was bullied and humiliated by one of the wardens. Towards the end of the film, the young Dury, who up until this point has spoken Standard English in a quiet and polite voice, stands up to the warden, bellowing 'I don't want no fucking fish. It's horrible' in a marked London English accent (complete with T-glottalization, H-deletion and double negation). It is not apparent, however, why it is a London accent he adopts or who he might be emulating in using it. However, the film suggests that this was a pivotal moment in Dury's life because it was at this point he discovered the mouthy 'Cockney geezer' persona that he would use throughout his career.

Another example of transformative style-shifting can be seen in Irvine Welsh's novel *Trainspotting* (1996), which tells the story of a circle of friends from a deprived inner city area in Leith, most of whom are heroin addicts. The story is told in the first person by Mark Renton. In the following extract, Renton is standing trial along with his friend Spud for shoplifting from a bookshop:

> The magistrate lets oot a sharp exhalation. It isnae a brilliant job the cunt's goat, whin ye think aboot it. It must git pretty tiresome dealin wi radges aw day. Still, ah bet the poppy's fuckin good, n naebody's asking the cunt tae dae it. He should try tae be a wee bit mair professional, a bit mair pragmatic, rather than showin his annoyance so much.
>
> – Mr Renton, you did not intend to sell the books?
> – Naw. Eh, no, your honour. They were for reading.
> – So you read Kierkegaard. Tell us about him, Mr Renton, the patronising cunt sais.
> – I'm interested in his concepts of subjectivity and truth, and particularly his ideas concerning choice; the notion that genuine choice is made out of doubt and uncertainty, and without recourse to experience or advice of others. It could be argued, with some justification, that it's primarily a bourgeois, existential philosophy and would therefore seek to undermine collective societal wisdom. However, it's also a liberating philosophy, because when such societal wisdom is negated, the basis for social control over the individual becomes

weakened and . . . but I'm rabbiting a bit here. Ah cut myself short. They hate a smart cunt. It's easy to talk yourself into bigger fine, or fuck sake, a higher sentence. Think deference Renton, think deference.

(Welsh 1996: 165–6)

Renton's dialect in the first person narration is very marked. There is considerable orthographical manipulation, including, for example, the respelling of vowels ('whin' for 'when', 'git' for 'get', 'ah' for 'I'), the respelling of consonants ('aw day' for 'all day' and 'showin' for 'showing') and the representation of rapid speech processes ('n naebody's asking' for 'and nobody is asking'). There are several dialectal vocabulary items, including 'radges' and 'poppy', as well as some general colloquial terms including 'cunt' and 'fuck', even though there is little in the way of non-standard grammar.

As this scene makes clear, however, Renton is a gifted linguistic chameleon who is capable of shifting style dramatically in order to impress the judge. This might be interpreted as Renton converging towards the speech style of the judge. Certainly his speech becomes more standard and therefore like the judge's as he shifts from saying 'tae' to saying 'to' and 'ah' to 'I'. However, there is more to it than that. Renton does not just speak like the judge, he speaks like a philosopher, deploying abstract Latinate terms such as 'subjectivity', 'bourgeois' and 'existential'. He also uses conjunctions and organizing phrases such as 'however', 'therefore' and 'it could be argued' which are more commonly found in a written rather than spoken English. By shifting style in this way Renton transforms the judge's perception of him, convincing him that he is not a hopeless drug addict and so he receives probation, not a custodial sentence. It is quite clear that this is down to language variety and the discriminatory practice of the judge. The judge is not prepared to show similar leniency because Spud is inarticulate in the courtroom, but he believes what Renton tells him because of the way that he speaks.

As these two examples suggest, in film and literature successful transformative style-shifting is often used to depict a wily and resistant character, who is capable of renegotiating the social situation in which they find themselves by projecting a new identity. In the next section I will consider an extended scene from the film *East is East* which contains examples of all three types of style-shifting.

Case study: style-shifting in East is East (O'Donnell 1999)

East is East is a film about an ethnically mixed family growing up in the 1970s in Manchester. The father, George Khan, is originally from Pakistan. He came to England in 1937 to find work, leaving behind his first wife. In 1946 he married Ella, an Englishwoman. Together they run a chip-shop. They have seven children: six boys (Nazir, Tariq, Abdul, Maneer, Saleem and Sajid) and one girl (Meenah). George is deeply concerned that his children are growing up with little or no connection to their Pakistani and Muslim heritage. Hoping to integrate them into the British Muslim community, he arranges marriages for his sons, first for Nazir (which ends in disaster when Nazir runs away in the middle of the ceremony), and then, with increased desperation, for Tariq and Abdul. Meanwhile, the Khan children enthusiastically embrace British culture in various forms. The film is the first full-length feature by Irish director, Damien O'Donnell. The screenplay was written by Ayub Khan-Din, based upon his own successful play of the same name. In interviews, Khan-Din describes the film as being autobiographical: he himself was one of ten children born to a chip-shop owning Pakistani father and an English mother.

In the following scene the Khans meet the Shahs, the family of Tariq and Abdul's prospective brides, for the first time. Mr and Mrs Shah are both of Pakistani origin, and live in Bradford with their two daughters. George and Ella greet them at the door. Abdul, Tariq, Meenah and Sajid are waiting in the front room.

George:	Salam alykum Mr Shah.
Mr Shah:	Alykum salam.
George:	Ella, Mr Shah.
Mr Shah:	Salam alykum.
Ella:	Alykum salam. Salam alykum, Mr Shah.
Meenah:	(*Listening at the door.*) What's she talking like that for?
Ella:	Would you like to come through to the parlour? (*She ushers them in.*)
Mr Shah:	Abdul, salam alykum. Alykum salam, Tariq, eh?

(*There are general salams all round. The prospective wives are extremely plain, and Abdul and Tariq struggle not to look horrified.*)

George:	Please. (*Gestures to Mr Shah to sit down.*)
Mr Shah:	Thank you.

George:	Is that too low? (*George energetically adjusts the chair.*)
Ella:	So, you found it all right Mr Shah?
Mr Shah:	Ah yes, no problem.
Mrs Shah:	The thing is, that all these little houses look the same. (*Pause*) To me.
Ella:	Meenah, would you fetch the tea love.
Meenah:	(*In an exaggerated accent*) Righty-ho. (*Leaves to get tea*).
Mrs Shah:	(*To Sajid*). And how old are you?
Sajid:	Not old enough to get married so don't ask me.
George:	(*Embarrassed*) Sajid!

(*Mr Shah laughs uproariously and pats Sajid on the top of his grubby parka. His laughter becomes a little less uproarious as he considers his fingers after.*)

Ella:	I'm sorry about him Mr Shah. He's um … He's just been circumcised.
Mr Shah:	(*Embarrassed pause.*) Indeed.
George:	Sajid, go see if Saleem here yet. (*Sajid scuttles out*).
Mr Shah:	Ah yes, your college student. (*To Mrs Shah*) Studying to be an engineer.
Mrs Shah:	Oh, really.

(*Meenah enters with the tea and starts passing it around*)

Ella:	Ah, here's the tea.
Mr Shah:	(*To Meenah*). Shukriya.
Mrs Shah:	Where did you get this … this sari?
Meenah:	Me Aunty Riffat in Pakistan.
Mrs Shah:	You should wear salwar kameez. It would look much better on you than this thing.
Ella:	Aunty Riffat said a lot of girls are wearing saris in Islamabad. And she's quite well-to-do, int she George?
George:	Riffat bloody stupid. Even in Pakistan, women are getting too bloody moderns.
Ella:	Well, I think it looks lovely.
Mr Shah:	Well, it's … it's just not traditional dress in Pakistan, Mrs Khan.
Mr Kahn:	(*Approvingly.*) Tradition sees, Ella.

(*Annie, a close friend of Ella's enters.*)

Annie:	Coo-eee, it's only me. Oh, didn't know you had visitors. (*This isn't true – she's just seen everyone arrive and she's being nosy.*)
George:	Annie, this is my friend Mr Shah. His daughters go be married Abdul Tariq.
Annie:	Is it these two? Oh, they're bleeding gorgeous. Well, you're lucky you two, aren't you, landing a couple of belters like these. (*Tariq and Abdul are not amused.*)
Ella:	Meenah. (*Meenah leaves, allowing Annie to sit down next to Ella.*)
Mr Shah:	Mrs Khan I'm very proud that your sons are joining my family. I can see you've brought them up to be very respectful.
Annie:	You're right there Mr Shah. They're a credit to her. (*Adds as an afterthought.*) And you George.
George:	Oh yeah, they're . . . they're good boys. Bring no trouble.
Annie:	They'd do anything for you Mr Shah. Good Samaritans they are, just like in t' Bible.

(*Pained looks from Mrs Shah to her daughters. A wail outside from Sajid.*)

| Ella: | (*To Maneer*) Go in there, cock, go and see what those two are up to. |

Perhaps the most noticeable linguistic aspect of this scene is the multiple different varieties of language that are in use. The characters greet one another in formal Urdu ('Salam alykum' was borrowed into Urdu from Arabic, Arabic being the language of the Qur'an) and Mr Shah also thanks Meenah for the tea in Urdu ('Shukriya'). The rest of the scene is in English, but there are multiple varieties of English at play. For example, George speaks in a Pakistani-Manchester dialect, Mrs Shah speaks in a Pakistani-RP dialect, and Annie speaks in a broad Manchester dialect. It is noticeable that several characters style-shift during the scene. Ella in particular continually shifts variety and I will focus on her in the following analysis.

Unlike the other three adults present throughout the scene, Ella appears to have been born and brought up in Manchester. In many situations this might give Ella a social advantage over the immigrant Shahs, but in this scene it is a disadvantage. George and the Shahs are planning to integrate the boys into the Shah family. Ella wants to resist this integration, but feels herself rendered powerless by her position outside Pakistani society and the Muslim religion. She therefore seeks other ways to assert herself. One of the ways she does this is by joining in with the exchange of Urdu greetings. Earlier in the film it has been made clear that this social nicety is compulsory for the children of the family, when the youngest child, Sajid, is taken to task for refusing to 'salam' one of his uncles. However, when Ella joins in, the listening Meenah immediately makes the metalinguistic comment 'What's she talking like that for?', suggesting that Ella does not normally greet people in this way. She is deliberately adopting the linguistic practices of her guests (arguably a case of interpersonal style-shifting). This can be interpreted in two ways. First, it is a marker of politeness: she welcomes the Shahs into her home in their own language. Second, it may also be understood as an attempt to integrate herself in the forthcoming discussion because as the only non-Pakistani of the four parents she is in danger of being marginalized. Her use of the Urdu greeting serves to implicitly stake her claim to participate in the discussion.

After the formal greeting, everyone switches back to English. However, the Pakistani English accents of George and the Shahs continue to mark their shared heritage, even though the Pakistani English that each uses is rather different (note too that Pakistan is a strongly multilingual nation, and it is not clear from the film what the first languages of these characters are). George's accent is characterized by features presumably carried over from his first language combined with Northern English features. For example, the fact that he realizes dental fricatives as aspirated dental stops is likely to result from the phonology of his first language (for example, in '**t**hey're … **t**hey're good boys'), but his consistent H-deletion and his use of the Northern [ʊ] (for example, 'Riffat bl**oo**dy stupid') demonstrates that his English has been acquired among the working classes of Northern English. Mrs Shah, by contrast, has some features associated with Pakistani English (for example, aspirated dental stops at the start of words in '**T**he **th**ing is, **th**at all **th**ese little houses look **th**e same'). However, she uses no Northern English features. This might be because she has acquired an RP accent on top of the phonological system of her first language, although it is not clear where she would have accessed RP in her Bradford community. It is therefore more likely that Mrs Shah learned her English in Pakistan and acquired a prestigious Indian English dialect, which was originally derived from RP. This suggests that she comes from a wealthy and socially advantaged background, a suggestion reinforced by her 'all these little houses' comment, which implies that she herself lives in a larger, unique house. Hence Mrs Shah's language variety suggests that there are socioeconomic issues at stake in this scene, alongside the cultural and religious issues

Ella thus finds herself at a double linguistic disadvantage to Mrs Shah. Her normal Manchester dialect marks her both as being excluded from the Pakistani-English community, and as rating poorly on the socioeconomic scale. After first greeting the Shahs in Urdu, she then attempts to speak Standard English with an RP accent. This is perhaps best described as an instance of transformative style-shifting, through which she attempts to position herself as Mrs Shah's social equal. She cannot simply converge towards Mrs Shah's Pakistani English because that could seem offensive, so she uses the most presti-gious variety she knows. However, Ella's ability to use Standard English and RP is limited, and it produces some odd results. For example, in the sentence 'Meenah, would you fetch the tea love' her pronunciation of Meenah's name is unlike any pronunciation heard in the rest of the film. George typically pronounces Meenah with a short first vowel and a schwa as [mɪnə]. Elsewhere in the film, Ella pronounces it with a long initial vowel (presumably because that is how it seems to be spelled to her) and a schwa as [mi:nɑ]. On this occasion, however, she pro-nounces it with two long vowels as [mi:na:]. This may be because Ella is aware that RP has a long /a/ vowel in some environments, and so intro-duces one in the second vowel here. However, no RP speaker would produce such a pronunciation as it is an unstressed vowel, and any-way, George's pronunciation of a Pakistani name is likely to be the more authoritative one. Meenah responds to her mother's attempted upward linguistic mobility by producing a stereotypically upper-class phrase: 'Righty-ho'. Here Meenah joins in with her mother's transformative shift, but does so for satirical purposes, lightly mocking her mother's attempts at linguistic upward mobility.

Despite Ella's best efforts elements of her Manchester dialect repeat-edly appear. Features of Ella's normal Manchester dialect include: dialectal vocabulary items including cock (a term of endearment), bleeding, bloody and bastard; H-deletion; glottalization of /p/, /t/ and /k/ in word-internal and word-final positions; pronunciation of the /a/ in words such as BATH as the short vowel [a], rather than the long RP vowel [ɑ:]; an absence of the distinction between [ʌ] and [ʊ] that is found in RP. All of these features appear periodically in her speech throughout this scene, particularly at moments where she feels herself wrong-footed. For example she deletes all three /h/ in, 'I'm sorry about him, Mr Shah. He's um . . . He's just been circumcised' but pronounces it in the less flustered 'Ah, here's the tea'. In other words, she cannot maintain her transformative shift, and demonstrates emotional style-shifting back to her more normal variety under the pressure of the encounter.

The arrival of their neighbour, Annie, signals the introduction of a new linguistic force into the group. Annie's linguistic strategy is very different from that of Ella, and from the start appears to be based on principles of divergence, or, at the very least, a determination not to converge. This is particularly noticeable in terms of the dialectal vocabulary that she employs: 'bleeding', 'landing' and 'belters' which is clearly incomprehensible to the polite Mrs Shah. It is reinforced at a phonological level, as Annie categorically deletes /h/ and produces solidly Northern vowels. The effect is to emphasize her solidarity with Abdul, Tariq and Ella, and to exclude the Shahs. Her expression of enthusiasm for the daughters also creates a shared joke: the Khans understand that she is insulting the daughters, but the Shahs seem to take it at face value; a reaction shot shows Mrs Shah looking pleased the praise.

Finally, it is worth considering the linguistic position of the Khan children in this scene, who are virtually silent. This can perhaps be partly accounted for by the fact that their Manchester dialect makes it difficult for them to participate given the dominant Pakistani-English environment established by George and the Shahs. However, it also appears to be because the dominant Pakistani-English environment makes it inappropriate for *any* of the children to speak unless spoken to. The only children who do speak (albeit briefly) during the scene are Sajid and Meenah. Both can be interpreted as offering linguistic resistance to the Shahs. Sajid responds to Mrs Shah's question about his age with 'Not old enough to get married so don't ask me'. This response is resistant at two levels. First, he refuses to answer the actual question, and instead implies that he believes that she is really assessing his suitability for the marriage market. Secondly, his accent is resolutely Mancunian: he glottalizes all three /t/ and pronounces 'ask' as [ask]. Meenah, as I have already discussed, initially mimics her mother's attempt at RP. When asked a direct question by Mrs Shah, however, she too switches to a divergent linguistic strategy, producing a brief response: 'Me Aunty Riffat in Pakistan'. Her use of the pronoun form [mɪ] instead of [maɪ] is a typical feature of the Manchester dialect, Aunty is pronounced as [anti] rather than the RP [ɑːnti], and there is some T-glottalization on 'Riffat'. Both children demonstrate linguistically their unwillingness to be absorbed into the Pakistani-English culture of the Shahs.

Although I have, for the purposes of length, only discussed part of this scene, it is worth watching to the end to see how the tensions that I have identified here play out. Annie's cheery rebellion ultimately proves no match for the stony-faced Mrs Shah, and she departs. George and the Shahs continue to dominate the conversation. Indeed, Ella is so effectively silenced that she too eventually removes herself from the room. In the next room, Saleem, who has just arrived home, displays his latest sculpture to her – a fleshy pink model of female genitalia ('It's an example of female exploitation in art' he explains, leaving it unclear as to whether he is reproducing the exploitation, or trying to critique it). An outraged Ella launches an attack on the sculpture, and the resultant scuffle bursts through into the front room, depositing the sculpture in Mrs Shah's lap. In the wake of Mrs Shah's horrified response, Ella shifts back to her normal dialect in the defence of her children, and she orders the Shahs off her property with bellows of 'Go on sling your bleeding hook. Go on piss off. Piss off out of my house.'

East is East is interesting for the subtle ways in which it explores a second-generation Pakistani-English experience, and its use of language variety to do so. The Khan children are shown to negotiate a range of identities, and the film critiques superficial understandings of Pakistani culture. However, a possible criticism of the film is that it unfairly weights the scales in the battle between East and West towards the West. George's violent and hypocritical traditionalism, along with the pantomime ugliness of the prospective brides, means that the ultimate rejection of the arranged marriages is presented as straightforwardly triumphant. Similarly, Mrs Shah is characterized as deeply unsympathetic, and Ella's final routing of her is clearly intended to provoke cheers (just for good comic measure, Mrs Shah is assaulted by a large dog upon leaving the Khans' house). Mrs Shah's language variety is a key part of that characterization, connecting her Pakistani identity to a socially privileged identity, so that it is Ella who is placed at a social disadvantage. If Mrs Shah spoke with a Northern accent, or if her grammar were non-standard, she might seem less privileged, and Ella's status as the oppressed underdog would not be as clear. As it stands, however, it is Ella who is shown to be attempting to negotiate her identity in response to Mrs Shah's double social advantage. Ella greets the Shahs in Urdu, attempts to modify her language variety towards RP in order to achieve social equality with them, and angrily reverts back to her own dialect in order to throw them out. In this case, style-shifting is shown to be symptomatic of the difficult social position that Ella is attempting to negotiate, and for that reason it elicits the audience's sympathy.

Conclusion

As I have demonstrated in this chapter, filmmakers and writers often make use of style-shifting in order to communicate information about the emotional state, relationships and identity of characters. As I have illustrated with my analysis of *East is East* this representation of style-shifting is often highly strategic: the question of which characters are shown to style-shift and why they do so can do much to colour perceptions of those characters.

In Chapter 10 I take a broader view of the role of dialect in a text or film as a whole. I investigate the relationship that dialect representation has to realism, arguing that the extensive representation of dialect in films and texts is often bound up with a desire to represent everyday life in a realistic manner.

Further reading

Allan Bell's chapter 'Style and the Linguistic Repertoire' offers a brief but informative overview of some of the different approaches to style-shifting (2007). For a more detailed treatment, see Nikolas Coupland's *Style* (2007), particularly Chapters 3 and 5. For examples of how style-shifting has been applied to literary texts see Roger Shuy, 'Code Switching in *Lady Chatterley's Lover*' (1975), J. O. Omole 'Code-switching in Soyinka's *The Interpreters*' (1987), Natalie Hess 'Code Switching and Style Shifting as Markers of Liminality in Literature' (1996).

Exercises

Exercise 1

Read through the texts below, all of which include one or more style-shifts. Identify as many style-shifts as you can, and for each think about:

- What type of style-shift do you think it is?
- What linguistic features change?
- Is there any metalinguistic comment upon the style-shift? If so, who makes it?
- What function does the style-shift serve? For example, what does it tell us about the characters, about the relationship between them?
- Do you think this style-shift serves any thematic purpose?

Text 1: Arlington *by Thomas Henry Lister, 1832*

In this extract a traveller is looking for Lord Arlington, who has become disillusioned with society and retired to his country estate in the North of England. The traveller proves to be Arlington's friend, Hargrave.

The traveller was obliged to her for the hint, and, conducted by Jem, he proceeded on his pedestrian pilgrimage to what was emphatically called 'the Hall.' On his way thither he was curious to extract from his conductor some information respecting Lord Arlington, and the light in which he was regarded in that neighbourhood. 'Is Lord Arlington popular hereabouts?' he asked.

'Sir?' was the exclamation of the uncomprehending Jem, a short, bandy-legged, ostlerlike looking youth of about twenty.

'I mean,' said the traveller, altering his phraseology, 'is he liked in this neighbourhood?'

'Oh—ay—yes, he's liked very well, for he's a very good gentleman, and spends a sight of money here. There's lots of hands as he employs one way or tother, and nobody hereabouts needs be out of work as wants to have it; only, you see, it would be better for the inn if he didn't live so quiet like, but had gentlefolks come and see him, just as other gentlefolks do; howsumever, that's partly his own consarn, for the inn is my Lord's, and master says he can't pay him hardly no rent if he don't do nothing for it'

'People would be sorry, I suppose, if Lord Arlington were to go away from here?'

'Ay, surely. It has been a rare thing for the parish him coming and living down here.'

'Is he charitable?' inquired the traveller; 'does he give away much money ?'

'He gives some sometimes to them as can't work, but he generally gives work to them as can.'

'Is he often seen?'

'Oh—ay—.you'll see him most days riding or walking somewhere abouts, but he don't go much off his own ground—but then that reaches a long way ; why it is all my Lord's as far as you can see, and a mile or two afore you came to the village.'

'Does he dislike being met or spoken to?'

'Eh! no—not at all—at least by them as live about here. He talks a deal to 'em, and knows them well nigh all, I reckon; there an't a gentleman in the land as is freer and pleasantspokener than my Lord, and he isn't stiff and high a bit, and not as they say lords is elsewhere.'

'Do any gentlemen of the neighbourhood ever call upon his Lordship?'

'No, Sir, none as I knows of; but there is no gentleman very nigh; Squire Grufferton is the nighest, and he is about twelve miles off.'

'Then Lord Arlington lives quite alone, doesn't he?'

'No, Sir.'

'No! and who lives with him?'

'Oh. there's Master Bennet the steward, and there's the butler, and—'

'Ah! his establishment, his servants; but is there anybody else?'

'No, Sir, nobody as I knows of.'

(Lister 1832, vol. 3: 69–72)

Text 2: Lady Chatterley's Lover *by D. H. Lawrence (1928)*

In one of the exercises for Chapter 8 we explored some of the metalanguage between Connie and Mellors. In this extract from later in the novel, Connie and Mellors have embarked upon an affair which has become a public scandal. Connie brings her sister Hilda to meet Mellors. For a full account of style-shifting in the novel see Robert Shuy 'Code Switching in *Lady Chatterley's Lover*' (1975).

'Do sit down, Hilda,' said Connie.

'Do!' he said. 'Can I make you tea or anything – or will you drink a glass of beer? It's moderately cool.'

'Beer!' said Connie.

'Beer for me, please!' said Hilda, with a mock sort of shyness. He looked at her and blinked.

He took a blue jug and tramped to the scullery. When he came back with the beer, his face had changed again.

Connie sat down by the door, and Hilda sat in his seat, with the back to the wall, against the window corner.

'That is his chair,' said Connie softly. And Hilda rose as if it had burnt her.

'Sit yer still, sit yer still! Ta'e ony cheer as yo'n a mind to, none of us is th' big bear,' he said, with complete equanimity.

And he brought Hilda a glass, and poured her beer first from the blue jug.

'As for cigarettes,' he said, 'I've got none, but 'appen you've got your own. I dunna smoke, mysen. – Shall y' eat summat?' – He turned direct to Connie. 'Shall t' eat a smite o' summat, if I bring it thee? Tha can usually do wi' a bite.' He spoke the vernacular with a curious calm assurance, as if he were the landlord of the Inn.

'What is there?' asked Connie, flushing.

'Boiled ham, cheese, pickled wa'nuts, if yer like.– Nowt much.'

'Yes,' said Connie. 'Won't you, Hilda?'

Hilda looked up at him.

'Why do you speak Yorkshire?' she said softly.

'That! That's non Yorkshire, that's Derby.'

He looked back at her with that faint, distant grin.

'Derby, then! Why do you speak Derby? You spoke natural English at first.'

'Did Ah though? An' canna Ah change if Ah'n a mind to 't? Nay, nay, let me talk Derby if it suits me. If yo'n nowt against it.'

'It sounds a little affected,' said Hilda.

'Ay, 'appen so! An' up i' Tevershall yo'd sound affected.' – He looked again at her, with a queer calculating distance, along his cheek-bone: as if to say: Yi, an' who are you?

He tramped away to the pantry for the food.

The sisters sat in silence. He brought another plate, and knife and fork. Then he said:

'An' if it's the same to you, I s'll ta'e my coat off like I allers do.'

And he took off his coat, and hung it on the peg, then sat down to table in his shirt-sleeves: a shirt of thin, cream-coloured flannel.

''elp yerselves!' he said. ''elp yerselves! Dunna wait f'r axin'!'

He cut the bread, then sat motionless. Hilda felt, as Connie once used to, his power of silence and distance. She saw his smallish, sensitive, loose hand on the table. He was no simple working man, not he: he was acting! acting!

'Still!' she said, as she took a little cheese. 'It would be more natural if you spoke to us in normal English, not in vernacular.'

He looked at her, feeling her devil of a will.

'Would it?' he said in the normal English. 'Would it? Would anything that was said between you and me be quite natural, unless you said you wished me to hell before your sister ever saw me again: and unless I said something almost as unpleasant back again? Would anything else be natural?'

'Oh yes!' said Hilda. 'Just good manners would be quite natural.'

'Second nature, so to speak!' he said: then he began to laugh. 'Nay,' he said. 'I'm weary o' manners. Let me be!'

(Lawrence 2006: 242–4)

Text 3: 'A Memory' short story by James Kelman (1991)

For copyright reasons I have not reproduced this very short story here. It can be found in Kelman's collection *The Burn* (1992: 85-6). In the story the first person narrator who is Scottish confuses the girl serving in an English cafe.

Exercise 2

Watch the film *Bhaji on the Beach* (Chadha 1993).

1. How many examples of cross-cultural pollination can you identify in the film? You might start with the title bhaji (an Indian food which has been anglicized), and include such things as the men who wear cowboy clothes to sell hotdogs, and the camel-racing betting game.
2. When they set off on their trip, Simi greets them by saying 'Hello. Namaste. Sat sir akal. Salam alykum.' Which languages do these different greetings come from? Consider what Simi's greeting implies about the ethnic mix of the group. Can you identify any other languages in the film?
3. Describe the accents of some of the different characters (particularly interesting people to think about are Simi, Ginder, Asha and Rekha). What do their accents indicate about them, and how do they relate to other aspects of their character, such as their age, dress and behaviour?
4. At two significant points in the film, the younger generation adopts the language of the older generation: Ladhu and Madhu mimic the Indian English accents of their aunties, and Ranjit speaks Hindi to Asha when asking her to help him. Analyse these scenes and consider why these younger characters switch language varieties.
5. Compare the speech communities of *Bhaji on the Beach* to those of *East is East*. What similarities and differences would you wish to note? How does the representation of multicultural Britain compare in the two films?

10

Realism

In Chapter 9 I looked at style-shifting, drawing on frameworks developed by linguists working on 'real world' conversations in order to analyse the language of films and literature. I made the point, however, as I have elsewhere in this book, that when doing this we must always bear in mind that dialect in films and literature function differently from dialects in the 'real world'. However, dialects in film and literature function at least in part because they bear some relationship to 'real world' dialects. In the two final chapters of this book, therefore, I address the relationship between 'real world' dialects and those found in film and literature. First, in this chapter, I focus on the issue of how and why the representation of dialect can have the effect of making films and texts seem more 'realistic'. In the next chapter, Chapter 11, I focus on the accuracy of dialect representation itself and consider to what extent it is important that the literary and filmic representation of dialect is linguistically authentic.

In this chapter I argue that the representation of dialect in films and literature is frequently used to signal a commitment to depicting the 'real world', and that dialects therefore have a particular association with realist modes. I begin by attempting to define 'realism'. I then focus on film and literature in turn, exploring the role that dialect representation has played in relationship to realism in each art form and offering two short case studies for each (*Adam Bede* and *How Late It Was How Late* for literature; *In Which We Serve* and *Ladybird, Ladybird* for film). Overall, I argue that while in each of these cases the presence of dialect is associated with a turn to 'the real', this has been achieved in very different ways and for very different ends.

What is realism?

Any attempt to define the term 'realism' must be prefaced by the warning that it is a notoriously difficult term to pin down, and that it has meant different things to different people at different times. One very broad way of approaching realism is to define it as any attempt to create a work of art which represents the world as it really is. Some of the problems with such a definition become apparent, however, as soon as we start to think about this idea of how the world 'really is'. From a philosophical point of view, the belief that the world is comprised of a single objective reality which is simply waiting to be observed and analysed is itself distinctly problematic. The question of how individuals perceive that world highlights some of these difficulties, because different individuals experience the world in very different ways: what I perceive as an unpleasant argument, for example, you may perceive as a lively debate. Our differing perceptions would lead us to film the same conversation in very different ways, but which one would be 'real'? Furthermore, any attempt to represent the world 'as it really is' in art is always a representation, not real life itself. In the case of literature, the 'real world' that individuals experience continually in their everyday lives through the five senses is represented solely through sight via strings of 26 characters printed on paper. In the case of film, the 'real world' is represented on a two dimensional screen via a strip of celluloid and an audio track. Hence, any text or film that claims to depict the world 'as it really is' must be treated with caution.

Realism and dialect in literature

Realism has a long history in literature, but in terms of its relationship to dialect a good starting point is *Lyrical Ballads*. In 1798 William Wordsworth and Samuel Taylor Coleridge published *Lyrical Ballads*, a collection of poems that challenged some firmly-entrenched conventions about what was appropriate 'poetic diction'. In 1800 Wordsworth oversaw a second edition of *Lyrical Ballads*, adding several new poems and a Preface, and he further edited the Preface in 1802. In this 'Preface to the *Lyrical Ballads*', Wordsworth set out to shape the way in which the language of *Lyrical Ballads* was understood, and in doing so he helped to shape new ways of thinking about the language of literature. The Preface can claim to be one of the most influential pieces of literary metalanguage to date in the history of English Literature. In Chapter 8 I offered a brief discussion of Alex Broadhead's article on metalinguistic aspects of *Lyrical Ballads* (Broadhead 2010).

In the 1802 version of the 'Preface' Wordsworth famously states that:

> The principal object then which I proposed to myself in these Poems was to chuse incidents and situations from common life, and to relate or describe them, throughout, as far as was possible in a selection of language really used by men; and, at the same time, to throw over them a certain colouring of imagination, whereby ordinary things should be presented to the mind in an unusual way; and, further, and above all, to make these incidents and situations interesting by tracing in them, truly though not ostentatiously, the primary laws of our nature: chiefly as far as regards the manner in which we associate ideas in a state of excitement. Low and rustic life was generally chosen, because in that condition, the essential passions of the heart find a better soil in which they can attain their maturity, are less under restraint, and speak a plainer and more emphatic language.
>
> (Wordsworth and Coleridge 1991: 244–5)

It is difficult to assess quite how revolutionary Wordsworth's statement really was. Much ink has been spilt in the two hundred years since the publication of the Preface debating exactly what Wordsworth meant by 'a selection of language really used by men' and, as he puts it elsewhere in the Preface, 'the real language of men' (1991: 241). Wordsworth's own position is at times rather hesitant; he adds the caveat, for example, that this 'real language of men' should be '(purified indeed from what appear to be its real defects, from all lasting and rational causes of dislike or disgust)' (1991: 245). Much debate has also gone into the relationship between Wordsworth's views as expressed in the Preface and the language of *Lyrical Ballads*, and it is true that *Lyrical Ballads* contains little in the way of outright dialect representation. It is also important to bear in mind that Wordsworth was not a lone pioneer when he wrote the Preface; Robert Burns, for example, was already an important figure on the literary landscape. But two key points remain. First, that throughout the Preface Wordsworth clearly and repeatedly articulates his view that there is such a thing as 'the real language of men', that it is a desirable medium for literature, and that it is best to be found in 'low' life. And second, that his articulation of this view has provided a touchstone for many later discussions of the language of literature.

In poetry, Wordsworth's Preface contributed to the rising popularity of dialect poetry, with writers such as John Clare, Alfred Tennyson and Thomas Hardy all finding success for their dialect works in the course of the nineteenth century. Less directly, Wordsworth's Preface also had an influence on the novel. Although dialect representation had appeared in novels in the eighteenth century, it had tended to be highly stereotyped and presented for comic effect. The burgeoning interest in 'the real language of men' from 1800 onwards encouraged a pioneering use of dialect in novels by Maria Edgeworth and Sir Walter Scott, which paved the way for dialect's central role in the great realist novels of the nineteenth century. Increasingly, writers became concerned to accurately portray the real patterns of speech found in real locations. In Emily Bronte's *Wuthering Heights* (first published 1847), for example, Joseph speaks with a dialect that is not just 'generic Yorkshire' but specific to the region around Howarth where the Bronte's lived, while Elizabeth Gaskell used the Manchester dialect to great effect in novels such as *Mary Barton* (1848) and *North and South* (1855) drawing on both her own experiences of living in the city, and her husband's scholarly expertise on the Lancashire dialect. Nevertheless, it remained the case – with a few notable exceptions – that during the nineteenth century dialect-speaking characters were confined to minor characters, to comedic roles, to peripheral figures observed from the outside.

By the turn of the twentieth century some writers were beginning to question the realist novel, with its omniscient third person narrator and faithful reporting of dialect speech. Innovators including James Joyce and Virginia Woolf developed new forms for the novel, exploring ways in which the immediate perceptions of characters could be represented, and developing techniques such as free direct speech and stream of consciousness in order to do so. As the relationship between narrator and character changed, so too did the handling of dialect. Writers began to blur the boundary between character and narrator, and in some cases to place dialect speaking characters at the centre of their novels. Experimentation with form – exploring the means by which dialect could be represented and the extent to which dialect could become a medium for representing the lived experience of characters on the margins of society – continued throughout the twentieth century.

It is important, however, to bear in mind that this turn towards dialect was not simply the result of writers becoming 'better' and developing new techniques. Norman Page makes the point that it is no coincidence that it was during the nineteenth and twentieth centuries that the representation of dialect took on this increasingly central role:

> In periods before widespread travel and promulgation of the spo-ken word by radio and other means made a variety of accents and dialects familiar to nearly all, the writer using dialect words or indi-cating regional pronunciations ran the risk of mystifying his reader if his representation went very far in the direction of realism.
>
> (Page 1988: 56)

This relates back to the point that I made in Chapter 5 when I noted that dialect representation works best when readers already have some idea of what the dialect sounds like. Before the advent of trains, radio, cars and television most people would have been familiar with a much narrower range of dialects than they are today. Literary use of dialect for purposes of 'realism' is dependent upon the readership having suf-ficient familiarity with both the dialect itself and the conventions of its representation to experience it as 'real'. Indeed, Sylvia Adamson argues that it is precisely because the reader is already familiar with the language variety in question, that the illusion of 'realism' is created through the incorporation of dialect and other varieties into the text:

> The existence of Varieties provides the linguistic resources for the act of literary illusionism by which the reader is persuaded that what s/he is reading is not a collection of words on a page but the tran-scription of a human voice endowed with a specific social identity. There are two aspects to this illusionist enterprise. First, since no real utterance takes place outside a social context, the presence of a recognisable Variety in a text persuades us of its authenticity as utterance or address. Secondly, the specificity of the Variety invoked allows us to categorise and characterise the utterance, to infer, that is, that we are hearing or overhearing a speaker of provenance X, performing role Y, or adopting attitude Z.
>
> (Adamson 1993: 232)

Hence it is not the case that writers became more skilled at accurately representing dialect on the page during the nineteenth and twenti-eth centuries, but rather that because readers were becoming more familiar with an increasing range of dialects, writers were able to use this knowledge to create the illusion of dialect speech in their texts, thereby making those texts seem more 'real' to readers.

In what follows I explore two instances of what might be described the 'realist' mode in novels, the first a 'classic realist' novel by George Eliot and the second a much more recent novel by James Kelman, which has been described as a 'social realist' novel.

Case Study 1: Adam Bede by George Eliot

First published in 1859, *Adam Bede* tells the story of the love affairs between a small group of characters living in the fictional village of Hayslope in 1799. It focuses on the eponymous Adam, who is in love with Hetty Sorrel, a beautiful but thoughtless girl. The novel opens as follows:

> With a single drop of ink for a mirror, the Egyptian sorcerer undertakes to reveal to any chance comer far-reaching visions of the past. This is what I undertake to do for you, reader. With this drop of ink at the end of my pen I will show you the roomy workshop of Mr Jonathan Burge, carpenter and builder in the village of Hayslope, as it appeared on the eighteenth of June, in the year of our Lord 1799.
>
> The afternoon sun was warm on the five workmen there, busy upon doors and window-frames and wainscoting. A scent of pine-wood from a tent-like pile of planks outside the open door mingled itself with the scent of the elder-bushes which were spreading their summer snow close to the open window opposite; the slanting sunbeams shone through the transparent shavings that flew before the steady plane, and lit up the fine grain of the oak panelling which stood propped against the wall. On the heap of those soft shavings a rough grey shepherd-dog had made himself a pleasant bed, and was lying with his nose between his fore-paws, occasionally wrinkling his brows to cast a glance at the tallest of the five workmen, who was carving a shield in the centre of a wooden mantelpiece. It was to this workman that the strong baritone belonged which was heard above the sound of plane and hammer singing –
>
> Awake, my soul, and with the sun
> Thy daily stage of duty run;
> Shake off dull sloth . . .

(Eliot 1980: 49)

The third person narrator describes the facts of the scene, giving the exact date and location of the scene. The scene itself is described with reference to several senses – the sunshine is warm, there is a smell of pinewood and elderberries, five workmen and a dog can be seen, and the sound of singing can be heard. The characters are initially intro-duced as a group from the perspective of the dog, then one workman (who proves to be the eponymous Adam) is singled out by his singing. The novel thus begins by describing the external appearance of the scene in its entirety, before focusing in to introduce the individual characters.

After a few paragraphs describing the external appearance of the characters they begin to speak, allowing the reader to eavesdrop on what they have to say:

> The concert of the tools and Adam's voice was at last broken by Seth, who, lifting the door at which he had been working intently, placed it against the wall and said –
>
> 'There! I've finished my door to-day, any how.'
>
> The workmen all looked up; Jim Salt, a burly red-haired man, known as Sandy Jim, paused from his planing, and Adam said to Seth, with a sharp glance of surprise –
>
> 'What I dost think thee 'st finished the door?'
>
> 'Ay, sure,' said Seth, with answering surprise, 'what's awanting to 't?'
>
> A loud roar of laughter from the other three workmen made Seth look round confusedly. Adam did not join in the laughter, but there was a slight smile on his face as he said, in a gentler tone than before – 'Why, thee 'st forgot the panels.'
>
> (Eliot 1980: 50–1)

In keeping with conventions of the realist novel, direct speech is rep-resented within speech marks and purports to capture exactly how the words were uttered. The workmen are all shown to be dialect speakers, as evidenced in particular by their use of the pronoun 'thee' for 'you', the verb forms 'dost' and 'hast' (shortened to ''st' by Adam), and the use of a-prefixing in 'awanting'. Each of these features is regional, but also by the time of writing possibly somewhat archaic, which chimes with the nostalgic feel to these opening paragraphs. Overall, this opening demonstrates a firm commitment to portraying the world as it really is and conveying to the reader what can be recorded by an observant spectator to the scene. Dialect is at the heart of this contract with the reader.

It is, nevertheless, worth pointing out that from the opening sentence Eliot demonstrates that she is very well aware that this is not 'real life' *per se* but the illusion of 'real life' created with 'a single drop of ink'. Thus while this can be thought of a 'classic realist' novel, it is not one that is unaware of its own artistic enterprise. It is also noticeable that Eliot is here upturning contemporary literary conventions by making a dialect speaking character the eponymous hero of her novel (even if, as the novel progresses, Adam's dialect is less strongly marked than that of other villagers). While Victorian realist novels may appear staid and conventional, particularly when compared to more experimental twentieth century texts, that does not mean that they were conventional in their own time. In the case of *Adam Bede*, Eliot innovates by putting rural characters at the centre of her novel and making them the focus of serious drama, rather than placing them at the fringes of her novel, and giving them comic roles. The representation of dialect is central to this, making the characters sound 'real' by drawing on a limited range of linguistic features in order to signal that these are people who speak something other than neutral Standard English.

Case Study 2: James Kelman *How Late It Was, How Late* (1994)

A very different form of realism is offered by the opening of James Kelman's *How Late It Was, How Late*, which was first published in 1994. This novel narrates a single day in the life of Sammy, an alcoholic Glaswegian who awakes one morning to find that he has gone blind after a beating:

> Ye wake in a corner and stay there hoping yer body will disappear, the thoughts smothering ye; these thoughts; but ye want to remember and face up to things, just something keeps ye from doing it, why can ye no do it; the words filling yer head: then the other words; there's something wrong; there's something far far wrong; ye're no a good man, ye're just no a good man. Edging back into awareness of where ye are: here, slumped in this corner, with these thoughts filling ye. And oh christ his back was sore; stiff and the head pounding. He shivered and hunched up his shoulders, shut his eyes, rubbed

into the corners with his fingertips; seeing all kinds of spots and lights. Where in the name of fuck . . .

He was here, he was leaning against auld rusty palings, with pointed spikes, some missing or broke off. And he looked again and saw it was a wee bed of grassy weeds, that was what he was sitting on. His feet were back in view. He studied them; he was wearing an auld pair of trainer shoes for fuck sake where had they come from he had never seen them afore man auld fucking trainer shoes. The laces were-nay even tied! Where was his leathers? A new pair of leathers man he got them a fortnight ago and now here they were fucking missing man know what I'm saying, somebody must have blagged them, miserable bastards, what chance ye got.

(Kelman 1995: 1)

The novel opens with a series of second person pronouns, which sound as though the reader is either being addressed directly ('Ye wake in a corner') or, more plausibly, that the speaker is talking to himself in the second person. The dialect representation continues with non-standard grammar such as 'why can ye no do it'; respellings such as 'yer' and 'auld' (although this second one might be considered Standard Scottish English); and dialectal and colloquial vocabulary including 'wee' and 'blagged'. Indeed, the fact that the character is a dialect speaker is really the only thing that is established for certain in these opening paragraphs because there is a great deal of uncertainty about everything else: who is this character? where are they? and what is happening? This uncertainty arises because the reader has been dropped straight into the character's ongoing thought processes and the character in question is not in an agile mental state. This means that the narrative cannot access privileged external information about place, date and appearances.

As the first paragraph progresses, it shifts from the second person pronoun to the third person, revealing the fact that the novel is told at least partly by a third person narrator: 'He shivered and hunched up his shoulders, shut his eyes, rubbed into the corners with his fingertips; seeing all kinds of spots and lights.' At the same time, a shift occurs from the present tense of the opening few sentences to the simple past tense, again marking a shift between the opening interior monologue of the character and a third person narrator. This third person narrator uses a language variety closer to Standard English (although it would be a mistake to assume that it is Standard English) and is able to offer some external perspective on events, but is unable to offer the kind of broad perspective date, place and time information of the narrator of *Adam Bede*. Furthermore, unlike the boundaries between dialect character and third person narrator which are clearly delineated by speech marks in *Adam Bede*, the boundaries between narrator and character speech and thought are often difficult to determine in *How Late It Was, How Late*. Consider, for example, the sentence that opens 'He studied them; he was wearing an auld pair of trainer shoes for fuck sake'. The opening clause is in Standard English and appears to mark the external perspective of the narrator, but the use of 'auld' in the phrase 'an auld pair of trainer shoes' belongs to the vocabulary of the character, suggesting that the sentence is slipping into free indirect speech, a suspicion that is further confirmed by the expletive 'for fuck sake'. The novel thus moves between the third person narrative voice and the speech and thought of the central character in a way that is reminiscent of passage from *Saturday Night and Sunday Morning* but much more thorough-going in its execution. Sue Vice, in a detailed reading of the novel informed by Bakhtinian theory notes how Kelman subverts the normal clear distinction between narrator and character: 'Confusion arises in Kelman's novel because narrator and character sound so alike, *and* so non-standardly, that they may be one entity' (Vice 1997: 100). Similarly, in his detailed chapter on the novel, Jeremy Scott argues that Kelman's technique narrows the gap between character voice and narrative voice 'so that the character and narrator (inasmuch as these two entities can be separated in *HLIW*) speak as one' (Scott 2009: 116). Scott argues that Kelman has a distinct political purpose in this, striving to achieve 'a mode of demotic representation which simulates transparency, giving an authentic voice to a constituency from which that voice had previously been denied' (Scott 2009, 118).

In some senses, therefore, it can be argued that *How Late It Was, How Late* offers a much more 'realistic' account than *Adam Bede*: after all, we all experience life from within the confines of our own head, rather than observing the lives of others at a privileged distance. Nevertheless (as Scott's description of Kelman's technique as one which '*simulates* transparency' recognizes) *How Late It Was, How Late* relies upon a series of literary techniques and conventions in order to create this impression of verisimilitude, not least in its weaving together of Standard English and Glaswegian English. There are also important points of similarity between the two novels: both focus on characters from lower down the social scale than was customary at the time of writing, and both share a concern with demonstrating the daily lives of those characters. Their techniques may be different, but within the constraints of the traditions within which they wrote, both sought to extend the boundaries of existing conventions in order to represent something more 'real'.

Realism and dialect in film

Within the history of film it is possible to identify a number of movements which have attempted to make films that can lay claim to faithfully representing real life. In their book *Realism and Popular Cinema*, for example, Julia Hallam and Margaret Marshment select five key moments 'when realism was the subject of intense critical attention and reflection' (Hallam and Marshment 2000: 24). For Hallam and Marshment these moments are: Soviet filmmakers in the 1920s; British wartime cinema; the Italian neorealist movement of the 1940s; British 'New Wave' cinema of the 1950s and 1960s; and American Black urban cinema of the 1990s (Hallam and Marshment 2000, ch. 2). One striking point to note about this list is how disparate the filmmaking practices are that it represents: there is no single way to invoke 'realism' in film. As I have already shown in relation to literature, this points to the essential fact about any artistic practice that takes 'realism' as one of its goals: it will always result in a particular set of conventions and practices that may from other perspectives seem anything but 'realistic'. A second striking point to note is how central dialect is to all of these realist moments, with the sole exception of the Soviet films of the 1920s which were produced in the days of silent film. British wartime cinema attempted to depict the struggles of ordinary people during the war, and so depicted a much greater range of dialects onscreen than had existed before in British films. The Italian neorealist movement worked with untrained actors in their home surroundings and as such presented a much broader range of accents to Italian movie-goers than they were accustomed to. British 'new wave' cinema of the 1950s and 60s frequently took Northern working-class heroes as its central subject (as I discussed in relation to *Saturday Night and Sunday Morning*). American urban cinema of the 1990s brought extensive use of African American Vernacular English in gritty, urban environments to the screen to an extent that had never been seen before. In each case, the decision to portray life 'as it really is' resulted dialects being used in film in innovative ways.

In the next two sections I explore two films which can be claimed as 'realist' but which use language variety in very different ways and to very different ideological ends. First I consider a British wartime film, Noel Coward's *In Which We Serve*, which follows the fortunes of the crew of a Royal Navy Ship. My discussion here is heavily indebted to Stephanie Marriott's article 'Dialect and Dialectic in a British War Film' (1997). Second I examine Ken Loach's *Ladybird, Ladybird* which follows the story of a woman whose children are taken into care by the social services. Overall, I argue that examining the way in which these films depict the interaction of language varieties can help us to understand their broader social and political themes.

Case Study 3: In Which We Serve (Coward and Lean 1942)

In a groundbreaking article Stephanie Marriott analyses the representation of language variety in the Second World War film *In Which We Serve* (Coward and Lean 1942). This film takes as its starting point the sinking of a ship during the Battle of Crete, which results in the three principal male characters awaiting rescue in a lifeboat together. Episodes from their lives leading up to the ill-fated voyage are told in flashback, which serve to sketch in their family backgrounds and commitments. The three men come from very different social milieus: Able-Bodied Seaman 'Shorty' Blake (played by John Mills) is working class, Chief Petty Officer Hardy (Bernard Miles) is lower-middle class and Captain Kinross (Noel Coward) is upper-middle class. As Marriott discusses, the social dimensions of the three sets of families and friends are mapped out through a careful contrasting of space, props and physical action as well as, she argues, through 'the systematic deployment of speech markers'. Upper-middle-class speakers use 'standard forms', 'U features' and 'High forms' of language including 'careful articulation, elaborate syntax and "High" or "H" vocabulary'. Working-class and lower-middle-class speakers use 'non-standard forms, non-U features and "Low" forms such as speech simplifications, relatively non-complex syntax and L vocabulary' (Marriott 1997: 182).

In Which We Serve can be claimed as a realist film, fitting tidily within Hallam and Marshment's identification of British wartime film as one of the 'key moments' of realist filmmaking. As Jonathan Rayner notes, the 'influence of documentary filmmaking upon the film's conception [is] apparent from the opening voice-over, accompanying a rapid montage of the ship's construction and launching, and the subsequent incorporation of newsreel footage of destroyers at sea' (Rayner 2007: 40). In terms of personal narrative, the film shares the concerns of many other British wartime films to reflect back to the wartime audiences a range of their own experiences. The film therefore includes a much more socially diverse range of characters than those typically found in pre-war films, and Shorty Blake's story is given equal prominence and treated with equal seriousness as Captain Kinross's.

One aspect of the film that Marriott finds noticeable, however, is that despite the fact that the film depicts a broad range of language varieties, the speakers of these varieties each tend to stick to a single variety. This can be seen, for example, in the scene where Blake and his new wife unexpectedly encounter Captain Kinross and his wife. We might expect to see some interpersonal style-shifting here as Blake attempts to impress his superior, while Kinross attempts to put his subordinate at ease. In practice, however, all of the characters stick resolutely to their habitual variety.

Marriott observes:

> Speakers from each class command a narrow and monolithic repertoire, with little evidence of style-shifting or accommodation to mark formality or 'audience design' (Bell 1984). The speech of working-class characters is invariably non-standard, casual and colloquial, no matter who the addressee or what the situation ... Only Captain Kinross commands a range of styles, switching from High to Low whenever he addresses his crew. But Kinross's simple noun phrases and Germanic vocabulary function less as tokens of downwards convergence reducing the distance between officer and men, than as echoes of the 'plain bareness' with which Churchill had two years earlier appealed 'to the hearts and minds of the English-speaking people' (McCrum et al. 1992:58).
>
> (Marriott 1997: 173–93, 182)

One possible explanation for this lack of sociolinguistic nuance can be found in the working methods for the making of the film. The dialogue was carefully scripted by Coward, and the lower-class characters are played by upper-middle-class actors who deliberately adopt a London accent. Natural linguistic phenomenon such as style-shifting are unlikely to happen under such conditions. Nevertheless, the filmmakers could have attempted to represent style-shifting if they had desired to do so. We only need to look at the character of Leonard in *Howards End* to see that an actor working to a script and performing in a dialect different from his natural one is capable of showing style-shifting.

Marriott contends that the lack of style-shifting is tied up with the ideological position of the film. She argues that while the film is keen to celebrate sociolinguistic diversity, it is also at pains to defend the status quo:

> This happily hierarchical world-view is conveyed not only by means of the occasionally overtly didactic speech but also by means of textual strategies and representational devices which work towards the neutralisation of class-based conflicts and contradictions. In the case of *In Which We Serve*, the systematic deployment of speech markers as signifiers of particular stereotyped class positions, together with the emphatic use of socio-spatial conventions to differentiate one group from another, have the effect of reproducing class difference as cultural difference, thus essentialising the divisions between the different social groups.
>
> (Marriott 1997: 187)

In other words, the ficto-linguistic patterning to be found in the film provides space for different dialects to be heard, and yet at the same time keeps those different varieties carefully separate from one another. As Marriott puts it, the film portrays 'a fundamentally Churchillian paternalistic view of British culture' in which the working classes are shown to be 'complacent and freely-consenting citizens of a community dedicated to service' (1997: 174). This illustrates a further important point to bear in mind about the relationship between dialect and realism: while in many instances the desire for a 'realistic' representation of non-RP speaking characters will be allied with a politically progressive agenda, this is not necessarily the case.

Case Study 4: Ladybird, Ladybird (Loach 1994)

My final case study is *Ladybird, Ladybird*, which follows the life of Maggie, a single mother living in Manchester who has four children, each by different fathers. She herself comes from a dysfunctional family, and she has a history of abusive relationships. The film traces Maggie's attempts at getting her life together, and her battles with the social services. Owing to her inability to provide the children with a stable and safe home, her first four children are taken into care. She then meets Jorge, an immigrant from South America, who begins to provide some stability in her life. Maggie becomes pregnant again, but, when the child is born, the social services step in once more and take it away. The film itself attempts to be even-handed in its portrayal of events, and it is more interested in exploring why these things happen, rather than in assigning blame. Maggie is shown to be a loving and protective mother, but also at times unwise and impulsive. The social workers are shown as attempting to act for the best, but they have to work within an inflexible institutional structure and they have only an outsider's understanding of Maggie's life. Much of the conflict arises because once Maggie has come to the attention of the system, it is almost impossible for her to prove definitively that her children are no longer at risk.

The scene I analyse here is a confrontation between Maggie and two social workers. Maggie moved into a hostel with her children in order to escape her most recent relationship. While staying there, she went out one night, leaving her children locked in their room so that the other residents would not disturb them. A fire broke out while she was away and her eldest son, Sean, was injured in it. Sean has now been taken into care and Maggie is meeting with the social workers to discuss his future, and the future of her other children. The scene starts at 31 minutes 20 seconds. I have used | to indicate interruptions.

Male S.W.	We've already explained to you Maggie. You can only get Sean home under certain conditions. Now, under the circumstances you're lucky that we haven't already started care proceedings.
Maggie	I'm not going into no detention centre. O.K.|
Female S.W.	|Maggie
Maggie	|I'm not going.
Female S.W.	Maggie, it's not a detention centre. It's what we call a family centre. It's to help you rehabilitate and, and cope. We're not trying to punish you or anything. It's a centre that, we'd, we'd be able to help you there.
Male S.W.	We just want to assess how you're getting on.

Maggie   I'm not going. I'm not going to the detention centre. If you want to help me, get me a flat. Not stick me in a doss house.

Male S.W. We just want to assess how you're getting on. Make sure you're coping.

Maggie   I'll cope much better if my son's home. Do you know what it's like? I went up there last week and he didn't even want to come to me because you're trying to turn him against me. I know what your little games are.

Male S.W. The thing is Maggie, Sean nearly died.

Maggie   I know Sean nearly died. And how do you think that makes me feel? So rub it in, eh? Let's all rub it in.

Male S.W. Maggie, Maggie. Listen to me please. Your children are on the 'at- risk' register. Now we need some reassurance that you're working with us on this.

Maggie   They're only there because of yous. Why don't you just get off me back. Why don't you just leave me alone and give me me son back. But no, you can't do that can you?

Male S.W. No, we can't do that. It's because it's our statutory duty to provide safe accommodation for you and your kids. And your kids' best interest is what we are concerned with.

Maggie   My kids' best interest is to have their brother back. My best interest is to have my son back. My son's best interest is to be home with us not with someone playing fucking happy families.|

Male S.W. | Are we? Maggie, please listen. We want you to have Sean back. But unfortunately the law says that we have to send you to this place. Now if you don't go then you don't co-operate then we will have to take all your children into care.

                                                    (Loach 1994)

In broad terms, this scene shows a conflict between three speakers who all use different varieties of English. Maggie speaks with a Liverpudlian accent, the female social worker speaks with an RP accent, and the male social worker speaks with a lightly marked Northern accent.

Maggie's English has a lot of dialect features. She uses some non-standard grammar, most notably the double negative 'I'm **not** going into **no** detention centre' and the plural second person pronoun 'because of yous'. She uses colloquial vocabulary, including 'stick me' and 'doss house'. Her accent is Northern. She categorically deletes /h/ (e.g. 'a doss **h**ouse'), frequently realizes /ŋ/ as [n] (e.g. 'fucki**ng** happy families') and regularly glottalizes both word-final and word-middle /t/ (e.g. 'your li**tt**le games'). There are also a number of consonants which mark her accent as being specifically Liverpudlian. For example, /k/ at the end of words often receives some frication (see particularly 'give me me son ba**ck**' and 'have their brother ba**ck**') and intervocalic /t/ is occasionally realized as [r] (e.g. 'ge**t** off me back'). In terms of vowels, it is noticeable that Maggie, as with most Northern accents, does not have the distinction between /ʌ/ and /ʊ/ that is found in RP, hence both of these vowels are consistently realized as [ʊ] (e.g. 'with **u**s not with s**o**meone playing f**u**cking happy families').

In this scene, Maggie is very angry, and she is unwilling to cooperate with the social workers. It is obvious to the viewer that Maggie is mishandling the situation and making matters worse rather than better. However, it can also be argued that she is being very verbally effective. Her aggressive use of non-standard forms can be seen as a way of rejecting everything that the social workers stand for. She is skilful at picking up their jargon and either throwing it back at them (as with 'best interest' and 'cope') or replacing their words with her own (e.g. she insists upon using 'detention centre' and 'doss house' where they use 'family centre'). She also shows herself to be adept at phrasing her argument in rhetorically striking ways. For example, she produces the triad 'My kids' best interest... My best interest... My son's best interest'. Ken Loach himself has commented on Maggie's verbal skills, noting that 'She is, in fact, very witty and uses language in a very sharp way' (Fuller 1998: 97). In addition, in this scene she gains power by standing while the social workers are sitting and speaking much more loudly than they are. She literally dominates the conversation.

By contrast with Maggie, I cannot detect any non-standard elements in the speech of the female social worker. Her accent is RP and as such unmarked for geographical background. She uses standard syntax, and lots of high-register social work jargon, for example, 'family centre', 'rehabilitate' and 'cope'. Overall, her speech sounds painfully different to Maggie's, and it is telling that she speaks so little. After her first turn is so unsuccessful, she gives up trying to communicate with Maggie and allows her colleague to take over. Arguably her failure here to be able to accommodate towards Maggie at all means that she is ineffective as a social worker. The male social worker's dialect is somewhere between the two. His grammar and vocabulary are entirely standard. Like the female social worker, he regularly uses social work terms, including 'care proceedings', 'reassurance' and 'statutory duty'. However, his accent is Northern. He does not delete /h/, but he does frequently glottalize /t/ and realize /ŋ/ as /n/ (see both, for example in 'how you're **getting** on'). Some of his vowels in particular mark him as a Northerner. For example, like Maggie he uses a single Northern /ʊ/ (e.g. 'you're **lucky**').

One aspect of the male social worker's speech that is particularly noticeable is that he does attempt to accommodate towards Maggie, particularly in the middle of the scene. For example, he starts out talking about 'children' but then uses 'kids' when he is trying to be conciliatory. In a similar way he increases his degree of glottalization around the middle of the scene, and he hesitates in the middle of the word 'statutory', as though he starts saying it but then cannot work out where to glottalize (alternatively we might interpret it as him becoming conscious of the fact that he is using an unnecessarily high register word). He also gets rather lost in his syntax, hesitating in the middle of the unwieldy 'your kids' best interest is what we are concerned with'. However, despite his attempts to make his syntax, vocabulary and accent converge towards Maggie's, he is unable to break through Maggie's defences. She responds angrily to his attempts at linguistic convergence, shouting and swearing. He then diverges away from her speech again, returning to using 'children' and ceasing to glottalize word-final /t/. Simultaneously, his gentle attempts to persuade Maggie to go to 'the family centre' become outright threats: if she does not cooperate, they will take all of her children away from her. The male social worker's final utterance serves to make evident the real power relationships underlying the interview. Although Maggie is achieving verbal dominance, it is the social workers who will decide whether or not she is a fit mother and the underlying message of the interview is that it is only by gaining their cooperation and consent that she will regain the custody of her son.

Critic John Hill has commented on the way in which the film does not allow the viewer to simply identify with Maggie: she is shown as being a complex and difficult person. He adds, '*Ladybird, Ladybird* nonetheless refuses to indict her as a bad mother and pinpoints how the obstacles to her achievement of happiness result from her lack of social and economic power' (Hill 2000: 183). The film repeatedly demonstrates that Maggie's lack of social and economic power is inextricably linked to the language variety she speaks. Because of her socially and economically deprived background, Maggie lacks both a prestigious language variety and the social communicative competence necessary to speak to the social workers in a manner they would find appropriate. Despite the fact that she is shown to be verbally dextrous, she is rendered linguistically powerless within the framework of the social services. This then is a film in which dialect is present not only to make the film seem 'realistic', but also as a subject of the film. The film suggests that this failure cannot be blamed solely on Maggie herself; it is a structural failing of the system as a whole.

The story of Maggie is based on the real case of a woman who had several children taken into care. As a director, Ken Loach favours naturalism and improvisation. He cast Crissy Rock, a Liverpudlian comic with no previous acting experience, in the lead role of Maggie. She used her own accent for the role. Some of the other actors in the film were professionals, but many of the cast were coming to acting for the first time. Loach also used unconventional directing techniques. In an interview he described his working methods on the film as follows:

> When something was going to come as a shock to Maggie in the story, then I'd want it to come as a shock to Crissy, so obviously she wouldn't see the script beforehand. Where she'd be reacting to something that wasn't a surprise, where it was a question of some development, then she'd perhaps get the script a day or two before. I wouldn't rehearse it with the other actors so that she'd always hear the lines spoken to her freshly. It's a commonplace to say it, but acting is about reacting isn't it? The first time you hear something, you respond to it in a way that you never would if you were to hear it again.
>
> (Fuller 1998: 96)

Loach describes how Rock was encouraged to improvise the first take of some scenes, after which he would suggest ways in which the scene could be developed, and these suggestions would then be incorporated into the improvisation for the next take. Overall, these comments suggest that although a script certainly existed (it is credited to Rona Munro, a Scottish playwright), the actors were at times speaking spontaneously, or at least basing their performance upon spontaneous responses. Some of the results of these working methods have been identified in my analysis of the scene, including, for example, more naturalistic performances of style-shifting than are commonly found in films. Nevertheless, we must not assume that the dialogue is entirely natural: it is still a staged interaction in front of a camera and director, and Loach has still made decisions about how to develop the scene with the actors, and editorially, which versions of any given scene make it into the final film. The scene may feel 'realistic', but as director Loach is creating that sense of realism for specific artistic and political purposes. We may (or may not) prefer Loach's more radical political agenda to Coward's Churchillian agenda, but that does not mean Loach is capturing an unmediated slice of 'real life' on film.

Conclusion

In this chapter I have argued that across a number of different creative movements a commitment to greater realism has entailed a commitment to depicting people hitherto ignored by film or literature, and that a representation of their speech has been deemed central to that depiction. As such, 'real life' has been equated with 'real speech', and 'real speech' has meant dialect speech. Nevertheless, it is important to recognize that these representations of dialect rely upon specific literary and filmic techniques and that they are being used by writers and directors to achieve specific artistic and ideological goals. In Chapter 11, I turn finally to the question of 'authenticity', asking whether authenticity in dialect representation is desirable, or indeed even possible.

Further reading

Pam Morris's *Realism* (2003) provides an excellent introduction to the complex topic of realism. Chapter 5 of Geoffrey Leech and Mick Short's *Style in Fiction* (Leech and Short 2007) explores the relationship between the language of literature and 'real life'. Julia Hallam and Margaret Marshment's *Realism and Popular Cinema* (2000) provides a useful survey of the different ways in which 'the real' has been invoked on screen.

Exercises

Exercise 1

The passage below is the opening of Thomas Hardy's *Tess of the D'Urbervilles* (first published 1891). Read through it and think about the following:

- What about the passage makes it feel 'real'? Think about issues such as: from whose perspective is the scene narrated? What aspects of the scene are described? How does the reader know where the scene is and what is happening?
- How does the narrator represent the speech of John and the parson? What about the language feels 'real'?
- Are there any features of this passage which seem less 'real' to you?
- What is the purpose of the 'realism' in this scene? You might find it helpful to explore how the novel was received by critics and readers.

On an evening in the latter part of May a middle-aged man was walking homeward from Shaston to the village of Marlott, in the adjoining Vale of Blakemore, or Blackmoor. The pair of legs that carried him were rickety, and there was a bias in his gait which inclined him somewhat to the left of a straight line. He occasionally gave a smart nod, as if in confirmation of some opinion, though he was not thinking of anything in particular. An empty egg-basket was slung upon his arm, the nap of his hat was ruffled, a patch being quite worn away at its brim where his thumb came in taking it off. Presently he was met by an elderly parson astride on a gray mare, who, as he rode, hummed a wandering tune.

'Good night t'ee,' said the man with the basket.

'Good night, Sir John,' said the parson.

The pedestrian, after another pace or two, halted, and turned round.

'Now, sir, begging your pardon; we met last market-day on this road about this time, and I said 'Good night,' and you made reply *'Good night, Sir John'*, as now.'

'I did,' said the parson.

'And once before that—near a month ago.'

'I may have.'

'Then what might your meaning be in calling me 'Sir John' these different times, when I be plain Jack Durbeyfield, the haggler?'

The parson rode a step or two nearer.

'It was only my whim,' he said; and, after a moment's hesitation: 'It was on account of a discovery I made some little time ago, whilst I was hunting up pedigrees for the new county history. I am Parson Tringham, the antiquary, of Stagfoot Lane. Don't you really know, Durbeyfield, that you are the lineal representative of the ancient and knightly family of the d'Urbervilles, who derive their descent from Sir Pagan d'Urberville, that renowned knight who came from Normandy with William the Conqueror, as appears by Battle Abbey Roll?'

'Never heard it before, sir!'

'Well it's true. Throw up your chin a moment, so that I may catch the profile of your face better. Yes, that's the d'Urberville nose and chin—a little debased. Your ancestor was one of the twelve knights who assisted the Lord of Estremavilla in Normandy in his conquest of Glamorganshire. Branches of your family held manors over all this part of England; their names appear in the Pipe Rolls in the time of King Stephen. In the reign of King John one of them was rich enough to give a manor to the Knights Hospitallers; and in Edward the Second's time your forefather Brian was summoned to Westminster to attend the great Council there. You declined a little in Oliver Cromwell's time, but to no serious extent, and in Charles the Second's reign you were made Knights of the Royal Oak for your loyalty. Aye, there have been generations of Sir Johns among you, and if knighthood were hereditary, like a baronetcy, as it practically was in old times, when men were knighted from father to son, you would be Sir John now.'

'Ye don't say so!'

'In short,' concluded the parson, decisively smacking his leg with his switch, 'there's hardly such another family in England.'

'Daze my eyes, and isn't there?' said Durbeyfield. 'And here have I been knocking about, year after year, from pillar to post,

as if I was no more than the commonest feller in the parish...
And how long hev this news about me been knowed, Pa'son
Tringham?'

(Hardy 1978: 43–44)

Exercise 2

In *The Observer*, Miranda Sawyer described the film *Kidulthood* (Huda
2006) as containing 'the slang-filled youth vernacular that you hear
every day on buses across urban Britain' (Sawyer 2006). Watch the
opening five minutes of the film and think about the following:

- What makes the film feel 'real'? Think about *mise en scene*,
  cinematography, editing, sound.

- What about the language feels 'real'? How does it differ from the
  language of other films? Which features are particularly dialectal
  or colloquial?

- Are there any features of either the filmmaking or language which
  seem less 'real' to you?

- What is the purpose of the 'realism' of the film? You might find
  it helpful to explore how the film was received by critics and
  audiences.

11

Authenticity

In the previous chapter I explored the association that frequently exists between 'realism' in film and literature and the representation of dialect. I argued that in both film and literature a commitment to portraying life 'as it really is' often goes hand-in-hand with a commitment to portraying language 'as it really is', by extending the range of dialects represented on the page or screen. In this chapter, I turn my focus to the 'realism' of the dialect representation itself, asking: how can we judge the authenticity of dialect representation in film and literature, and does authenticity matter in any case?

At first glance, the issue of authenticity is the flipside of the issue of stereotyping that I examined in relation to film in Chapter 4 and in relation to literature in Chapter 6. After all, it would appear to follow that if a representation of dialect is not stereotyped then it must be authentic, and if it is not authentic then it must be stereotyped. Literary critics have sometimes made this assumption, drawing the conclusion that the more authentic a dialect representation can be shown to be, the better that dialect representation must be. Nevertheless, as I began to explore in Chapters 4 and 6, the relationship between stereotyping and dialect representation is more complex than it initially seems. In particular, as I argued in those chapters, it is important to be aware of the very real limitations that are placed on accurate dialect representation in both literature and film. In film, both production factors and audience comprehension place limits on the extent to which 'real world' dialects are represented. In literature, the fact that the spoken dialect is being transferred to the written page means that the representation will be partial and evocative at best. Once we accept that completely authentic dialect representation cannot be achieved in film or literature additional questions begin to emerge: how do we compare degrees of authenticity? And what is authenticity anyway?

In this chapter I start by surveying the study of literary dialect across the twentieth century, arguing that although the fictional and artistic aspects of dialect representation have long been recognized, the desire to validate some works of literature by asserting that their dialect representations are particularly 'authentic' has been strong. I trace this desire in part to the founding influence of dialectology, where for many years the ideal of 'the authentic speaker' was central to linguistic approaches to language variation. I then explore how linguists such as Nikolas Coupland, Mary Bucholtz and Penny Eckert have more recently begun to scrutinize the ideal of 'the authentic speaker', questioning its validity and emphasizing the role of speaker choice and speaker performance. This, I argue, makes now a particularly good time to reassess the relationship between authenticity and literary dialect. Following the work of Coupland in particular, I argue that discourses of authenticity are powerful in their own right and have frequently been mobilized in order to assign value to specific literary works and films. I explore some recent work that has been undertaken on authenticity in relation to dialect and literature: Taryn Hakala on two Lancashire dialect writers and Philip Leigh on nineteenth-century representations of African American Vernacular English. I then turn to examine the way in which 'authenticity' functions in relationship to film, exploring the role of dialect and authenticity in two film versions of the Robin Hood story, and in the TV series *The Wire*. In conclusion, I argue that authenticity is not an objective quality inherent in specific dialect representations, but that the perception of authenticity is nevertheless important.

A brief history of the study of literary dialect

The question of whether or not authenticity is an appropriate yardstick by which to judge literary dialects has been the subject of debate for almost a century. In the nineteenth century, literary reviewers would often provide impressionistic appraisals of the accuracy of dialect representation in works under review, approving of those representations which they felt to be authentic, and condemning those they felt to be inauthentic. In 1926 the first serious attempt to put the study of literary dialect on an academic footing was made by George Krapp with the publication of his essay 'The Psychology of Dialect Writing'. Krapp is emphatic that literature cannot and should not accurately represent real dialects:

A genuinely adequate representation of a living dialect could be made only with the help of a phonetic alphabet, and such a record would contain an enormous amount of detail which would merely distract and puzzle the literary reader. The writer of a literary dialect is not concerned with giving an exact picture of the folklore of speech. As an artist he must always keep his eye on the effect, and must select and reject what the scientific observation of his material reveals to him according as it suits or does not suit his purpose.

(Krapp 1971: 24)

Much of what Krapp proposes has been influential through to the present day, and in some areas his ideas are in line with modern thinking. For example, it is Krapp who first coins the term 'eye dialect' and he describes its effect very cogently: 'To the scientific student of speech, these misspellings of words universally pronounced the same way have no significance, but in the literary dialect they serve a useful purpose as providing obvious hints that the general tone of the speech is to be felt as something different from the tone of conventional speech' (Krapp 1971: 24). He also comments on the fact that some linguistic features may have long disappeared from everyday speech but still have an important role to play in literary dialects, for example 'gwine' for 'going': 'Such pronunciations are philologically interesting, and for the dialect artist they are as symbolic as a bandana handkerchief; but it would be fatal to look at them too critically from the point of view of truth to reality' (Krapp 1971: 26). Krapp's identification of the symbolic value of key linguistic features thus to some extent anticipates the concept enregisterment (Johnstone et al. 2006). However, other parts of Krapp's argument have stood the test of time less well. Several of his claims have not been borne out in the intervening years, for example: 'Negro English is [. . .] a disappearing speech' (Krapp 1971: 25) or 'Literary dialects do not flourish in England' (Krapp 1971: 28). The modern reader is also likely to take issue with Krapp's insistence that all literary dialect is 'a highbrow literature, the work of persons who stand superiorly aloof from popular life and picture it amusedly, patronizingly, photographically, satirically, sentimentally, as their tastes incline them' (Krapp 1971: 27). Even taking into account the literary period during which Krapp was writing, it is difficult to agree with his dismissive attitude towards the potential of literary dialects for representing the voices of lower-class characters seriously and sympathetically.

In 1950 Sumner Ives published 'A Theory of Literary Dialect' (rev. edn. 1971) in response to Krapp's article, which was at that time still considered a reliable treatment of the topic. Ives takes particular exception both to Krapp's repeated assertion that 'it is beside the point to apply the test of truth to reality too stringently' when assessing literary dialect, as well as to his claim that '[t]he main conclusion to be drawn from this analysis of passages from American dialect literature is that all local dialects of this kind are at bottom merely general colloquial or low colloquial American English, with a slight sprinkling of more characteristic words or pronunciations' (quoted in Ives 1971: 149). Ives states at the outset 'I have assumed that the authors of literary dialects have been seriously concerned with the validity and justice of their representations'. He develops a methodology for studying these dialects, drawing on 'the teachings of linguistic geography' whilst also recognizing 'limitations in the conventional orthography' (Ives 1971: 149). Ives insists that a proper appraisal of literary dialect depends upon the recognition that dialect is not 'a homogenous set of speech conventions that differs from other homogenous sets of conventions in each feature', but that it is 'a combination of features which are individually diverse in their distribution but which are found in a particular combination in only one limited area' and further that individual speakers will use some individual subset of those features (Ives 1971: 152). From the total range of possibilities, Ives argues, the writer 'selects those features that seem to be typical, to be most representative of the sort of person he is portraying' and 'generalizes so that the literary dialect is likely to be more regular in its variants than the actual speech which it represents' (Ives 1971: 153). Ives surveys the various means by which dialect can be represented on the page, and offers a detailed procedure by which critics can analyse literary dialect. The steps include: ascertaining the dialect that the author spoke; analysing the respellings in the text; verifying the existence of the individual features so identified; determining whether the combination of features present in the literary dialect corresponds with a geographical region where this combination occurs. Ives concludes that:

> If it can be shown that the region of overlapping features includes the locale of the story, and if this region of overlapping features is relatively limited, then the literary dialect has regional significance. The more narrowly the region of overlapping can be delimited from the features in the literary dialect, the more regional significance the literary dialect has. It follows, of course, that the dialect does not

have regional validity if there is no area where its features overlap. It may then be nothing more than a social dialect with features applicable to its social level anywhere in the country, and it may be nothing more than a mess of spurious and generally meaningless re-spelling.

(Ives 1971: 175–6)

It thus requires a substantial and specialized piece of research in order to ascertain the validity of a literary dialect and it is only at the end of all of this research that a proper judgement of the author as a writer of literary dialect can be formulated. Once all of the evidence has been properly sifted, Ives notes, 'the problem of the linguist is over, further evaluation of the author is a problem of literary criticism and is based on nonlinguistic criteria' (Ives 1971: 176).

As Norman Blake has pointed out, however, there are problems with this approach:

> modern scholars have often tried to suggest that authors were indeed trying to create a realistic non-standard speech and that they had a good ear to catch the various tones. Chaucer, Emily Bronte and Dickens, to name but a few, have all been praised in his way. They can be made to appear competent phonetically because a scholar can always interpret their spellings in accordance with what he knows of the dialects they are trying to represent. But the accuracy of their dialect portrayals may well be exaggerated in this way.

(Blake 1981: 17)

There are thus at least two factors which may compromise the linguist's neutrality: first, the desire to vindicate particular authors; and second, the linguist's existing familiarity with the dialect in question. The first factor returns us to a point I made in Chapter 6 where I noted that the identity of the author is important, and that authors who are not authentic speakers are always subject to more scrutiny than those who are. Yet this makes no logical sense when dialect is approached in Ives's terms: if authenticity really can be ascertained objectively by examining the linguistic facts then it should not matter who wrote it. The second factor is also problematic. In Chapter 5 I argued that dialect representation might be likened to a puzzle, and I noted that if the reader already has a good idea of what the answer to the puzzle is then semi-phonetic respellings may prove effective at indicating the intended accent. Philip Leigh states this in stronger terms, arguing that 'literary histories which attempt to delineate differences between literary dialect texts, genres, and periods based on authorial interest and skill in authentic representation of speech have not realized the constitutive role their own imaginations have played in the drawing of those lines' (Leigh 2011: 10). In short, once we recognize the active role that the reader plays in interpreting dialect representations, finding an objective methodology by which authenticity might be gauged becomes impossible.

Ives's article has been referenced by almost all writings on the broad subject of dialect representation over the last 50 years, including studies on Hawai'i Creole as a literary language (Romaine 1994), the literary representation of dialect in Spanish and Portuguese (Azevedo 2002), and SMS text messaging as a language variety (Tagg 2012). Of course, not everyone who cites Ives endorses his position on authenticity, and Ives himself recognizes the difficulties of deciding which phonological feature is being represented by any given semi-phonetic respelling. Nevertheless, Ives's central formulation – that the best way of determining the value of literary dialects is in terms of their linguistic authenticity and that the scholars best placed to determine authenticity are linguists – has proved remarkably influential. As Ives himself insists: 'a valid theory of literary dialect must be based on linguistic evidence, especially that supplied by dialect geography' (Ives 1971: 174). One result of this has been that many of the scholars who have engaged extensively with literary dialects have come from a dialectological background and have brought with them their disciplinary perspectives. As dialectology itself has only recently begun to interrogate 'authenticity', this has served to reinforce further the view that authenticity is the key to properly assessing literary dialects.

Authenticity and dialectology

The concept of the 'authentic speaker' has long been a cornerstone of attempts to study language variation. Mary Bucholtz notes that 'the emphasis on the authentic is in part a residue of Romanticism. The roots of dialectology lie in late nineteenth and early twentieth century European efforts to document the speech of the *Volk*' (Bucholtz 2003: 399). This residue can, for example, be seen in the Survey of English Dialects which was undertaken in Britain 1950–1961 and involved fieldworkers travelling round Britain, using a questionnaire to elicit responses from members of the public. As the project was primarily concerned with capturing traditional rural speech which was perceived to be under threat, fieldworkers aimed to capture the most conservative forms of speech. They therefore sought out older, less educated male speakers, most typically farm labourers, on the basis that such speakers were likely to speak the 'purest', most authentic form of the dialect (Orton 1962). The development of sociolinguistic approaches to studying language variation language in the 1960s and 1970s brought with it a commitment to studying a much broader range of speakers and social settings. Nevertheless, there was an emphasis on recording the most 'natural' and authentic speech. As Bucholtz has noted, 'authenticity underwrites nearly every aspect of sociolinguistics, from our identification of socially meaningful linguistic phenomena, to the definition of the social groups we study, to the methods we use to collect our data, to the theories we draw on in our analysis' (Bucholtz 2003: 398).

But what exactly is 'authenticity' and why is it given such pre-eminence within dialectology? Penny Eckert notes that 'Authenticity implies stasis – the 'real' peasant is just like the peasant that came before. But neither social locations and identities, nor language, are static. Is the person who remains centrally located in what is viewed as prototypical practice more authentic than the person who is pushing the envelope?' (Eckert 2003: 393). A focus on 'authenticity' requires that the analyst ignores many aspects of social interaction that do not fit within a framework of 'stasis'.

In his 2007 book *Style* Nikolas Coupland identifies five different qualities of authenticity:

> The first is *ontology*, meaning that things we consider authentic have a real existence, as opposed to a spurious or derived existence. The second is *historicity*. Because they are not 'made to order', authentic things generally have longevity; they have survived . . . A third quality of authentic things is their *systemic coherence*. Authentic things are 'properly' constituted in significant contexts . . . Fourthly, there needs to be degree of *consensus* in judging something to be authentic. So authenticity relates to the process of authorisation and to a particular source of authority . . . Fifthly and most obviously, an authentic object has *value*. Because authentic

things are ratified in a culture, they have definite cultural value. They are anchoring points – things one can hold on to.

(Coupland 2007: 180–1)

Coupland goes on to argue that any given example of 'vernacular speech' possesses all of these qualities of authenticity: (1) it has a real existence, (2) it has a long-established existence, (3) it has systemic coherence within the social groups who use it, (4) there is consensus about its existence among speakers and experts, and (5) it is valued by speakers as well as by the experts who study it. But the problem is that 'standard speech' – often set up by linguists as 'inauthentic' in opposition to the authenticity of 'vernacular speech' – also possesses these qualities (2007: 182). Standard English (1) has a real existence, (2) it has a long-established history that can be traced back to the chancery scribes of the fourteenth century, (3) it has a systemic coherence within society, (4) there is a consensus among many commentators – teachers, journalists, politicians – that it has a real existence, (5) it is valued by a significant portion of the population. Coupland argues that this reveals that authenticity is not a neutral quality that resides innately within certain forms of speech, but rather a subjective judgement. He writes: 'when we start to unpack the ideological politics of linguistic authenticity, we can't avoid seeing authenticity, in this field at least, as a discursive construction' (2007: 182). Coupland concludes *Style* by arguing that what is required is 'not a simple 'new authenticity' but a new footing for reassessing value, historicity, coherence and so on – the various qualities of authentic experience' (2007: 184) and he places style at the heart of this endeavour. Within this context, the representation of dialect in literature and film is no longer a topic marginalized by its own inauthenticity, but has the potential to become a genuine sociolinguistic concern. But what might this 'new footing' look like in relation to literature and film?

Authenticity, dialect and literature

As should be clear by this point in this book, representations of dialect in literature score poorly with regard to the qualities of authenticity identified by Coupland: (1) literary dialects are by definition 'made to order' and do not have a 'real existence' beyond the pages of the book; (2) although there are ongoing traditions of dialect representation, literary dialects lack the well-established historicity of real-world dialects; (3) literary dialects lack systemic coherence within society as a whole, and even within an individual literary work they may be inconsistently presented; (4) there is often little consensus as to how 'authentic' any given dialect representation is (consider, for example, the debates about *Huckleberry Finn*); and (5) while the texts within which the literary dialects appear may have cultural value, the literary dialect itself may have a marginal status (how many readers value the representation of Joseph's speech in *Wuthering Heights*?). Where claims are made about the authenticity of a specific literary dialect, this is always achieved by demonstrating that the features of the literary dialect correspond to the features of a 'real world'. In other words, a literary dialect is always what might be termed an authenticity parasite, deriving its authenticity at one remove from real-world dialects which have clearer claims to authenticity.

In his article 'The Mediated Performance of Vernaculars' Coupland uses the term 'mass-mediated vernacular speech' to describe the representation of a vernacular dialect or accent for a popular audience in film, television, literature, advertising, etc. (Coupland 2009: 284). He points out that any mass-mediated vernacular entails the representation of the original language variety in an entirely new context; the language that was originally used to a small group of people in the home, field or factory is now used for a mass audience in a film, television programme, novel, poem or advert. In one of the articles that appear in the same volume, Ruth King and Jennifer Wicks explore the reception of a television advertisement that made 'humorous' use of Newfoundland dialect, analysing what the subsequent debate reveals about the ownership and commodification of regional dialect. As they discuss, some of their informants offered the opinion that the problem with the advert was that the dialect performance just was not very good: if only the advertisement had used a real Newfoundlander, their informants argued, then the advertisement as a whole would have been less offensive (King and Wicks 2009). Coupland takes issue with this view, arguing: 'If we take the fact of mediated recontextualization seriously, then "accuracy" is irrelevant. This is the familiar Bakhtin-type argument, that a phrase repeated is not the same phrase'(Coupland 2009: 298). In other words, whatever set of social meanings a dialect may have had in its original context, the fact that it is now appearing in a different context gives that dialect a different set of meanings. This offers a new way of understanding the argument that

I made in Chapter 4, where I separated out linguistic stereotyping from character stereotyping, and argued that it was possible for a particular representation to avoid linguistic stereotyping and yet still function as character stereotyping. This is because even if a particular dialect is represented in a film or text with exactly the same linguistic features as it would have when used among a group of friends on a bus, the very fact that that dialect has been recontextualized from a bus to a film or text means it takes on a different set of meanings. In the case of the advert, even if the actor had been born and raised in Newfoundland, the problem would have remained that he was performing a particular 'Newfoundlander' identity, and that identity was being played for laughs.

If authenticity is meaningless for mass-mediated vernaculars, does this mean, then, that we should abandon it as a meaningful quality altogether? Coupland suggests not. He proposes that 'Instead of either glorifying authenticity or dismissing it out of hand, we can approach it in other ways. Authenticity could be a powerful concept to use *within* the analysis of style' (Coupland 2007: 25). With reference to dialect literature, Hakala similarly notes that 'Any attempt to locate a true or authentic working-class voice in these texts would be futile. We should not, however, discount the importance of the *idea of authenticity* in identity formation' (Hakala 2010a: 14). In other words, authenticity matters because people believe that it matters. Filmmakers and writers work hard to position their work as authentic, and audiences and readers often find that a perception of authenticity enhances their appreciation of a work of art or justifies their preference for a particular author and director. In the case of dialects, there is a tendency to admire writers and performers who represent dialects 'well', and to castigate writers and performers who are 'bad' at dialects. At the same time, we should not assume that readers and audiences are naïve about authenticity. Indeed, the fact that there is so much popular interest in judging performances of dialect should alert us to the very fact that readers and audiences do not passively accept what is presented to them on the page or screen. Coupland proposes that in late modernity authenticity is becoming 'harder to find' and he proposes that we find new ways to think about authenticity:

So we can think of 'authenticity in performance', or the construction of *second-level authenticities*. Performers often 'earn' degrees of authenticity precisely through their disavowal of first-order authenticities. Indeed it is an interesting speculation that, in late modernity, authenticity needs to be earned discursively rather than automatically credited.

(Coupland 2007: 184)

Here we can return to paratexts and metalanguage, which provide an important way – through prefaces, footnotes and back-of-book blurbs – for authors and publishers to lay claim to authenticity. But rather than taking them at their word and seeking to judge whether or not authenticity has been accomplished, a better approach is to consider these paratexts and metalinguistic comments as part of the literary text. This is one way to move us beyond the easy assumption that authenticity and stereotyping are inverse opposites of each other.

Taryn Hakala provides a good example of such an approach in her article 'A Great Man in Clogs: Performing Authenticity in Victorian Lancashire' (2010b). She examines how two nineteenth-century Lancashire dialect writers, Ben Brierley and Edwin Waugh, performed regional authenticity in different ways. Taking her cue from the work of Coupland, Eckert and Bucholtz, Hakala also explores the way in which Lancastrians felt invested in Brierley and Waugh's dialect performances, arguing that 'Lancastrians, regardless of whether or not they themselves could approximate the traditional vernacular, could identify with the local values, norms and mores indexed by it' (2010b: 389). She demonstrates how the representation of the men themselves within their network of supporters functioned to present them to audiences as inherently 'authentic':

It is worth noting that Turner refers to Brierley as 'Owd Ben' and quotes him as using the dialectal 'fra' rather than the Standard English 'from.' Though Brierley and Waugh quoted themselves as speaking Standard English, their middle-class supporters often cite them as speaking in the Lancashire dialect. This is not to say that Brierley and Waugh did not embrace their linguistic roots, for indeed they did, but it provides further evidence of their social network's promotion and circulation of the writers as representative Lancashire men and the pressure they must have felt to provide both visible and audible proof of their authenticity.

(Hakala 2010b: 395)

Hakala concludes that we should 'cease attempting to pass off Lancashire dialect writers as something they are not – authentic representations of the working class – and instead acknowledge their remarkable negotiation of subject positions, understanding their authenticity as performance'(2010b: 407). This conclusion underlines the fact that the discursive construction of authenticity is by no means a twenty-first-century phenomenon.

Philip Leigh also interrogates discourses of authenticity in the second half of the nineteenth-century literature in his doctoral dissertation *A Game of Confidence: Literary Dialect, Linguistics and Authenticity*. Leigh takes American dialect literature as his object of investigation, with chapters on Herman Melville, James Russell Lowell, Mark Twain and plantation fiction. By analysing the production and reception of a range of texts from this period, he finds that literary 'authenticity' was 'the product of extratextual transactions between writers and readers rather than the result of any objective assessments of verisimilitude', and he describes these transactions as '"games of confidence"' (Leigh 2011: 41). He summarizes the underlying questions of each of his chapters as follows:

> In my first chapter I asked, 'What is the nature of the confidence game that readers intent on proving authenticity play?' In my second chapter I asked 'What effect has this confidence game had on our literary histories of the nineteenth century?' In my third chapter I asked, 'What effects has this confidence game had on efforts to bring linguistics and literary criticism together to study dialect texts?' In my final chapter I asked 'How can the trials and errors of efforts to mine quantitative data from dialect texts help us to move beyond this confidence game?'
>
> (Leigh 2011: 153)

These four questions are worth asking in relation to any examples of dialect representation where 'authenticity' has been invoked, and they provide productive lines of future enquiry for work in relation to many different types of dialect literature.

Authenticity, dialect and film

In film issues of authenticity have been obscured to a much greater degree than in literature because dialogue can be recorded directly.

There have also been historical factors at play: because much dialect writing occurred before the technological capacity existed to record sound directly, dialectologists have long been interested in assessing what information can be derived from literary dialects about the historical development of real-world dialects (see for example Sullivan 1980; Troike 2010). By definition, by the time 'talkies' were being filmed, the capacity to record speech directly already existed, and so no one looks to film to recover information about historical dialects.

Despite this lack of academic interest in film dialect, the general public have always been fascinated by the question of which actors do a good accent. An important factor to bear in mind is that the only section of an audience who will be in a position to judge whether or not a film accent is any good is that section of the audience who speak with the accent themselves. This fact has not, however, discouraged audiences from voicing their opinion. In 2008, for example, the *Radio Times* conducted a poll inviting its readers to vote for the worst American accents used by British actors. The results were widely reported, including in *The Guardian* (Martin 2008). The odd thing about the poll, of course, was that if you really want to find out who has a poor American accent, you should ask American not British viewers. Even then, American viewers are likely to struggle when the accent is not one with which they are personally familiar: Minnesotans are unlikely to be very good at judging the authenticity of Alabama accents, and vice versa. What was further noticeable about the *Radio Times* list was that all of the actors named were very well known to UK audiences for English roles before they were cast into their American roles: Michelle Ryan, Eddie Izzard, Anna Friel, Hugh Laurie, Ian McShane. In other words, what might be considered relevant is not the success or failure of the actor to master an American accent – which British viewers were poorly placed to judge – but rather the extent to which the British viewer was conscious of the fact that the actor was really British and that therefore the accent must be fake. This suggests that the situation in films is not as dissimilar from the situation in literary texts as it might first appear. The audience accepts the illusion that a 'good' accent is being performed and does not think about it further unless something (such as personal familiarity with the variety, or knowledge of the actor's natural accent) triggers more careful attention.

An interesting case in point is the TV series *The Wire* (2002–8), which was created by David Simon. The series was set and filmed in Baltimore and was notable for casting a lot of local residents among the supporting cast. For the central performances, however, Simon wanted seasoned professional actors, but ones whose faces would not be distractingly familiar to US audiences. The result was that several key roles were played by foreign actors. These included Dominic West (born in Sheffield, educated at Eton) as police detective Jimmy McNulty, Idris Elba (born and raised in Hackney) as high-level drug dealer Russell 'Stringer' Bell and Aiden Gillen (born and raised in Dublin) as mayoral candidate Tommy Carcetti. Audiences seem to have found their accents convincing, albeit with the occasional lapse (there is, for example, a popular clip on YouTube where McNulty's accent becomes noticeably English during a heated argument). In making these casting decisions, Simon was trading on the fact that it is easier for audiences to accept an accent as authentic when they have no preconceptions about the actor's natural accent. The success of this strategy is attested by the fact that when a journalist for the *LA Times* interviewed West at the end of the show's five seasons, he commented on 'West's still-surprising native British accent that sounds light-years removed from Baltimore' (Barton 2008). Having become accustomed first to Jimmy McNulty's Baltimore accent, it was Dominic West's British accent that seemed unnatural.

An example of how invocations of authenticity can backfire is provided by a recent film version of *Robin Hood*. The story of Robin Hood is very specifically located in medieval England, but a Hollywood movie requires a big-name star, and many big-name stars are not English. For example, *Robin Hood: Prince of Thieves* (Reynolds 1991) starred California-born Kevin Costner who used a mid-Atlantic accent throughout. This version received some critical censure for this decision, but it proved to be a popular piece of light entertainment on both sides of the Atlantic, not least because it is difficult to engage in a sustained critique of a film for its lack of authenticity when it makes little attempt to appear authentic in the first place. By contrast, the marketing of Ridley Scott's 2010 *Robin Hood* starring Australian Russell Crowe placed much more emphasis on authenticity. The tagline for the film was 'The untold story behind the legend' and in interviews both Ridley and Crowe talked about how historical research had informed decisions about the movie (see for example McLean 2010). An interview by a local Nottingham newspaper with an actress who did dubbing work on the film provides some specific insights into the issue of accent in the film:

'Both Russell Crowe and Cate Blanchett are attempting a North Notts accent,' she said. 'I was really pleased about it because I found Kevin Costner's American Robin Hood was quite frustrating. I was saying to the producer, 'Why make another Robin Hood?' but this one seems more historically accurate. And having the Notts accents gives it an authentic feel.'

('Ey up Mi Duck – Russell Crowe's Talking Notts in New Film' 2010)

However, when the film was released, some British reviewers specifically criticized Crowe's accent:

The accents, meanwhile, suffer from Hollywood Drift (Crowe's goes from Leeds to Sheffield via Edinburgh — although anything's better than Kevin Costner's 'Notting-ham' drawl). *Empire*

(Jolin 2010)

His accent ping-pongs from sing-song Oirish to angular Aussie-Scottish until it finally settles on fookin' Northern/Nottingham for t'film's inevitable inspirational-speech moment. *Total Film*

(Lowe 2010)

The issue became news when Crowe responded badly to a question from the BBC's Mark Lawson during a radio interview for 'Front Row' (broadcast BBC Radio 4, 7:15PM Wed, 12 May 2010). Lawson asked 'The accent that you've given him, there are hints to me of Irish, but what ... were you thinking in those terms?' Crowe accused Lawson of having 'dead ears' and later stormed out of the interview. The spat was quickly reported across the globe. There are three important aspects to this story. First, filmgoers were already primed to consider the authenticity of Crowe's accent because he was a well-known Australian actor who had hitherto shown great skill at acquiring different accents. Moreover, Crowe's public persona – bad-tempered and arrogant – made him a good candidate for what might be termed the 'tall poppy syndrome' of bad accent spotting (just as in everyday life, criticizing someone's language can provide a superficially objective way of undermining them, so with acting criticizing someone's dialect performance can provide a superficially objective way of undermining their acting ability). Second, the film was being marketed as authentic in ways that the 1991 version was not, meaning that from the outset the value of the film was explicitly tied to the discursive construction of its authenticity. Third, despite the fact that both the audience and the filmmakers were so willing to invoke notions of authenticity in talking about the film, the ensuing media coverage gave very little consideration to what an authentic Medieval Nottingham accent would have sounded like. Indeed, given that all accents of English were rhotic until at least Tudor times, an accent that mixed features of Irish or Scottish with features of Northern English may not have been very far off the mark. Lawson's tentative question ('were you thinking in those terms?') could theoretically have been answered with an authoritative 'Well, Mark, in the Medieval period everyone in the British Isles would have used /r/ much more extensively than English speakers do today, so yes we were aiming to combine Northern vowels with Celtic rhoticity.' Few listeners would have been well enough versed in phonetics to judge whether that was a good description of Crowe's performance, and an even smaller number would have been able to answer the question of whether such a characterization of Medieval Nottingham English was valid. It is unlikely that such an exchange would have garnered international attention, although of course it might not have done much to alter the popular perception of Crowe as someone who takes himself and his acting far too seriously.

The point I wish to make is that it is perfectly possible to analyse dialect in film in terms of authenticity, applying the techniques outlined by Sumner Ives for the study of literature to the study of film. We can research what a Nottingham accent would have sounded like in the thirteenth century and compare it to Russell Crowe's performance in *Robin Hood*. We can identify the features of a contemporary Baltimore accent, and compare them to the performances of Dominic West, Idris Elba and Aidan Gillen in *The Wire*. We can rate the accents assayed by Michelle Ryan, Eddie Izzard, Anna Friel, Hugh Laurie and Ian McShane in their various American roles, and compare our findings to the rankings of *Radio Times* readers. However, none of this would really help us to understand what these performances are doing or how audiences respond to them. Instead, as with approaches to literary representations of dialect, we must recognize that dialect is frequently part of a much broader construction of authenticity both within the film or television programme itself and the discourses that surround it (marketing, interviews, reviews, etc.). Finally, we need to be aware that writers and directors are sometimes engaging playfully with issues of authenticity through dialect performance.

We might, for example, turn our attention to a scene from the second series of *The Wire* where McNulty goes undercover by posing as a customer of a brothel. McNulty's colleague, Lester Freamon, advises him to adopt an overseas accent in order to persuade the brothel that he is not a policeman, and McNulty assumes a terrible, cliché-strewn English dialect that swerves rapidly between Cockney, RP and Baltimore. The scene is of course an in-joke because by this point in the series most fans of *The Wire* were well aware that Dominic West was really English. It is worth bearing in mind Coupland's observation that 'Performers often "earn" degrees of authenticity precisely through their disavowal of first-order authenticities'(2007: 184). McNulty's bad English accent signals that, despite all the ways in which *The Wire* repeatedly invokes authenticity with reference to location, casting, storyline, etc., it is nevertheless highly conscious of the fact that it lacks any first-order authenticity. Indeed, in interviews Simon has explicitly stated that 'Authenticity is only a tool in the toolbox like any other thing you have when you're trying to get people to believe in the story ... If you don't put enough of it in, you're in trouble. If you put too much in and you don't tell the story that ought to be told, then you're defeating your narrative' (Rawls 2010). This strategy of using interviews and performance in-jokes to disavow authenticity permits Simon to circumvent some of the difficulties that *Robin Hood* ran into where, having claimed authenticity, any evidence of inauthenticity became problematic. McNulty's bad English accent in *The Wire* strategically highlights the inauthenticity of its central character, thereby opening up a space where other degrees of authenticity can be recognized.

Conclusion

In this chapter I have shown that, although authenticity has often been assumed to be a significant criterion by which the success of dialect representation is to be measured, there are significant problems in defining and establishing authenticity. Drawing on the work of Nikolas Coupland I have suggested an alternative approach: that we recognize that authenticity is constructed through the discourses that surround dialect representation, and that we analyse these discourses in their own right. This is a complex issue and I am not proposing that we simply dispense with any notion of stereotyping and authenticity. There clearly is space for approaches which attempt to assess how close specific literary or filmic representations are to 'real world' dialects. However, we need to abandon the idea that such judgements can ever be absolute, as well as the idea that representations which lay claim to some to real-world 'authenticity' are therefore inherently 'better'. Instead we need to explore how authenticity is being constructed in particular instances, and investigate who gets to decide what is authentic and what is not.

Further reading

The three articles that focused sociolinguistic discussions of 'authenticity' at the start of the twenty-first century are worth reading in order to understand the broader debate on this topic. These are Penny Eckert's 'Sociolinguistics and Authenticity: An Elephant in the Room' (2003), Nikolas Coupland's 'Sociolinguistic Authenticities' (2003), Mary Bucholtz's 'Sociolinguistic Nostalgia and the Authentication of Identity' (2003). Nikolas Coupland's 'The Mediated Performance of Vernaculars' (2009) offers some valuable thoughts on performances of dialect and authenticity and it introduces a special edition of *Journal of English Linguistics* which contains other useful articles. Taryn Hakala's 'A Great Man in Clogs: Performing Authenticity in Victorian Lancashire'(2010b) provides a good example of how the construction of authenticity can become an object of study in relation to dialect literature.

Exercises

Exercise 1

Choose a novel published in the last twenty years that contains a substantial amount of dialect representation. Use a search engine to gather together material that discusses the dialect representation in terms of its authenticity (search for some combination of the title and author, 'dialect', 'language', 'authentic', 'authenticity', 'inauthentic', etc.). Think about:

- Who is writing the piece? Who does the intended readership seem to be?
- How is the language of the novel described?

- Is the idea of dialect authenticity invoked in the discussion? If so how is it judged? Is it always a positive quality? Are there any problems with authenticity?

If you can't think of a suitable text here are some suggestions to get you started: *Buddha Da* by Anne Donovan (2003), *Londonstani* by Gautam Malkani (2006), *Pigeon English* by Stephen Kelman (2011).

Exercise 2

Choose a film where an actor has performed in a dialect different from his or her natural one. Use a search engine to gather together material that has been written about the dialect performance; this might include interviews with the actor, reviews, blogs, newspaper articles, online discussion boards, etc. Think about:

- Who is writing about the dialect performance? Who does their intended readership seem to be?
- How is the discussion framed? Is it about authenticity, performance, artistry? Who gets to judge the dialect performance? How is its success measured?
- What is at stake in this discussion of dialect performance? Why does it matter to the writer of the piece?

If you can't think of a suitable film here are some suggestions to get you started: Renée Zellwegger in *Bridget Jones* (2001), Matt Damon and Morgan Freeman in *Invictus* (2009), Daniel Day Lewis in *Lincoln* (2012).

Concluding thoughts

I first became fascinated by dialect representation when I encountered Norman Blake's *Non-Standard Dialect in Literature* (1981) as an undergraduate. Since the publication of that comprehensive survey there have been some excellent articles, chapters and books on specific periods and authors, but there has been no single text attempting to give an overview of the subject of dialect representation as a whole. This is the gap that I set out to fill with this book. I have not attempted a chronological survey like Blake's, but rather a primer of some of the issues and ideas that I think are essential in preparing the student or scholar to undertake further research.

Above all, what I hope I have shown in this book is that there is a lot of exciting work still to be done on dialect and literature and dialect and film. With regards to dialect and film the field is almost entirely untouched. With regards to dialect and literature, despite almost a hundred years of formal study, there is much still to be done. I know from my own research how revealing it can be to look in detail at a single period, genre, author or dialect. On my AHRC-funded 'Dialect in British Fiction 1800–1836' project I explored what was happening to dialect representation during a period when both the novel and language attitudes were undergoing rapid change. On my 'Sheffield Voices' project I worked with undergraduate students to uncover the history of the representation of one specific dialect, identifying several innovative but forgotten writers along the way. In both cases I found that what might appear from a distance to be a narrative of steady progress marked out by landmark texts becomes on closer inspection a much more complex and hard-fought process of innovation and experimentation.

One question I have frequently had occasion to ask myself while writing this book is why the subject of dialect in film and literature has not been more intensively studied in recent years. I am tempted to suggest that it is perhaps because it seems both marginal and rather fusty. Dialect by its nature is regional, and in literature it is often nostalgic. But at its heart the representation of dialect in film and literature is often (although not always) about writers and filmmakers trying to give voice to people in communities who are more frequently spoken about than allowed to speak. As I have tried to show, the question of how these voices are communicated on the screen and in print is far from straightforward. Nevertheless, the question is an important one, and recent developments within dialectology mean that now is a particularly good time to investigate it. Choose a text or film, choose a period or genre, choose a framework or approach and ask: what dialect is represented here? How is it represented? And what purpose does it serve?

References

Adamson, Sylvia (1993), 'Varieties, Stereotypes, Satire – and Shakespeare', in Y. Ikegami and M. Toyota (eds), *Aspects of English as a World Language* (Tokyo: Maruzen), pp. 225–45.

Adamson, Sylvia (1998), 'Chapter 7: Literary Language', in Suzanne Romaine (ed.), *The Cambridge History of the English Language Volume IV 1776–1997* (Cambridge: Cambridge University Press), pp. 589–692.

Archerd, Army (1997), 'Lee Has Choice Words for Tarantino', *Variety*. http://www.variety.com/article/VR111779698, date accessed 1 March 2013.

Audiard, Jaques (2009), *A Prophet*. Writers: Thomas Bidegain and Jacques Audiard (screenplay); Abdel Raous Dafri and Nicolas Peufailit (original screenplay).

Azevedo, Milton M. (2002), 'Considerations on Literary Dialect in Spanish and Portuguese', *Hispania*, 85.3, 505–14.

Bakhtin, Mikhail (1981), *The Dialogic Imagination: Four Essays*, translated by Caryl Emerson and Michael Holquist, edited by Michael Holquist (Austin: University of Texas Press).

Barber, Charles, Joan C. Beal and Philip A. Shaw (2009), *The English Language: A Historical Introduction* (Cambridge: Cambridge University Press).

Barton, Chris (2008), '"The Wire": The Dominic West Perspective – Latimes.com', *Los Angeles Times*. http://latimesblogs.latimes.com/showtracker/2008/02/the-wire-react.html, date accessed 1 March 2013.

Beal, Joan C. (2000), 'From Geordie Ridley to Viz: Popular Literature in Tyneside English', *Language and Literature*, 9.4, 343–59.

Beal, Joan C. (2009), '"You're Not from New York City, You're from Rotherham": Dialect and Identity in British Indie Music', *Journal of English Linguistics*, 37.3, 223–40.

Beal, Joan C. (2010), *An Introduction to Regional Englishes: Dialect Variation in England* (Edinburgh: Edinburgh University Press).

Bell, Allan (1984), 'Language Style as Audience Design', *Language in Society*, 13.2, 145–204.

Bell, Allan (2007), 'Style and the Linguistic Repertoire', in Carmen Llamas, Louise Mullany and Peter Stockwell (eds), *The Routledge Companion to Sociolinguistics* (Abingdon: Routledge), pp. 95–100.

Blake, Norman Francis (1981), *Non-standard Language in English Literature* (London: Deutsch).

Bordwell, David and Kristin Thompson (2008), *Film Art: An Introduction*, 8th edn (New York: McGraw Hill).

Bourdieu, Pierre (2003), *Language and Symbolic Power* (Cambridge: Polity Press).

Bourhis, Richard Y. and Howard Giles (1977), 'The Language of Intergroup Distinctiveness', in *Language, Ethnicity, and Intergroup Relations* (London: Academic Press), pp. 119–35.

Bowdre Jr, Paul Hull (1971), 'Eye Dialect as a Literary Device', in Juanita Williamson and Virginia Burke (eds), *A Various Language* (New York: Holt, Rinehart and Winston, Inc.), pp. 178–86.

Boyle, Danny (1996), *Trainspotting*. Writers: Irvine Welsh (novel) John Hodge (screenplay).

Broadhead, Alex (2010), 'Framing Dialect in the 1800 Lyrical Ballads: Wordsworth, Regionalisms and Footnotes', *Language and Literature*, 19.3, 249–63.

Bucholtz, Mary (2003), 'Sociolinguistic Nostalgia and the Authentication of Identity', *Journal of Sociolinguistics*, 7.3, 417–31.

Bucholtz, Mary (2011), 'Race and the re-embodied voice in Hollywood film', *Language & Communication*, 31.3, 399–416.

Bucholtz, Mary and Qiuana Lopez (2011), 'Performing blackness, forming whiteness: Linguistic minstrelsy in Hollywood film', *Journal of Sociolinguistics*, 15.5, 680–706.

Carkeet, David (1979), 'The Dialects in Huckleberry Finn', *American Literature 1*, 51.3, 315–32.

Carter, Angela (1985), *Nights at the Circus* (London: Picador).

Catford, J. C. (2001), *A Practical Introduction to Phonetics* (Oxford: Oxford University Press).

Cattaneo, Peter (1997), *The Full Monty*. Writer: Simon Beaufoy.

Chadha, Gurinder (1993), *Bhaji on the Beach*. Writers: Gurinder Chadha and Meera Syal.

Chapman, Raymond (1994), *Forms of Speech in Victorian Fiction* (London and New York: Longman).

Cole, Roger W. (1986), 'Literary Representation of Dialect: a Theoretical Approach to the Artistic Problem', *The University of South Florida Language Quarterly*, 24.3–4, 3–8.

Conrad, Joseph (1984), *The Nigger of the 'Narcissus'* (Oxford: Oxford University Press).

Coupland, Nikolas (2007), *Style: Language Variation and Identity* (Cambridge: Cambridge University Press).

Coupland, Nikolas (2009), 'The Mediated Performance of Vernaculars', *Journal of English Linguistics*, 37.3 (July 23), 284–300.

Coupland, Nikolas (2003), 'Sociolinguistic Authenticities', *Journal of Sociolingusitics*, 7.3, 417–31.

Coward, Noel and David Lean (1942), *In Which We Serve*. Writer: Noel Coward.

Curtis, Richard (2006), *Six Weddings and Two Funerals: Three Screenplays by Richard Curtis* (London: Michael Joseph).

Dabydeen, David (1984), *Slave Song* (Sydney: Dangaroo Press).

Dickens, Charles (1966), *Oliver Twist* (Harmondsworth: Penguin).

Dickens, Charles (2003), *Great Expectations* (London: Penguin Books).

Eckert, Penelope (2003), 'Sociolinguistics and Authenticity: An Elephant in the Room', *Journal of Sociolinguistics*, 7.3, 392–7.

Eckert, Penelope (2000), *Linguistic Variation as Social Practice: The Linguistic Construction of Identity in Belten High* (Oxford: Blackwell).

Edwards, John R. (1979), *Language and Disadvantage* (London: Arnold).

Edgeworth, Maria (1992), *Castle Rackrent and Ennui* (London: Penguin).

Eliot, George (1980), *Adam Bede* (London: Penguin).

'Ey up Mi Duck – Russell Crowe's Talking Notts in New Film' (2010), *This Is Nottingham*. http://www.thisisnottingham.co.uk/Ey-mi-duck-8211-Russell-Crowe-s-talking-Notts-new-film/story-12249621-detail/story.html, date accessed 1 March 2013.

Ferguson, Susan L. (1998), 'Drawing Fictional Lines: Dialect and Narrative in the Victorian Novel', *Style*, 32.1, 1–17.

Fishkin, Shelley Fisher (1994), *Was Huck Black?: Mark Twain and African-American Voices* (New York: Oxford University Press).

Forster, E. M. (1973), *Howards End* (London: Edward Arnold).

Fuller, Graham (ed.) (1998), *Loach on Loach* (London: Faber & Faber).

Genette, Gerard (1997), *Paratexts: Thresholds of Interpretation* (Cambridge: Cambridge University Press).

Giaimo, Genie (2010), 'Talking Back through "Talking Black": African American English and Agency in Walter Mosley's Devil In a Blue Dress', *Language and Literature*, 19.3, 235–47.

Gilbert, Lewis (1983), *Educating Rita*. Writer: Willy Russell.

Giles, Howard and Nikolas Coupland (1991), *Language Contexts and Consequences* (Milton Keynes: Open University Press).

Giles, Howard and Philip Smith (1979), 'Accommodation Theory: Optimal Levels of Convergence'. In Howard Giles and Robert St. Clair (eds) *Language and Social Psychology* (Baltimore: Basil Blackwell), pp. 45–65.

Gottleib, Bruce (1999), 'The Merchant of Menace', *Slate*. http://www.slate.com/articles/news_and_politics/hey_wait_a_minute/1999/05/the_merchant_of_menace.html, date accessed 1 March 2013.

Gray, Alasdair (1991), *Something Leather* (London: Picador).

Griffin, Kate (2011), *The Neon Court* (London: Orbit).

Hague, Tom (1976), *Totley Tom: Tales of a Yorkshire Miner* (Kineton, Warwick: Roundwood Press).

Hakala, Taryn (2010a), 'Working Dialect: Nonstandard Voices in Victorian Literature', PhD Thesis: University of Michigan, Ann Arbor.

Hakala, Taryn (2010b), 'A Great Man in Clogs: Performing Authenticity in Victorian Lancashire', *Victorian Studies*, 52.3, 387–412.

Hall, Stuart (2010), 'Send for the Elocutioneer', *Radio Times*, 7-13 August, 65.

Hallam, Julia and Margaret Marshment (2000), *Realism and Popular Cinema* (Manchester: Manchester University Press).

Hardy, Thomas (1978), *Tess of the D'Urbevilles* (London: Penguin).

Hardy, Thomas (1996), *The Complete Stories* edited by Norman Page (London: J.M. Dent).

Harrison, Tony (2006), *Selected Poems* (London: Penguin).

Heller, Zoe (2003), *Notes on a Scandal* (London: Penguin).

Hermeston, Rod (2011), '"The Blaydon Races": Lads and Lasses, Song Tradition, and the Evolution of an Anthem', *Language and Literature*, 20.4, 269–82.

Hess, Natalie (1996), 'Code Switching and Style Shifting as Markers of Liminality in Literature', *Language and Literature*, 5.1, 5–18.

Higson, Andrew (2003), *English Heritage, English Cinema* (Oxford: Oxford University Press).

Hill, John (2000). 'Failure and Utopianism: Representations of the Working Class in British Cinema of the 1990s', in Robert Murphy (ed.), *British Cinema of the 90s* (London: British Film Institute), pp. 178–87.

Hornby, Nick (1995), *High Fidelity* (London: Victor Gollancz).

Huda, Menhaj (2006), *Kidulthood*. Screenwriter: Noel Clarke.

Hudson, Richard A. (1980), *Sociolinguistics* (Cambridge: Cambridge University Press).

Hughes, Arthur, Peter Trudgill and Dominic Watt (2012), *English Accents and Dialects: An Introduction to Social and Regional Varieties of English in the British Isles* (London: Hodder Education).

IMDb (2013a), 'Sam West', http://www.imdb.com/name/nm0922335/?ref_=fn_al_nm_1, date accessed 1 March 2013.

IMDb (2013b), 'Nicola Duffett', http://www.imdb.com/name/nm0240440/, date accessed 1 March 2013.

Ingham, Patricia (1970), 'Dialect in the Novels of Hardy and George Eliot', in George Watson (ed.), *Literary English Since Shakespeare* (London: Oxford University Press), pp. 347–63.

Ives, Sumner (1971), 'A Theory of Literary Dialect', in Juanita Williamson and Virginia Burke (eds), *A Various Language* (New York: Holt, Rinehart and Winston, Inc.), pp. 145–77.

Ivory, James (1992), *Howards End*. Screenwriters: E.M. Forster (novel); Ruth Prawer Jhabvala (screenplay).

Jaffe, Alexandra and Shana Walton (2000), 'The voices people read: Orthography and the representation of non-standard speech', *Journal of Sociolinguistics*, 4.4, 561–87.

Jaworski, Adam, Nikolas Coupland and Dariusz Galasiński (2004), 'Metalanguage: Why Now?', in Adam Jaworski, Dr Nikolas Coupland and Dariusz Galasiński (eds), *Metalanguage: Social and Ideological Perspectives* (Berlin and: Walter de Gruyter), pp. 3–8.

Jeffries, Richard (1939), *"After London" and "Amaryllis at the Fair"* (London: J M Dent).

Johnstone, Barbara, Jennifer Andrus and Andrew E. Danielson (2006), 'Mobility, Indexicality, and the Enregisterment of "Pittsburghese"', *Journal of English Linguistics*, 34.2 (June 1), 77–104.

Jolin, Dan (2010), 'Robin Hood', *Empire*. http://www.empireonline.com/reviews/reviewcomplete.asp?FID=134778, accessed 1 March 2013.

Joseph, John Earl (1987), *Eloquence and Power: The Rise of Language Standards and Standard Languages* (London: Frances Pinter).

Kelman, James (1992), *The Burn* (London: Minerva).

Kelman, James (1995), *How Late It Was, How Late* (London: Minerva).

Kerswill, Paul (2006), 'Standard English, RP and the standard/non-standard relationship', in David Britain (ed.), *Language in the British Isles*, 2nd edn (Cambridge: Cambridge University Press), pp. 22–33.

King, Ruth and Jennifer Wicks (2009), '"Aren't We Proud of Our Language?": Authenticity, Commodification, and the Nissan Bonavista Television Commercial', *Journal of English Linguistics*, 37.3, 262–83.

Kortmann, Bernd and Clive Upton (2008), *Varieties of English 1: The British Isles* (Berlin; New York: Mouton de Gruyter).

Kozloff, Sarah (2000), *Overhearing Film Dialogue* (Berkeley and Los Angeles: University of California Press).

Krapp, George Philip (1971; 1st published 1926), 'The Psychology of Dialect Writing', in Juanita Williamson and Virginia Burke (eds), *A Various Language* (New York: Holt, Rinehart & Winston Inc.), pp. 22–9.

Labov, William (1966), *The Social Stratification of English in New York City* (Washington, DC: Center for Applied Linguistics).

Lawrence, D.H. (2006), *Lady Chatterley's Lover, A Propos of 'Lady Chatterley's Lover'* (London: Penguin).

Le Page, Robert B. and Andree Tabouret-Keller (1985), *Acts of Identity: Creole-based Approaches to Language and Ethnicity* (Cambridge: Cambridge University Press).

Lean, David (1948), *Oliver Twist*. Writers: Charles Dickens (novel); David Lean and Stanley Haynes (screenplay).

Lee, Harper (2010), *To Kill a Mockingbird* (London: Arrow Books).

Leech, Geoffrey N. and Mick Short (2007), *Style in Fiction: A Linguistic Introduction to English Fictional Prose*, 2nd edn (Harlow: Pearson Education).

Leigh, Philip John (2011), 'A Game of Confidence: Literary Dialect, Linguistics and Authenticity', PhD Thesis, University of Texas at Austin, USA.

Levy, Andrea (2004), *Small Island* (London: Headline Review).

Lippi-Green, Rosina (1994), 'Accent, Standard Language Ideology, and Discriminatory Pretext in the Courts', *Language in Society*, 23, 163–98.

Lippi-Green, Rosina (1997), *English with an Accent: Language, Ideology and Discrimination in the United States* (London: Routledge).

Lister, Thomas Henry (1832), *Arlington, a Novel. In Three Volumes* (London: Henry Colburn and Richard Bentley).

Loach, Ken (1969), *Kes*. Writers: Barry Hines (book); Barry Hines, Ken Loach and Tony Garnett (adaptation).

Loach, Ken (1994), *Ladybird, Ladybird*. Writer: Rona Munro.

Lowe, Andy (2010), 'Robin Hood', *Total Film*. http://www.totalfilm.com/reviews/cinema/robin-hood-1/page:2, date accessed 1 March 2013.

Lucas, George (1999), *Star Wars: The Phantom Menace*. Writer: George Lucas.

Lyon, John M. (2005), '"What Are You Incinerating?": Geoffrey Hill and Popular Culture', *English*, 54.209, 85–98.

Macaulay, Ronald K. S. (1991), '"Coz It Izny Spelt When They Say It": Displaying Dialect in Writing', *American Speech*, 66.3, 280–91.

Marriott, Stephanie (1997), 'Dialect and Dialectic in a British War Film', *Journal of Sociolinguistics*, 1.2, 173–93.

Martin, Daniel (2008), 'Have People Had Enough of British Actors Playing Americans?', *The Guardian*. http://www.guardian.co.uk/culture/tvandradioblog/2008/may/28/havepeoplehadenoughofbrit, date accessed 1 March 2013.

McCrum, Robert, William Cran and Robert MacNeil (1992), *The Story of English* (London: Faber & Faber/BBC Books).

McFarlane, Brian (1996), *Novel to Film: An Introduction to the Theory of Adaptation* (Oxford: Clarendon Press).

McLean, Craig (2010), 'Cannes Film Festival 2010: Ridley Scott Interview', *The Telegraph*. http://www.telegraph.co.uk/culture/film/cannes-film-festival/7692902/Cannes-Film-Festival-2010-Ridley-Scott-interview.html, date accessed 1 March 2013.

McMillan, Ian (2011), *This Lake Used to Be Frozen: Lamps* (Sheffield: Smith/Doorstop).

Meek, Barbara A. (2006), 'And the Injun goes "How!": Representations of American Indian English in white public space', *Language in Society*, 35.1, 93–128.

Milroy, James and Lesley Milroy (1999), *Authority in Language: Investigating Standard English*, 3rd edn (London and New York: Routledge).

Minnick, Lisa Cohen (2001), 'Jim's Language and the Issue of Race in *Huckleberry Finn*', *Language and Literature*, 10, 111–28.

Morris, Chris (2010), *Four Lions*. Writers: Chris Morris, Sam Bain and Jesse Armstrong.

Morris, Pam (2003), *Realism* (London: Routledge).

Morrison, Toni (2005), 'This Amazing, Troubling Book', in Stephen K. George (ed.), *Ethics, Literature, and Theory: An Introductory Reader*, 2nd edn (California: AlaMira Press), pp. 279–88.

Mugglestone, Lynda (2003), *Talking Proper: The Rise of Accent as Social Symbol*, 2nd edn (Oxford: Oxford University Press).

Myers, Caren (1994), 'Review of Four Weddings and a Funeral', *Sight and Sound*, May, 47.

Newell, Mike (1994), *Four Weddings and a Funeral.* Writer: Richard Curtis.

Nobbs, David (1983), *Second from Last in the Sack Race* (London: Methuen).

O'Donnell, Damien (1999), *East is East.* Writer: Ayub Khan-Din.

Oldman, Gary (1997), *Nil by Mouth.* Writer: Gary Oldman.

Omole, James O. (1987), 'Code-switching in Soyinka's *The Interpreters*', *Language and Style*, 20.4, 385–95.

Ong, Walter J. (1988), *Orality and Literacy: The Technologizing of the Word* (London: Routledge).

Orton, Harold (1962), *Survey of English Dialects: An Introduction* (Leeds: E. J. Arnold & Son Ltd).

Orwell, George (1954), *A Collection of Essays* (New York: Doubleday).

Page, Norman (1988), *Speech in the English Novel*, 2nd edn, Vol. 2 (Basingstoke: Macmillan).

Park, Ji Hoon, Nadine G. Gabbadon and Ariel R. Chernin (2006), 'Naturalizing Racial Differences Through Comedy: Asian, Black, and White Views on Racial Stereotypes in *Rush Hour 2*', *Journal of Communication*, 56.1, 157–77.

Pickering, Michael (2001), *Stereotyping: The Politics of Representation* (Basingstoke: Palgrave Macmillan).

Preston, Dennis R. (1982), ''Ritin' Fowklower Daun 'Rong: Folklorists' Failures in Phonology', *The Journal of American Folklore*, 95.377, 304–26.

Preston, Dennis R. (1985), 'The Li'l Abner Syndrome: Written Representations of Speech', *American Speech*, 60.4, 328–36.

Preston, Dennis R (2000), 'Mowr and Mowr Bayud Spellin': Confessions of a Sociolinguist', *Journal of Sociolinguistics*, 4.4, 615–21.

Rankin, Ian (1998), *Tooth and Nail* (London: Orion Books).

Rawls, Alex (2010), 'Music Brings Authenticity to HBO's "Treme"', *Los Angeles Times.* http://articles.latimes.com/2010/may/01/enter tainment/la-et-trememusic-20100501, date accessed 1 March 2013.

Rayner, Jonathan (2007), *The Naval War Film* (Manchester: Manchester University Press).

Reisz, Karel (1960), *Saturday Night and Sunday Morning.* Writer: Alan Sillitoe.

Relph, Josiah (1747), *A Miscellany of Poems: Consisting of Original Poems, Translations, Pastorals in the Cumberland Dialect, Familiar Epistles* (Wigton: printed by Robert Foulis for Mr Thomlinson).

Reynolds, Kevin (1991), *Robin Hood: Prince of Thieves*. Writers: Pen Densham and John Watson.

Roddick, Nick (1995), 'Four Weddings and a Financial Reckoning', *Sight and Sound*, January.

Romaine, Suzanne (1994), 'Hawai'i Creole English as a Literary Language', *Language in Society*, 23.4, 527–54.

Rowling, J. K. (2004), *Harry Potter and the Order of the Phoenix* (London: Bloomsbury).

Russell, Willy (2007), *Educating Rita* (London: Methuen Drama).

Ryan, Ellen Bouchard, Howard Giles and Richard J. Sebastian (1982), 'An Integrative Perspective for the Study of Attitudes Towards Language Variation', in Ellen Bouchard Ryan and Howard Giles (eds), *Attitudes Towards Language Variation: Social and Applied Contexts* (London: Edward Arnold), pp. 1–19.

Salinger, J. D. (1994), *The Catcher in the Rye* (London: Penguin).

Saro-Wiwa, Ken (1998), *Sozaboy* (Harlow: Addison Wesley Longman Ltd; 1st published 1985).

Sawyer, Miranda (2006). 'The film that speaks to Britain's youth in words they understand'. http://www.guardian.co.uk/film/2006/feb/26/features.mirandasawyer, date accessed 1 March 2013.

Scott, Jeremy (2009), *The Demotic Voice in Contemporary British Fiction* (Basingstoke: Palgrave Macmillan).

Sebba, Mark (1997), *Contact Languages: Pidgins and Creoles* (Basingstoke: Macmillan).

Sheridan, Thomas (1780), *A General Dictionary of the English Language* (London: Dodsley).

Shorrocks, Graham (1996), 'Non-standard Dialect Literature and Popular Culture', in Juhani Klemola, Merja Kyto and Matti Rissanen (eds), *Speech Past and Present: Studies in English Dialectology in Memory of Ossi Ihalainen* (Frankfurt am Main: Peter Lang), pp. 385–411.

Short, Mick. (1996), *Exploring the Language of Poems, Plays, and Prose* (London and New York: Longman).

Shuy, Roger W. (1975), 'Code Switching in *Lady Chatterley's Lover*', *Working Papers in Sociolinguistics*, 22. The Social Council Committee on Sociolinguistics, Southwest Development Laboratory, Austin, Texas.

Sillitoe, Alan (1985), *Saturday Night and Sunday Morning* (London: Panther; 1st published 1958).

Simpson, Paul (1999), 'Language, Culture and Identity: With (another) Look at Accents in Pop and Rock Singing', *Multilingua*, 18.4, 343–67.

Smith, Murray (2002), *Trainspotting* (London: BFI Publishing).

Smith, Zadie (2001), *White Teeth* (London: Penguin).

Stone, Alan A. (1999), 'A New Hope', *Boston Review*. http://boston review.net/BR24.5/stone.html, date accessed 1 March 2013.

Stone, Jeff, Zachary W. Perry and John M. Darley (1997), '"White Men Can't Jump": Evidence for the Perceptual Confirmation of Racial Stereotypes Following a Basketball Game', *Basic and Applied Social Psychology*, 19.3, 291–306.

'Subtitle Decision "Puzzles" Scots' (2006), *BBC Website*. http://news.bbc.co.uk/1/hi/entertainment/5244738.stm, date accessed 1 March 2013.

Sullivan, James P. (1980), 'The Validity of Literary-Dialect – Evidence from the Theatrical Portrayal of Hiberno-English Forms', *Language in Society*, 9.2, 195–219.

Taavitsainen, Irma and Gunnel Melchers (1999), 'Writing in Non-standard English: Introduction', in Irma Taavitsainen and Gunnel Melchers (eds), *Writing in Nonstandard English* (Amsterdam and Philadelphia: John Benjamins), pp. 1–26.

Tagg, Caroline (2012), *Discourse of Text Messaging: Analysis of SMS Communication* (London and New York: Continuum).

Tarantino, Quentin (1992), *Pulp Fiction*. Writers: Roger Avary and Quentin Tarantino.

Toolan, Michael (1992), 'The Significations of Representing Dialect in Writing', *Language and Literature*, 1.1, 29–46.

Traugott, Elizabeth Closs and Mary Louise Pratt (1980), *Linguistics for Students of Literature* (San Diego: Harcourt Brace Jovanovich).

Tricomi, Albert H. (2006), 'Dialect and Identity in Harriet Jacobs's Autobiography and Other Slave Narratives', *Callaloo*, 29.2, 619–33.

Troike, Rudolph. C. (2010), 'Assessing the Authenticity of Joel Chandler Harris's Use of Gullah', *American Speech*, 85.3 (October 4), 287–314.

Trudgill, Peter (1972), 'Sex, Covert Prestige and Linguistic Change in the Urban English of Norwich', *Language in Society*, 1, 179–95.

Trudgill, Peter (1983), 'Acts of Conflicting Identity. The Sociolingistics of British Pop-Song Pronunciation', in *On Dialect: Social and Geographical Perspectives* (Oxford: Blackwell), pp. 141–60.

Twain, Mark (1985), *The Adventures of Huckleberry Finn* (London: Penguin).

Vice, Sue (1997), *Introducing Bakhtin*. Manchester and New York: Manchester University Press.

Wales, Katie (2006), *Northern English: a Cultural and Social History* (Cambridge: Cambridge University Press).

Wells, J C. (1982a) *Accents of English I: An Introduction*. Cambridge: Cambridge University Press.

——— (1982b) *Accents of English 2: The British Isles*. Cambridge: Cambridge University Press.

——— (1982c) *Accents of English: Volume 3: Beyond the British Isles*. Cambridge: Cambridge University Press.

Welsh, Irvine (1996), *Trainspotting* (New York and London: W.W. Norton & Company).

Wheat, Alynda (2000), 'George Lucas' Jedi Mind Trick', *Salon*. http://www.salon.com/2000/03/22/lucas_2/, date accessed 1 March 2013.

Whitecross, Mat (2010), *Sex & Drugs & Rock & Roll*. Writer: Paul Viragh.

Wordsworth, William and Samuel Taylor Coleridge (1991), *Lyrical Ballads*, edited by R.L. Brett and A.R. Jones (London and New York: Routledge).

Wright, Edgar (2007), *Hot Fuzz*. Writers: Edgar Wright and Simon Pegg.

Zahn, Christopher J. and Robert Hopper (1985), 'Measuring Language Attitudes: The Speech Evaluation Instrument', *Journal of Language and Social Psychology*, 4.2 (June 1), 113–23.

Index